Food Lovers' Guide to Chicago

First Edition

Best Local Specialties, Markets, Recipes, Restaurants, & Events

Jennifer Olvera

gPP

Guilford, Connecticut

To buy books in quantity for corporate use
or incentives, call **(800) 962–0973**
or e-mail **premiums@GlobePequot.com**.

Editor: Amy Lyons
Project Editor: Lynn Zelem
Layout Artist: Mary Ballachino
Text Design: Sheryl Kober
Illustrations: © Jill Butler with additional art by Carleen Moira Powell
Map: Sue Murray © Morris Book Publishing, LLC

ISBN 978-0-7627-7015-1

Printed in the United States of America
10 9 8 7 6 5 4 3 2

All the information in this guidebook is subject to change. We recommend that you call ahead
to obtain current information before traveling.

I dedicate this book to my son, Hayden—an intelligent, inquisitive companion. May the seeds I sow someday guide you to the pleasures of food. It's also for my husband, Chris. You have been my steady—from the kitchen of our first rickety, third-floor apartment to the backyard garden we tend today. We discovered our places in life side by side, and I thank you for everything you've done.

Contents

About the Author

Jennifer Olvera holds an English degree from DePaul University and began covering Chicago food and dining over a decade ago. Having spent years as a restaurant reviewer for *Chicago* magazine, she went on to pen international culinary travel stories for the *Los Angeles Times, Chicago Tribune,* and Frommers.com. Jennifer contributed to the *Zagat 2010/2011 Chicago Restaurants Survey,* regularly tests and develops recipes for the *Chicago Sun-Times,* and oversees Midwest and Chicago dining for Gayot.com. Her work has been published everywhere from *Women's Day Special Interest Publications* to Orbitz .com, *Edible Chicago,* and *Time Out Chicago.*

Jennifer lives in the Chicago suburbs with her husband, Chris, and son, Hayden Greer. When she's not plucking heirloom tomatoes from her backyard garden, you'll find her canning, sourcing ingredients from local farms, or kicking back over an ice-cold martini.

Follow her edible adventures at web.mac.com/olverajennifer and via Twitter @olverajennifer.

Acknowledgments

As a kid, I favored the darkest, moodiest spots—Harvey's Prime Rib, for example, where the walls were newsprint-papered, the servers were sassy, and burgers on pumpernickel arrived alongside raw onions on rough-hewn metal plates. Coming in a close second: the Saddle Club, where song requests—scribbled on cocktail napkins— were *de rigueur*. (Personally, I favored the tacos over the rousing renditions.)

Looking back, most all of my early memories involve food. I practiced penmanship on recipe cards and prepared microwave "snacks" to fortify my mom after she mowed the lawn.

It's no coincidence, really, that I ended up covering food and dining as a profession. That said, I'm grateful to love what I do, whether it's writing about biltong in South Africa, Bora Bora's impossibly fresh *poisson cru,* or—quite honestly—local farms.

But all those wisps of Aragonese *jamón,* Berliner wurst, and Swedish meatballs don't change a simple fact: I am a Midwestern girl at heart. Chicago feels like home, and that's because of the people who inhabit it.

I therefore want to acknowledge the family and friends who believed in me through the years, and I offer my gratitude to respected colleagues who lent their assistance—especially Carly Boers. Her attention to detail, patience, and keen eye helped bring this book to fruition.

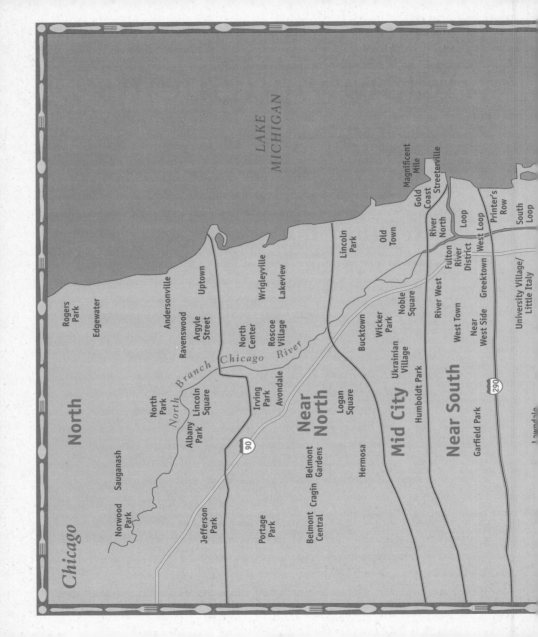

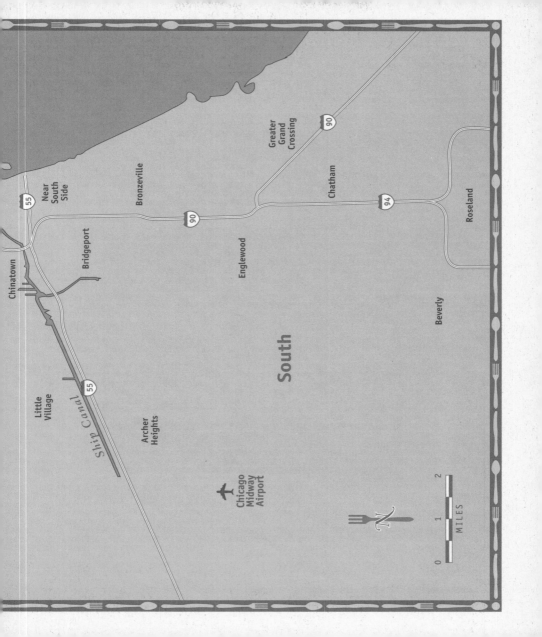

Introduction

Chicago gets pegged as a brawny, broad-shouldered place, filled with deep-dish-devouring types, who garble the word "tree" (instead of "three") between bites of relish-slathered hot dogs and swigs of "pop." Let's, once and for all, put these descriptors to rest. Chicago is a food city—and it's a sophisticated, multifaceted one at that.

According to the Chicago Historical Society's "Encyclopedia of Chicago," its name nods to the Miami and Illinois people's word for ramp, a wild onion that signals the coming of spring. Today, ramps are celebrated on Chicago menus and also preserved.

As a city of industry, Chicago attracted an immigrant population with edible traditions—from corned beef to brats—intact. Some ethnic enclaves arose, though a handful—Little Italy, Argyle Street, Devon Avenue, and Chinatown, for example—remain. More often, the influence can be found in neighborhood gems, tucked into strip malls or located off the beaten track.

From Chicago's historic, defunct stockyards to its heyday as a candy-making juggernaut, food has always been a strong, pervasive undercurrent. Flaming saganaki, chicken Vesuvio, and shrimp de Jonghe—not to mention the brownie—are said to have gotten their start right here. And the cafeteria as we know it? Consider that—inspired by the smorgasbord—homegrown, too.

Admittedly, the economic downturn has left its mark.

Chicago—long a bastion of fine dining—hasn't exactly changed its tune. Haute haunts, such as Alinea and L20, offer proof of that. What has shifted, however, is notable chefs are opening casual, cost-conscious spots. Paul Kahan, Bill Kim, Rick Bayless, and Stephanie Izard are among the examples. Not one compromised culinary integrity to do so. Emphasizing quality ingredients—often local and sustainable—their menus have been a revelation for the food-enthused.

There is one thing that proves problematic for Chicagoans, however: its growing season—or lack thereof. Thankfully, hoop houses (greenhouses) are sprouting up, extending the availability of farm-fresh fare.

Of course, when it's warm, Chicagoans revel in it. Many restaurants grow produce on rooftops; apiaries produce honey in the unlikeliest of places; and garden-flanked sidewalks and beer gardens emanate with the joviality winter inhibits.

In the pages that follow, I'll share the big-flavored, food-loving spirit of Chicago as I know it. Here, the classics appear alongside that which is lesser known and emerging.

This is a guidebook—make no mistake—so you'll find greatest hits. But it also offers inspiration beyond roads well-traveled.

This isn't a visitor's guide in the traditional sense—it's for the culinary community; curious, longtime residents; *and* the expense account–wielding suit as well as the traveling family. It's for all those who share a love of good eating.

Most notably, though, this is a book for those respectful—and supportive—of small farms, appreciative of artisanal products, and intoxicated by the simple things, like a steaming bowl of morning *pho*.

Navigating the City

Exploring Chicago is relatively easy. The city's layout is based on a grid system, and its block numbers—increasing 100 per block—are generally uniform throughout. The origin is at the intersection of State Street (0W/E) and Madison Street (0N/S). In most cases, individual blocks are approximately an eighth of a mile long. A secondary street typically appears every four blocks, or half-mile. Even addresses are located on the North and West side of the street, while odd numbers are found on the South and East. Certain streets—such as Lincoln Avenue, Clark Street, and Milwaukee

Avenue—run diagonally, but their addresses are numbered the same as North-South and East-West thoroughfares.

Chicago is serviced by two major airports: O'Hare International Airport and Midway Airport; the former is situated 17 miles north-west of downtown Chicago, while the latter is located approximately 10 miles southwest. O'Hare is far more frenetic, though it hosts the largest number of domestic and international carriers. Midway tends to experience fewer delays, but it doesn't serve as many airlines.

The easiest—and most cost-effective—way to get around Chicago is to take public transportation because garages, valet service, and, increasingly, metered parking are costly. The city's Regional Transportation Authority (RTA) encompasses the Chicago Transit Authority (CTA) bus and elevated rail systems (referred to locally as the "L") as well as Metra commuter trains and the Pace suburban bus system. Check out the online trip planner at rta chicago.com; alternately, plan itineraries by calling (312) 836-7000. The current CTA fare when paying cash is $2.25 per single ride; however, transit cards, purchased at www.transitchicago.com and at rail stations, allow for transfers and—in some cases—slightly reduced fares.

The CTA Blue Line runs between O'Hare and Chicago's epicenter, the Loop; it takes upwards of an hour to get from point A to point B. The Orange Line connects Midway and the Loop, with a ride time ringing in at about 30 minutes one way.

Unfortunately, public transportation in the 'burbs as well as the city's outlying areas leaves something to be desired. If you're heading outside of the city proper, plan on driving or renting a car.

How to Use This Book

In the pages that follow, you'll find entries organized for easy navigation. The front half of the book is dedicated to restaurants, while the back highlights everything from gourmet shops and ethnic grocers to farms worth visiting. Throughout the book, sidebars point to edibles of interest, growing trends, and tales of those doing interesting things in Chicago and beyond.

Organization

Each locale is followed by its address and designated neighborhood within the city of Chicago. The establishments in this book are categorized in chapters by proximity—**North, Near North, Mid City, Near South,** and **South**—and listed alphabetically within chapters to keep things tidy. To clarify the neighborhood division, communities are listed at the beginning of the chapters and are as follows:

North: Albany Park, Andersonville, Argyle Street, Devon Avenue, Edgebrook, Edgewater, Edison Park, Jefferson Park, Lincoln Square, North Park, Norwood Park, Ravenswood, Rogers Park, Sauganash, Uptown

Near North: Avondale, Belmont Cragin, Hamlin Park, Hermosa, Irving Park, Lakeview, Logan Square, North Center, Portage Park, Roscoe Village, Wrigleyville

Mid City: Bucktown, Gold Coast, Humboldt Park, Lincoln Park, Noble Square, Old Town, Streeterville, Ukrainian Village, Wicker Park

Near South: East Village, Fulton River District, Garfield Park, Greektown, Loop, Near West Side, River North, River West, West Loop, West Town

South: Archer Heights, Ashburn, Beverly, Bridgeport, Bronzeville, Chatham, Chinatown, Englewood, Far South Side, Greater Grand Crossing, Hyde Park, Lawndale, Little Italy, Little Village, Near South Side, Pilsen, Printer's Row, Roseland, South Deering, South Loop, University Village

Price Code

Each locale is followed by its address and designated neighborhood within the city of Chicago. Restaurants follow a pricing guide so you have some idea of what to expect. Dollar signs point to the following price ranges for a dinner and single drink:

$	**less than $10**
$$	**$10 to $30**
$$$	**$30 to $50**
$$$$	**$51 or more per plate**

Suburban Stunners, Stalwarts & Surprises

Suburban restaurants appear in a separate, but collective, chapter.

Cocktail Culture

Chicago's burgeoning cocktail and brewery culture continues to spark interest—with good reason. Within these pages, learn of sublime sips, hops havens, and lounges serving noshes of note.

Specialty Stores, Gourmet Shops & Purveyors/Farm Fresh

A chapter on purveyors—including gourmet grocers, specialty stores, butchers, and fishmongers—gives way to one on farm-fresh locales. Page through to find an edited list of farmers' markets, local farms, and farmstands.

Recipes

Before the feast winds down, a handful of recipes from Chicago chefs (plus two from the author), give you something to savor—in hands-on fashion.

Culinary Instruction

Because many food enthusiasts don't just eat, but also cook, there's a chapter dedicated to cooking schools and classes that help hone skills.

> ### HELPFUL TIP
>
> In the back of the book are Appendices to help you find a restaurant by cuisine or a food purveyor by type.

Food Fests & Events

It seems there's always something food-related happening in Chicagoland. Look to the chapter dedicated to food fêtes, including festivals and events.

Keeping Up with Food News

In this city, food journalists and bloggers abound. Each covers Chicago's cuisine scene from a slightly different angle.

Edible Chicago (www.ediblechicago.com) is published four times a year and is available at farmers' markets and gourmet food stores, with the goal of connecting readers with their food, telling stories of local producers, and providing inspiration for those interested in sustainable living.

LTHForum.com is an Internet-based culinary chat site and virtual "dining society" moderated by David Hammond, a WBEZ-FM (91.5) contributor. It skews toward undiscovered, mom-and-pop destinations and features a weekly roundup of food media. A definitive resource for food lovers, LTHF's highly anticipated Great Neighborhood Restaurants guide is available in downloadable, pocketbook format.

The *Chicago Reader*—hipsters' alt weekly of note—covers Chicago's dining scene through Mike Sula's journalistic eye.

Venerable food writer Michael Nagrant's online **Hungry** (www .hungrymag.com) takes a witty—though downright approachable—

look at food and cooking, striking a balance between the farm-to-table sensibility and guilty pleasures. The 'zine's food imagery, features, dining reviews, and chef-centric podcasts deserve props.

Sky Full of Bacon (www.skyfullofbacon .com/blog) is the launching pad for Michael Gebert's blog and thought-provoking video food podcasts on Chicago and Midwestern food.

Dana Joy Altman's blog, **Real Food Rehab** (www.realfoodrehab .blogspot.com), provides salt-of-the-earth advice and recipes that promote "authentic" living and the pleasures of good food.

Little Locavores (www.littlelocavores.blogspot.com) is a blog from Melissa Graham, attorney-turned-caterer and membership chair of Green City Market. It's dedicated to living sustainably in Chicago.

Digging In (www.blogs.suntimes.com/food), the *Chicago Sun-Times'* food blog, is speared by Food Editor extraordinaire Janet Fuller. It's loaded with inspiring recipes and tidbits on Chicago's dining scene. The paper's food section proper appears each Wednesday; turn to it for tempting recipes and info on food-related festivities.

The Stew (www.chicagotribune.com/features/food/stew) is penned by the *Chicago Tribune*'s Good Eating and Dining staffs, and it's loaded with timely food- and drink-related news. Its most interesting commentary comes from Monica Eng, an intrepid reporter whose pieces have stirred up many a spirited discussion. Phil Vettel is the *Chicago Tribune*'s respected dining critic.

Restaurants to Watch For:

GT Fish & Oyster, 531 N. Wells St., River North, Chicago, IL 60654; (312) 929-3501; www.gtfishandoyster.wordpress.com. The BOKA Group's small plates venture with Giuseppe Tentori. (See recipe on p. 344.)

Grant Achatz's by-advance-ticket dining establishment, Next (www.nextrestaurant.com), and redefined cocktail bar, Aviary (www.theaviarychicago.com), located adjacent to one another at 953-955 W. Fulton Market, West Loop, Chicago, IL 60607.

The Doughnut Vault, 401 N. Franklin St., River North, Chicago, IL 60654. A River North doughnut shop from restaurateur Brendan Sodikoff (Gilt Bar, Maude's Liquor Bar), located in the building that houses sib, Gilt Bar.

Slurping Turtle, 116 W. Hubbard St., River North, Chicago, IL 60654. An izakaya-style spot for Japanese tapas and noodles from Takashi Yagihashi.

If you eat and/or drink in the city, you're bound to encounter *Time Out Chicago* magazine (http://chicago.timeout.com), a source for restaurant reviews, news, chef interviews, and dining trends. Food-types also turn to its reader-generated Eat Out Awards and the staff's annual "100 Best Things We Ate (and Drank)."

Chicago magazine's **Dish** (www.chicagomag.com/Radar/Dish), overseen by Penny Pollack, is a weekly food newsletter that may be viewed online or delivered via e-mail. The food section in the magazine proper is worth a look, too.

Chicagoist (http://chicagoist.com) is a city-centric website and blog covering Chicago happenings, which, naturally, includes food.

Chicago Bites (www.chicagobites.com) is a destination for independent restaurant reviews, food-related podcasts, and food-related news and events from Bridget Houlihan and Tammy Green, who also custom-design dining tours for food-curious locals and tourists.

Grub Street Chicago (http://chicago.grubstreet.com) is the local offshoot of nymag.com/Menupages. It's an entertaining resource for daily food news, including openings and closings, as well as industry observations.

Steve Dolinsky (a.k.a. "The Hungry Hound," www.stevedolinsky .com) is a Chicago food-broadcaster-turned-avid-eater, occasional *Iron Chef* judge, and blogger who also creates podcasts.

Chicago Gapers Block: Drive Thru (www.gapersblock.com/ drivethru) is the food and drink arm of the Chicago-minded web pub, delivering news and observations on Chicago food.

Serious Eats dispenses food news and commentary on Chicago at www.seriouseats.com/tags/Chicago.

Adding local content to Curbed Network's snarky national food blog, **Eater Chicago** (http://chicago.eater.com) provides food coverage, news niblets, and commentary courtesy of Ari Bendersky.

For a humorous—okay, downright irreverent—take on the food scene, check out **Chicago Gluttons** (www.chicagogluttons.com).

Providing a wealth of information on restaurants and hotels both nationally and abroad, **Gayot.com** is packed with dining reviews, travel guides, and helpful themed best-of lists.

Metromix (www.chicago.metromix.com) is an online entertainment guide covering dining, nightlife, music, and events.

312 Dining Diva (www.312diningdiva.com) is Audarshia Townsend's dining and drinking blog, a source for of-the-moment info on openings, closings, and happenings around town.

A free e-mail daily, **Tasting Table** (www.tastingtable.com) uncovers unique food, dining, and libations in Chicago.

North

Albany Park, Andersonville, Argyle Street, Devon Avenue, Edgebrook, Edgewater, Edison Park, Jefferson Park, Lincoln Square, North Park, Norwood Park, Ravenswood, Rogers Park, Sauganash, Uptown

Chicago has more than 200 neighborhoods and 75-plus communities (some sharing the same name). Confusingly, boundaries are often open for interpretation, sometimes redefined and—admittedly—fluid.

That said, the city's densely populated northern reaches are home to culinarily rich, ethnic enclaves. Among them: Devon Avenue—Chicago's so-called "Little India"—and Argyle Street in Uptown, with its bounty of Vietnamese foodstuffs. Not to be overlooked is charming Andersonville, once an epicenter of Swedish culture. These days its cheery, hip—not to mention, diverse—restaurants hold court with funky bars and LGBT-friendly businesses.

Whatever your speed—heartwarming Thai, glistening barbecue duck, or aromatic *chile en nogada*—find it right here.

Agami, 4712 N. Broadway, Uptown, Chicago, IL 60640; (773) 506-1845; www.agamisushi.com; Sushi/Japanese; $$$. Nestled in the historic Goldblatt's building, this thoroughly modern Japanese den turns out wacky rolls amid underwater-themed surrounds. Grab a curvaceous, semiprivate booth, and make short work of the spicy tuna "rice crispy," crisped rice, topped with tuna tartare and a shard of fresh jalapeño. Of the specialty maki, the Ocean Drive—spicy mayo-swathed tuna, yellowtail, avocado, cilantro, and peppers in cod sheets with chile oil and lime—shines. The kitchen turns out competent cooked dishes, too.

Al Primo Canto, 5414 W. Devon Ave., Edgebrook, Chicago, IL 60646; (773) 631-0100; www.alprimocanto.com; Brazilian/Italian; $$$. A chicken lover's answer to the *churrascaria,* this handsome *galeteria* with a fixed-price approach serves never-ending, marinated, cooked-over-hardwood rotisserie birds, plus leg of lamb and beef, in family-style fashion. Ordering a la carte is an option, too. Though all they'll do is fill you up prematurely, a selection of sides come with all-you-can-eat meals. Meanwhile, bruschetta (try the ricotta, pistachio, and honey) and other Italian-esque add-ons distract from the main event.

Anteprima, 5316 N. Clark St., Andersonville, Chicago, IL 60640; (773) 506-9990; anteprimachicago.net; Italian; $$$. Cute as a button, this rustic, regional Italian restaurant from Marty Fosse (ex-Spiaggia, Carlucci) goes well beyond what's red-sauced. The comfort-driven, highly seasonal selections—tangy, thyme-scented sweet-and-sour cipollini; peppery *strascinati* amatriciana tossed with tomatoes, pancetta, and chiles; tender, roasted rabbit with pickled peppers, rabbit conserva, and shelly beans—are extra-enjoyable when eaten on the flower-filled patio. Many atypical, affordable— but topnotch—Italian wines are offered by the quartino.

Argo Georgian Bakery, 2812 W. Devon Ave., Rogers Park, Chicago, IL 60659; (773) 764-6322; Bakery; $. Piping hot, crisp-crusted flatbreads, pastries, and flaky, mozzarella- and feta-filled *hachapuri* are the draw at this simple, honest Georgian bakery, where delights are turned out from domed ovens. Time things just right, though: bites are extra-ethereal when sampled fresh. Sweet tooths should finish with a *tapluna*—a sweet, honey-nut pie.

Arya Bhavan, 2508 W. Devon Ave., Rogers Park, Chicago, IL 60659; (773) 274-5800; www.aryabhavan.com; Indian/Pakistani; $$. Indian cuisine takes center stage at this vegetarian enclave, which features raw food on Monday evenings and a bountiful weekend buffet wafting with aromatic curries. On the menu, classic starters like samosas and cilantro-flecked *uthappam* team with paper-thin *dosa*, *jeera* rice and fragrant, complexly flavored North and South Indian curries and lentils.

Mobile Mayhem

At press time, one hurdle remained for food truck–frenzied Chicagoans: Law in the city proper dictates food cannot be prepared on board. Follow the debate—and any progress that ensues—at www.chicagofoodtrucks.com and via Twitter @chicagofoodtrux. However, plenty of trucks sure load up with prepared fare. Keep in mind some among the ever-growing list are seasonal, most are cash-only, and whereabouts are best followed via Twitter.

Matt Maroni's gaztro-wagon (www.gaztro-wagon.com/@wherezthewagon) specializes in signature naan-wiches.

Happy Bodega (www.happybodega.com/@happybodega) makes its way along the boulevards filled with coffee, tea, gelato, and sweet and savory "happy pockets," including one filled with Italian sausage, fennel, and feta.

Chicago All Fired Up (773-708-4561/@ chgoallfrup) turns out everything from jerk chicken to baby back ribs.

The area's first true mobile food truck with grub prepared on board is **Hummingbird Kitchen** in Evanston (www.hummingbirdkitchen.com/@hummingbirdtogo). It features oft-changing, laid-back fare, such as black-bean soup with cheddar, onions, and crème fraîche.

Three J's (773-667-1360) is a go-to for jerk chicken and catfish, smothered pork chops, and beef patties. Call the number to receive the truck's coordinates for pickup.

Sweet Miss Givings (www.sweetmissgivings.com/@SMGFoodTruck) donates half its profits to Chicago House—an organization helping the formerly homeless, who suffer from HIV/AIDS. Somehow, the red velvet cupcakes, biscotti, and brownies taste all the better for it.

Phillip Foss's Meatyballs Mobile (www.phillipfoss.net/@FossFood Trucks) divvies up glam sliders, including cola-bourbon BBQ Balls (pulled pork shoulder with red cabbage and apples).

Taking the prize for weirdest food truck is **tamaleria Tamalli Space Charros** (@tamalespaceship). Raúl Arreola, formerly of Mixteco Grill, consulted on the menu, which includes serrano-spiked guacamole and a shredded-pork tamale covered in black mole.

Cupcakes are being doled out by several spots at a rapid-fire rate. Options include **Flirty Cupcakes** (www.flirtycupcakes.com/@FlirtyCupcakes), **More Cupcakes** (www.morecupcakes.com/@themoremobile), and **The Cupcake Gallery** (www.cupcake-gallery.com/@webakecupcakes).

Sweet Ride (www.sweetridechi.com/@SweetRideChi) dispenses saccharine treats, such as whoopie pies, old-fashioned banana pudding, and Belgian dark-chocolate mousse.

Soul Vegetarian teams with Ste Martaen (www.stemartaen.com/food-truck/@stemartaen) to turn out meatless cheesesteaks, buffalo pitas, and tofu wraps.

Cary Taylor of The Southern hits the streets with **The Southern Mac** (www.thesouthernchicago.com/@thesouthernmac) serving mac and cheese, including a white cheddar take with caramelized onions and sun-dried tomatoes.

Ba Le, 5014 N. Broadway St., Uptown, Chicago, IL 60640; (773) 561-4424; www.balesandwich.com; Vietnamese/Bakery; $. When ordering from the counter of this bustling, modern storefront, plan ahead—you'll long for leftovers. The *banh mi* sandwiches are in a league of their own. Go with the lemongrass-marinated barbecue pork, particularly when nestled into a still-warm, house-baked baguette. When the mood strikes, add on spring rolls and sweet, layered *che* (pudding-like sweets) or *rau câu,* coconut jelly. Remember to procure extra loaves of baked bread to go—they freeze beautifully.

Bananas Foster Cafe, 1147 W. Granville Ave., Edgewater, Chicago, IL 60660; (773) 262-9855; www.bananasfostercafe.com; New American; $$. Come as you are to this relaxed nook, where full Irish breakfast and a hefty roster of creative hot cakes and French toast—such as lemon cheesecake and caramel apple—give way to a balsamic veg and Brie panini, British fish-and-chips, and skillet-fried chicken, served all day.

Big Jones, 5347 N. Clark St., Andersonville, Chicago, IL 60640; 773-275-5725; www.bigjoneschicago.com; Regional American; $$. Urbane yet inviting, Paul Fehribach (Shubas Tavern, Harmony Grill) puts grandma's cooking to shame. His coastal cuisine has farm-to-table leanings, and the quality ingredients show in the results. Fried green tomatoes, however they're served, are not to be missed. If you can, get them garnished with pickled shrimp. Other finds include pork belly, frisée and heirloom tomato cornbread panzanella; benne-crusted, honey-fig-glazed Gunthorp Farms chicken breast; and shrimp and Anson Mills cheese grits with tasso gravy. End with a pot of flowering chrysanthemum tea and pillowy, powder-sugared beignets.

Bistro Campagne, 4518 N. Lincoln Ave., Lincoln Square, Chicago, IL 60625; (773) 271-6100; www.bistrocampagne.com; French; $$$. Chef Michael Altenberg is committed to turning out dishes both classic and contemporary, crafted from seasonal, organic, and local ingredients. Whether your meal at this neighborhood bistro begins with escargots bathed in garlicky Pernod butter or ridiculously tender duck confit, beef short ribs with roasted bone marrow, or leg of lamb with flageolet beans and niçoise tapenade, the result is the same: comfort to the nth degree. When weather allows, ask for a seat on the lovely garden patio.

Blue Nile Ethiopian, 6118 N. Ravenswood Ave., Uptown, Chicago, IL 60660; (773) 465-6710; www.bluenilechicago.com; Ethiopian; $$. Blink and you'll overlook this simple strip-mall spot, where spongy, tangy *injera* "pancakes" stand in for silverware and service is well intentioned. Mouth-singeing *doro wat*—chicken stew with hard-boiled egg—is familiar and pleasing. *Yebeg alicha,* headily spiced, silken lamb stew redolent of garlic, and lentils simmered in fiery *berbere* sauce, are soul-soothing, too.

Broadway Cellars, 5900 N. Broadway, Edgewater, Chicago, IL 60660; (773) 944-1208; www.broadwaycellars.net; New American; $$. Date-perfect, this friendly eatery checks pretension at the door. Whether you sit in the dining room—all intimate with white-clothed tables—or on the outdoor patio, you'll be met with memorable, vino-minded dishes that are fairly priced. Get the yellowfin tuna puttanesca, its linguine studded with olives, capers, onions, and tomatoes. Likewise, the duck lasagna is fine.

Cafe Hoang, 1010 W. Argyle St., Uptown, Chicago, IL 60640; (773) 878-9943; www.cafehoang.com; Vietnamese; $$. It's requisite to begin with salads—lemony, basil-laden chicken; chile oil–laced duck; spicy, gingery lemon beef—when dining at this mainstay. The crispy pork, shrimp, and veg-flecked *ban xeo* pancake  and a bowl of noodle soup—such as *bun bo hue,* a meaty, spicy beef and pork-hock concoction enlivened by lime—are smart successors. When you don't want to trek to the Argyle strip, visit its Chinatown location: 232 W. Cermak Rd., (312) 674-9610.

Cafe Selmarie, 4729 N. Lincoln Ave., Lincoln Square, Chicago, IL 60625; (773) 989-5595; www.cafeselmarie.com; Bakery/Cafe; $$. A neighborhood institution (circa 1983) for light bites and breakfast—not to mention afternoon tea and early dinner—this popular bakery dishes up house-made granola and brioche French toast with berry compote, moving on to the more substantial croque Monsieur and Hungarian goulash as the day progresses. Both the lofty dining room and chill patio are populated by neighborhood types, many of whom like to linger.

Ceres' Table, 4882 N. Clark St., Edgewater, Chicago, IL 60460; (773) 878-4882; www.cerestable.com; New American; $$$. Composed and inviting at once, this blue-hued spot from Giuseppe Scurato (ex-Topaz Cafe) is named for the Roman goddess of agriculture and harvest. Appropriately, seasonality guides the contemporary—but never over-the-top—menu. Aromatic saffron risotto arancini with a gooey Taleggio core is a standout. Ditto the deftly prepared, shaved artichoke–mushroom salad, gone luxe with nutty wisps of Parmesan and lemon-truffle vinaigrette. Whether followed by pheasant with eggplant caponata, beans, and salsa verde or corzeti with fennel, anchovies, currants, and pine nuts, spot-on flavors prevail.

Chicago Brauhaus, 4732 N. Lincoln Ave., Lincoln Square, Chicago, IL 60625; (773) 784-4444; www.chicagobrauhaus.com; German; $$. It's always Oktoberfest at this buoyant *Biergarten,* one of the few remaining of its ilk. And while many of the Germans who settled in Lincoln Square are now gone, here at least the oompah lives on. Come famished and load up on rib-sticking fare, like onion and pickle-stuffed beef rouladen, wurst, schnitzel, and liver-dumpling soup. Expect free-flowing steins and plenty of kitsch—it all fuels the fun, especially when the Brauhaus Trio makes their nightly appearance, lederhosen and all.

Chopal Kabab & Steak, 2242 W. Devon Ave., Rogers Park, Chicago, IL 60659; (773) 338-4080; Pakistani; $. Artifacts and vibrant, intricately carved furniture adorn this Pakistani pad with a menu that yields grilled halal kebabs, spiced, yogurt-marinated lamb, and veal steaks. Buttery broccoli rabe and Chopal *lassi* are among the additional rewards.

City Provisions Deli, 1818 W. Wilson Ave., Ravenswood, Chicago, IL 60640; (773) 293-2489; www.cityprovisions.com; Deli; $. Healthy, ingredient-driven sandwiches and salads from caterer Cleetus Friedman highlight the bounty from area farms, while emphasizing product that is responsibly produced and humanely raised. That means everything from a TLT—a smoked, Rushing Waters trout sandwich with horseradish cream, leaf lettuce, and tomato on brioche—to Sriracha egg salad. Friedman also hosts supper clubs with distillers and brewers as well as farm dinners.

Demera Ethiopian, 4801 N. Broadway, Uptown, Chicago, IL 60640; (773) 334-8787; www.demeraethiopianrestaurant.com; Ethiopian; $$. This homey, casual Ethiopian eatery is a go-to for vegetarians and spice-seeking carnivores in equal parts. Start with crisp beef or spinach *sambussa*—both requisite precursors to communal platters (*messob*) of *doro wat;* wicked-hot, *berbere*-sauced chicken; *gomen* (greens); and *kitfo,* spiced beef tartare. Finish with house-roasted Ethiopian coffee—though not before sipping its homemade honey wine.

Dong Ky, 4877 N. Broadway St., Uptown, Chicago, IL 60640; (773) 989-5579; Vietnamese/Chinese; $. There's not much in the way of ambience at this goofily named hole-in-the-wall adjacent to Broadway Supermarket. Fortunately, the super-cheap, very fresh fare will leave you singing its praises right quick. Skip the *pho* in favor of *bun,* complex, salty-sweet—and, yes, a bit funky—rice-stick noodle dishes. Or, opt for the *quang,* a slightly brothy egg-noodle concoction. There are enough selections covering the rest of the Asian repertoire (Szechuan chicken, shrimp egg foo young) to sate less adventuresome diners.

The Elephant, 5348 W. Devon Ave. Edgebrook, Chicago, IL 60646; (773) 467-1168; www.the elephantthai.com; Thai; $. Thai classics, including chicken satay and pad Thai are on hand, but come for the home-style and special-menu offerings, which are cooked with devotion. The papaya salad, lovingly cut by hand, is bright and—upon request—fiery as all get-out, while *larb,* sprinkled with toasted, ground rice, practically sparkles.

Ethiopian Diamond; 6120 N. Broadway St., Edgewater, Chicago, IL 60660; (773) 338-6100; www.ethiopiandiamondcuisine.com; Ethiopian; $$. Bright, cheery and authentic, this stew lover's para-dise delivers Ethiopian classics, plenty of them vegetarian, which are scooped up with pleasantly sour *injera* flatbread. A safe, always satisfying bet, are the *wats,* stews simmered in spicy sauce, or *tibs,* cubed meats burnished with pepper and onion-flecked sauce. There is also a location at 7537 N. Clark St., (773) 764-2200.

Fat Cat, 4840 N. Broadway St., Uptown, Chicago, IL 60640; (773) 506-3100; www.fatcatbar.com; American; $$. A notch above your average pub, this perpetually packed, Art Deco–inspired tap turns out a house-made corn dog trio and a grilled jack-cheese sandwich with basil pesto, tomatoes, and roasted garlic. However, it's really the braised pork belly Cuban—stuffed with crunchy cabbage slaw, oozy Swiss, and pickles—that gives pause. An ample selection of craft beer and fun cocktails add to its festive feel.

First Slice Pie Cafe, 4401 N. Ravenswood Ave., Ravenswood, Chicago, IL 60640; (773) 506-7380; www.firstslice.org; Cafe; $. Dine for a cause at this nonprofit eatery from l'École des Arts Culinaires–trained Mary Ellen Diaz (North Pond, Printer's Row). Located in the Lillstreet Art Center, proceeds from its menu selections—whether chocolate–peanut butter pie, chopped salad, or fancified lasagna—go to community kitchens, which in turn prepare quality meals for families in need. There's also a shareholder program, for which subscribers receive weekly meals while contributing the same quality fare to the hungry. There are additional locations.

Furama, 4936 N. Broadway St., Uptown, Chicago, IL 60640; (773) 271-1161; www.furamachicago.com; Asian; $$. Expect a diverse, reliable, and brisk dim sum encounter at this cavernous place, where dumplings—chive-flecked pork, shrimp with green onion—chewy barbecue ribs, and panfried pot stickers are musts. Love goes to the silken egg custard, too.

Gale Street Inn, 4914 N. Milwaukee Ave., Jefferson Park, Chicago, IL 60630; (773) 725-1300; www.galestreet.com; American; $$. For over four decades, this legendary joint has doled out trademark tender barbecue ribs alongside soul-satisfying jambalaya, traditional steaks, chops, and seafood. Midweek specials court budget-conscious diners of the silver-haired persuasion, a fact that's furthered by early bird specials on London broil and half racks of baby backs. Waits can be long on weekends, so belly up to the bar.

gaztro-wagon, 5973 N. Clark St., Edgewater, Chicago, IL 60660; (773) 942-6152; www.gaztro-wagon.com; Eclectic; $. Matt Maroni—founder of chicagofoodtrucks.com—has been instrumental in mobilizing Chicago's burgeoning food truck scene. His casual storefront both sells and preps mobile "naan-wiches," which he then dispenses from a roving, converted UPS truck. But traditionalists also may visit Maroni's brick-and-mortar digs for hand-helds like sweetly piquant wild boar belly with dates, blue cheese, romesco sauce, and onions. Seasonal soups and in-house fish and oyster po' boys on Friday and Saturday nights are added boons.

Glenn's Diner, 1820 W. Montrose Ave., Ravenswood, Chicago, IL 60613; (773) 506-1720; www.glennsdiner.com; American/Seafood; $$. A reimagined diner from a Davis Street Fishmarket vet proves an easy option for eggy eats and over two-dozen types of cereal, served all day. However, it's the crazy-fresh Alaskan king crab legs and dozen-plus simply prepared, fresh fish options daily that steal the show. Keep your eye on the specials, which may include a colossal prawn "cocktail," blue striped marlin, Idaho brook trout, or potato-crusted walleye.

Great Lake, 1477 W. Balmoral Ave., Andersonville, Chicago, IL 60640; 773-334-9270; Pizza; $$. Queue up with diehards to wait—and wait—for Nick Lessins and Lydia Esparza's amazing, painstakingly handcrafted pies topped with the very best artisanal ingredients. Get the bubbly, blistered, chewy crust topped with zucchini, aged cheese, and generous turns of black pepper, adding pepperoni for flourish. Or swoon over the vibrant tomato-sauced take, dappled with homemade mozzarella and aged Wisconsin sheep and cow's milk cheeses, whirled with olive oil and finished with a sprinkle of sea salt. It's only open Wednesday through Saturday.

Hae Woon Dae, 6240 N. California Ave., Rogers Park, Chicago, IL 60659; 773-764-8018; Korean; $$. Pay no mind to the strip-mall setting. This campfire-scented Korean barbecue has the requisites right. Snack on a bevy of *panchan,* from pickled turnips to kim-chee. Then, roll up your sleeves for a DIY approach, sizzling quality meats—soy and sesame oil–marinated *kalbi,* pork *bulgogi*—for mere seconds atop white-hot coals. Wrap the charred results in lettuce leaves, zapped with sauce and accompanied by *soju* to temper the heat.

Hai Yen, 1055 W. Argyle St., Uptown, Chicago, IL 60640, (773) 561-4077; www.haiyenrestaurant.com; Vietnamese; $$. If you only get one thing at this newbie-friendly Argyle Street eatery, make it the *bo la lot,* grilled beef sausages, wrapped in betel leaves. Also a winner is the showy, lime-spurted *chao tom,* grilled, ground shrimp balls speared with sugarcane and served with a salt-pepper mix for dredging. Both the lotus root and banana blossom salads are sprightly and fresh, while roll-your-own rice paper dishes afford a customizable, DIY experience. Order a glass of *chanh,* bubbly lime soda, and finish with the sweet, battered bananas. Its sleek, Lincoln Park sister is at 2723 N. Clark St., (773) 868-4888.

Hamburger Mary's, 5400 N Clark St., Andersonville, Chicago, IL 60640; (773) 784-6969; www.hamburgermarys.com/chicago; American/Burgers; $$. An offshoot of the San Francisco original, this lively, gay-friendly hang is welcoming to all, its laughably named burgers the star of the show. Try the Queen Mary with cheddar and jack cheeses, grilled onions, bacon, and "special" sauce. Sandwiches—as well as a fried Twinkie, provided you don't have a heart problem— stave off hunger pangs. Next door, the Rec Room—an adjunct sports bar—serves house-brewed beers. Upstairs, Mary's Attic exudes a nightclub vibe, complete with karaoke, cabaret acts, and DJ beats.

Heartland Cafe, 7000 N. Glenwood Ave., Rogers Park, Chicago, IL 60621; (773) 465-8005; www.heartlandcafe.com; Vegetarian/ Eclectic; $$. On the scene since 1976, this community epicenter consists of a restaurant, bar, and general store stocked with kitschy, silly toys. Catering largely to vegetarians though its repertoire extends well beyond, the restaurant's focus is kept organic and local. Turn to the specials; if you're lucky they will include phyllo-encased, double-cream Brie with brandy-fig compote or vegan pasta primavera. But you can do no wrong with the substantial black-bean burger and pecan-crusted ruby-red trout with fruit salsa. Live acts—from singer-songwriters to rockabilly musicians—perform regularly. Sibling **Red Line Tap,** 7006 N. Glenwood Ave., (773) 274-5463, is a prime place to watch games.

Hema's Kitchen, 2439 W. Devon Ave., Rogers Park; (773) 338-1627; www.hemaskitchen.com; Indian/ Pakistani; $$. Crowds flock to Hema Potla's inviting Indian BYOB, where flaky, cilantro and pea–spiked vegetable or ground-lamb samosas are an onslaught of flavor. Meanwhile, chickpea flour–battered potato chips go beyond the norm. Sizzling tandoori chicken, devilish vindaloo, and lentils fragrant with cumin follow suit. There is a second location at 2411 N. Clark St., (773) 527-1705.

Hon Kee, 1064 W Argyle St., Uptown, Chicago, IL 60640; (773) 878-6650; Chinese; $. Lacquered barbecue ducks hang like beacons in the window, luring diners inside this bare-bones joint. Noodle-packed soups and crisp, roast pork with scrambled eggs are among the reasons to dawdle. Traditional dishes—from egg foo young to lo mein, chop suey, and fried rice—are packed with flavor, though it's the ethereal shrimp dumpling soup that is most likely to leave you hooked.

Hyderabad House, 2225 W. Devon Ave., Rogers Park, Chicago, IL 60659; (773) 381-1230; Indian; $. Score meat-centric South Indian dishes around-the-clock at this cabbie favorite, which dishes up chicken masala and chicken paratha that challenge your flame threshold—along with beef *boti*—for near-cents. Shoot a game of pool before heading out the door.

Icosium Kafé, 5200 N. Clark St., Andersonville, Chicago, IL 60648; (773) 271-5233; www.icosiumkafechicago.com; African; $$. Don't pass on this Algerian creperie, where organic veggies and halal meats burst from their signature, paper-thin confines. Get one jammed with toasted almonds, wilted spinach, raisins, caramelized onions, mint, sun-dried tomato tapenade, and a touch of cream cheese, adding some nicely spiced *merguez* into the mix. You may also customize your own, or get creations in salad form. Breakfast crepes, be they blueberry, rose petal jam, and Brie or pecan, fig jam, and feta, are tasty as well. Order honeyed mint tea alongside.

Jamaica Jerk, 1631 W. Howard St., Rogers Park, Chicago, IL 60626; (773) 764-1546; www.jamaicajerk-il.com; Caribbean; $$. These West Indies wonders will warm you up—and tide you over until that island escape. Bring your own hooch to mix with pineapple sorrel or limeade, and settle in the ocean-toned, lattice-flanked dining room, which is presided over by a Cooking and Hospitality Institute of Chicago–trained chef. By the time the curry goat, tangy, pickled escoveitched fish, and tolerably hot jerk chicken arrive, you'll have forgotten the outdoor temps. For a sweet finish, linger over homemade Grape-Nut or rum-raisin ice cream.

Jin Ju, 5203 N. Clark St., Andersonville, Chicago, IL 60640; (773) 334-6377; Korean; $$. The elevated, enjoyable fare served in these low-lit digs draws daters seeking a solid—albeit not particularly authentic—meal. This bodes well for those less than familiar with Korean cuisine. Still, the consensus agrees the *bulgogi,* bibimbap, and spirited *soju* cocktails are good.

J.K. Kabab House, 6412 N. Rockwell Ave., Rogers Park, Chicago, IL 60645; (773) 761-6089; www.jkkababhouse.com; Indian/Pakistani; $. Grilled kebabs in several forms (try the ground beef *seekh*), plus charcoal-grilled chicken *tikka,* lentils mingling with tender cubes of lamb, and *roti* attract a low-key clientele, both here and at 2402 W. Army Trail Rd., Hanover Park, (630) 830-6089.

Katsu, 2651 W. Peterson Ave., Rogers Park, Chicago, IL 60659; (773) 784-3383; Japanese; $$$. Standing head and shoulders above most sushi bars, this intimate eatery is a stalwart for staggeringly fresh sashimi platters, a deep-fried fish appetizer that is the stuff of dreams, and a generous sake selection perfect for pairing. Also memorable: the luxe super-white *toro maki*. Special touches, perhaps gold leaf or flower garnishes, give dining an extra-special feel, despite straightforward surroundings.

Khan BBQ, 2401 W. Devon Ave., Rogers Park, Chicago, IL 60659; (773) 274-8600; www.khanbbq.net; Indian/Pakistani; $$. Cheap eats and casual environs benchmark this Indo-Pak, a go-to for incomparable kebabs and chicken *boti*. From the charcoal-grilled tandoori chicken to fish and stewy riches, the endlessly flavorful finds—though it hardly seems fair—cost next to nothing.

La Cocina de Frida, 5403 N. Clark St., Andersonville, Chicago, IL 60640; (773) 271-1907; www.lacocinadefrida.com; Mexican; $$. Stick with the classics at this muraled, sister-run eatery named for—and decorated in homage to—Frida Kahlo. Chicken in smoky, silky *mole negro* and *carne asada* are solid, and the orange, pink and brown-hued space, ramshackle dishware, and Oaxacan pottery are nothing short of charming. Its more sedate sibling, **Frida's,** is located at 3755 N. Southport Ave., (773) 935-2330.

La Fonda Latino, 5350 N. Broadway, Edgewater, Chicago, IL 60640; (773) 271-3935; Colombian/Pan-Latin; $$. Colombian fare

Skip the Standards

Typically, when most "outsiders" think of Chicago, stalwarts—hot dogs, deep-dish pizza, Italian beef—come to mind. The thing is, there are far more interesting eats with Windy City roots.

The Mother-in-Law sandwich, available at **Ramova Grill** (see p. 190), consists of a corn tamale tucked into a hot dog bun and blanketed with chili.

The **Maxwell Street Polish,** championed by places like **Jim's Original** (312-733-7820; www.jimsoriginal.com), consists of a grilled or fried sausage, smothered in grilled onions, squeezed with yellow mustard, topped with sport peppers, and placed in a bun. It is believed to date back to the original **Maxwell Street Market** (see p. 292).

The Freddy, available at **Chuck's Pizza** (773-233-4282; www .chuckspizzachicago.com), is a griddled Italian sausage patty sandwich on French bread, topped with sautéed green peppers, red sauce, and mozzarella. It is thought to have originated on the city's Southwest Side.

dominates the menu, though the flavors of Mexico and Argentina shine through at this chill spot, where killer margaritas meet a menu of beef empanadas dotted with plump raisins, a *chimichurri*-bolstered *churrasco* and *sobrebarriga,* meltingly tender, slow-simmered flank steak with black beans and rice.

La Unica, 1515 W. Devon Ave., Rogers Park, Chicago, IL 60660; (773) 274-7788, Cuban/Latin; $. Stocked with Peruvian, Mexican, and Cuban necessities, this market also houses a hidden gem of a

The Jibarito, first realized at **Borinquen Restaurant**'s California Avenue location (see p. 76), is a garlicky, steak (or other meat), cheese, and lettuce sandwich, cradled by smashed plantains rather than bread.

The Big Baby, a specialty at **Nicky's Drive-Through** (773-238-2855), is a distinct style of hamburger, believed to hail from Greek restaurants on the Southwest Side. It consists of two griddled, greasy patties with gooey American cheese between. Topped with grilled onions, pickles, mustard, and ketchup, the tasty mess is held by a grilled, meat-juice-saturated sesame bun.

Shrimp de Jonghe, the brainchild of Belgian-born Henri De Jonghe at his namesake South Side restaurant in the late 1800s, is a butterflied, whole-shrimp casserole covered in garlic-laden breadcrumbs laced with sherry. Try it at **Krapils the Great Steak** (see p. 247).

cafe in back. Line up for the mustard-kissed Cuban, which delivers a dose of piquant pickles, tender pork, melty Swiss, and ham perfectly sandwiched between crisped bread. Also winning are the garbanzo soup, flavorful black beans, and arroz con pollo. For a real bargain, sample the crazy-cheap snacks, including croquettes.

LM Restaurant, 4539 N. Lincoln Ave., Lincoln Square, Chicago, IL 60640; (773) 942-7585; www.lmrestaurant.com. French $$$. The bistro concept gets a gastropub spin in the former Tallulah space, where Bradford Phillips (Blackbird, NoMI) prepares a frequently changing, three-course prix fixe as well as sautéed sweetbreads with sunchoke puree, brussels sprouts leaves, and vanilla brown butter; whitefish atop Burgundy snail *ragù;* and roasted leg of lamb with slow-roasted shoulder, green lentils, and tomato jam. A Parisian sandwich counterpart is located in the **Chicago French Market:** 131 N. Clinton St., (312) 575-0306.

Lutz Continental Cafe & Pastry Shop, 2458 W. Montrose Ave., Ravenswood, Chicago, IL 60618; (773) 478-7785; lutzbakery.com; Bakery/German; $$. You'll be tempted by the pastry case—as well you should. It's the flaky strudels, towering, multilayered cakes and tortes, marzipan, and delicate pastries that incite satisfied sighs. So, as passable as the butter-crusted quiche Lorraine, goulash, and senior citizen–style sandwiches may be, it's a slice of chocolate strawberry whipped-cream cake—accompanied by Viennese-style coffee—that's divine. In summer, seats in the flower-filled outdoor garden are prime real estate.

Marigold, 4832 N. Broadway, Uptown, Chicago, IL 60640; (773) 293-4653; www.marigoldrestaurant.com; Indian; $$$. Not your average Indian experience, this romantic, mosaic-accented dining room sparks excitement with cilantro-accented, mango powder and paprika-spiced corn salad; fragrant, silkily sauced *saag paneer;* and aromatic, spice-rubbed duck confit with sizzled green beans and tomato chutney. Naan-wiches cater to light eaters; inventive cocktails and frequent specials are perks.

Mekato's Colombian Bakery, 5423 N. Lincoln Ave., Lincoln Square, Chicago, IL 60625; (773) 784-5181; www.mekatos.com; Colombian/Bakery; $. Customers—many Colombian— file in to procure house-made, electric-yellow empanadas, *chicharrones,* and *arepas* with savory chorizo from this inviting bakery-cafe. Those in the know also save room for *dulce de leche*–laced sweets. Juices—from pas- sion fruit to oatmeal—and imported dry goods, such as guava paste, flour, and candy, fill a need.

m. henry, 5707 N Clark St., Edgewater, Chicago, IL 60660; (773) 561-1600; http://mhenry.net; New American; $$. Modernized, organic-leaning a.m. eats—dulce banana rumba French toast with raisins and toasted pecans, a heaping fried-egg sandwich with applewood bacon and Gorgonzola—attract loyalists to this sunlit daytime cafe. Later, opt for design-your-own grilled cheese (perhaps sour boule, stuffed with pears and walnut pesto), and consider grab- bing pies, muffins, and savory flatbreads on the fly. Sibling **m. hen- rietta** (1133 W Granville Ave., 773-761-9700) also serves dinner.

Moody's Pub, 5910 N Broadway St., Edgewater, Chicago, IL 60660; (773) 275-2696; www.moodyspub.com; Burgers; $$. Touted in equal parts are the burger and beer garden at this casual pub, where Goose Island 312 flows from the taps, sides are customarily deep-fried, and peanuts top the candlelit tables inside. When it's cold, grab a bench by the flickering fireplaces, order your half-pounder with cheese, and soak up the dark-cozy setting and convivial scene.

Mysore Woodlands, 2548 W. Devon Ave., Rogers Park, Chicago IL, 60659; (773) 338-8160; www.mysore woodlands.info; Indian/Vegetarian; $$. Vegetarians dig the massive *dosa,* available in over a dozen varieties, plus other familiar vegetarian fare (think *saag paneer*). Nibble to your heart's content with combination plates, which come with a host of accoutrements and dessert. Check out the *payasam,* raisin-and cashew-stippled vermicelli pudding.

Mythos, 2032 W. Montrose Ave., Lincoln Square, Chicago, IL 60618; (773) 334-2000; www.mythoschicago.com; Greek; $$$. Offering a refreshing change of pace, one that deviates from Greektown she-nanigans, this serene, sister-run taverna serves standbys. However, here the *saganaki* isn't flamed tableside; just-charred *loukaniko (Greek sausage)* is made for the restaurant by design; and the gently sauced *pastitsio* arrives in an individual crock.

Nhu' Lan's Bakery, 2612 W. Lawrence Ave., Ravenswood, Chicago, IL 60625; (773) 878-9898; www.nhulansbakery.com; Vietnamese/Bakery; $. It doesn't get much better than the *banh mi* from this mostly carryout bakery, where crusty loaves are made in-house and finished with texturally triumphant cilantro-flecked daikon, carrot, and jalapeño "slaw." (Try the pork belly and pâté or grilled pork versions.) Veering in a different though no less satisfying direction is its sticky rice with Chinese sausage, spring rolls, and the array of fresh-fruit smoothies dotted with tapioca pearls.

Noon-O-Kabab, 4661 N Kedzie Ave., Albany Park, Chicago, IL 60625; (773) 279-8899; www.noonokabab.com; Persian; $. This perpetually packed, authentic Persian restaurant is known for its tender, flame-grilled kebabs (it's but a fool who bypasses the chicken) as well as its downy, dilled long-grain basmati, studded with lima beans and garlic. Skewers of shrimp, steak, and ground beef are great alternatives; minted Persian salad, smoky baba ghannouj, and saffron-scented dolma set the gold standard, too.

Pho 888, 1137 W. Argyle St., Uptown, Chicago, IL 60640; (773) 907-8838; Vietnamese; $. Petite and free of embellishments, this somewhat under-the-radar Vietnamese serves one amazing, highly fragrant bowl of *pho*. Come for the house-made *cha* (sausage), *banh mi,* and fresh, tissue-thin spring rolls as well.

Pho 777, 1065 W. Argyle St., Uptown, Chicago, IL 60640; (773) 561-9909; www.pho777chicago.com; Vietnamese; $. The anise-scented *pho* with all the trimmings is sustaining, filling, and incredibly satisfying, but it has nothing on the bright, minty beef salad, showered with peanuts and topped with cloudlike, crackling rice crackers. However, don't leave this endearing Argyle Street eatery without ordering the veggie-laden pan-fried noodles, slick with sweet-salty sauce and offset by barbecue pork, beef, and shrimp. It's the breakfast of champions.

Pho Xe Tang (a.k.a. Tank Noodle), 4953 N. Broadway St., Uptown, Chicago, IL 60640; (773) 878-2253; Vietnamese; $. The number of available options at this Argyle fave are overwhelming. The good news is it provides the most reliable, point-and-pick experience on the Argyle strip. Start with the *banh xeo,* sizzling, crisped pancakes studded with shrimp, pork, and sprouts. Follow with a bowl of fragrant *pho,* the perfect restorative for winter chills.

Pho Xua, 1020 W. Argyle St., Uptown, Chicago, IL 60640; (773) 271-9828; www.phoxuarestaurant.com; Vietnamese/Chinese; $. The most stylish option along the Argyle stretch, this noodle house does its namesake proud. Other winners include ramen soup bolstered by fried duck; tangy tamarind soup; and *bun bo hue.* It's not entirely about brothy bowls, however; the smoky-sweet, grilled beef wrapped in betel leaves and nest of citrus-y, julienned kohlrabi salad with shards of pork, shrimp, and cilantro sing with flavor.

Pizza D.O.C., 2251 W. Lawrence Ave., Lincoln Square, Chicago, IL 60625; (773) 784-8777; www.mypizzadoc.com; Pizza; $$. Neapolitan pies, both straightforward (Margherita) and sophisticated (*quattro stagioni* with prosciutto, mushrooms, olives, and artichokes) arrive from the wood-burning oven lightly charred. The pastas—carbonara specked with guanciale and homemade spinach gnocchi with blue cheese–mascarpone sauce—as well as classic 'tizers also merit consideration.

Reza's, 5255 N. Clark St., Andersonvlle, Chicago, IL 60640; (773) 561-1898; www.rezasrestaurant.com; Persian; $$. This popular mini-empire with River North and Oak Brook outposts serves no brainer Persian plates, including many vegetarian options. Most memorable on the super-sized menu: grilled, garlic-buttered mushrooms; ground beef *koobideh* and moist-but-charred chicken skewers; and fluffy, generously dilled rice.

RoPa Restaurant & Wine Bar, 1146 W. Pratt Blvd., Rogers Park, Chicago, IL 60626; (773) 465-6500; www.roparestaurant.com; Wine Bar/Mediterranean; $$. Filling a neighborhood niche, this tiled, wood-trimmed Mediterranean haunt attracts residents with affordable, vino-friendly small and large plates. Start with flaky, egg roll–like feta *burek,* dolma filled with pine nut-studded rice, or homey lentil soup, followed by *kofta* or kebabs, of which there are several kinds.

Sahara Kabob, 6649 N. Clark St., Rogers Park, Chicago, IL 60618; (773) 262-2000; www.saharakabob.com; Middle Eastern/Assyrian; $. Smoky, chunky baba ghannouj, fall-apart, tender lamb shank, flavorful falafel, *lahmim beajin*—a spicy, meat-topped flatbread—they're all good at this simple Assyrian storefront with serious following. Bountiful portions and budget-conscious prices make any question of dining here a done deal.

Salam, 4634 N. Kedzie Ave., Albany Park, Chicago, IL 60625; (773) 583-0776; www.salamchicago.com; Middle Eastern; $. Get the crisp outside, crumbly inside falafel while it's hot and you'll be met with some of the best in town. The no-frills establishment also hits high notes for its silky hummus; sprightly *fattoush* and Jerusalem salads; and tasty kebabs and kofta.

San Soo Gab San, 5247 N. Western Ave., Lincoln Square, Chicago, IL 60625; (773) 334-1589; Korean; $$. Wildly popular with late-night boozehounds, this classic Korean barbecue allows you to sear your own grub on tabletop grills, munching on a generous array of *panchan* practically around the clock. Though you'll leave its wood confines smelling of smoke, the *kalbi* certainly is worth its weight in coals—even when served by a not so welcoming staff.

Semiramis, 4639 N. Kedzie Ave., Albany Park, Chicago, IL 60625; 773-279-8900; www.semiramisrestaurant.com; Lebanese; $$. Airy and cheery, this cute, from-scratch cafe deserves accolades for its fresh salads (try the lemony, parsley-packed tabbouleh), meze (including the minty, slatherable fava mash called *foul*), and garlicky *toum*. The rotisserie chicken, which comes with *lavosh* and salad or rice, has its own fan club; then again, so does the lamb and beef shawarma, which is offset by hunks of eggplant and pickles. Be sure to order cinnamon-scented *maamoul,* too.

Silver Seafood, 4829 N. Broadway St., Uptown, Chicago, IL 60640; (773) 784-0668; www.silverseafoodrestaurant.com; Chinese/Seafood; $$. Specializing, not surprisingly, in fare from the watery deep, this popular Cantonese kitchen delivers a spot-on experience, provided you order right. Regulars make fast tracks for the Chinese menu (translated), which bypasses Americanized standards in favor of the more exotic: shark's fin soup, pigeon with planks of green onion, and birds nest. Once tried, though, it's hard to order beyond the salt-and-pepper squid or fried flounder.

Smak Tak, 5961 N. Elston Ave., Jefferson Park, Chicago, IL 60646; (773) 763-1123; www.smaktak.com; Polish; $$. An Old-World vibe permeates this hidden-but-hyped Polish "lodge," where the hearty—and, yes, heavy—sustenance is downright sublime. No one can resist the glistening, lacy potato pancakes, which are garnished with sour cream and applesauce. Plump, perfect pierogies and meaty, vibrantly sauced cabbage rolls have no rival, while the Hungarian-style potato pancake—bursting with goulash goodness—justifies a bit of waistline expansion.

Spacca Napoli, 1769 W. Sunnyside Ave., Ravenswood, Chicago, IL 60640; (773) 878-2420; www.spaccanapolipizzeria.com; Pizza; $$. Devotees can't get enough of the thin, oak-fired Neapolitan pizzas topped with quality ingredients. Running faves include the basil-flecked Margherita and Funghi e Salsiccia, crowned with Fior di Latte mozzarella, basil, mushrooms, and fennel-perfumed Italian sausage. For something a bit more luxe, though, go with the Bianco Nero, a Pecorino, porcini, and black truffle-topped beauty. The wine and beer list get the job done.

Spoon, 4608 N. Western Ave., Lincoln Square, Chicago, IL 60625; (773) 769-1173; www.spoonthai.com; Thai; $$. Go outside of your comfort zone at this authentic, top-tier restaurant with a traditional and translated Thai menu. Order some items from the latter, perhaps the Isaan-style pork-rice sausage and jerky with flaming, tangy tamarind sauce. From the fabulous fried chicken to bracing banana blossom salad, sour, spicy tamarind shrimp curry, and explosively flavorful *naem khao thawt*—rice salad dotted with ham—there are reasons for repeat visits.

Sunshine Cafe, 5449 N. Clark St., Andersonville, Chicago, IL 60640; (773) 334-6214; Japanese; $. As unassuming as a home-style Japanese kitchen, this quaint cafe isn't much to look at. However, the perfect sukiyaki, filled with glass noodles and shards of rib eye and topped with an optional cracked egg; crisp-skinned, flaky grilled mackerel; and *tonkatsu* command attention. Even the potato croquettes, *musubi,* and miso are more memorable than most.

Sun Wah Bar-B-Q Restaurant, 5041 N. Broadway, Uptown, Chicago, IL 60640; (773) 769-1254; www.sunwahbbq.com; Chinese/

Barbecue; $. Get the duck—make that anything with duck or pork—at this stellar, Hong Kong–style Chinese barbecue, where you can customize your own brothy, chewy noodle-filled bowls. Roast duck on rice is eminently satisfying—likewise the duck with pan-fried noodles, the glimmering barbecued pork, and the barbecue duck. The setting is simple, but the food is anything but ho-hum.

Superdawg Drive-in, 6363 N. Milwaukee Ave., Norwood Park, Chicago, IL 60646; (773) 763-0660; www.superdawg.com. Hot Dogs; $. This neon-lit, car hop-equipped red-hot stand—dating back to 1948—is larger than life. And while it holds court among Chicago-style dogs, here a pickled green tomato topper stands in for tomato. Add in crinkle-cut fries and straw-defying, pint-sized milkshakes, and it's easy to see how the kitsch caught on. There is a second locale at 333 S. Milwaukee Ave., Wheeling, (847) 459-1900.

Swedish Bakery, 5348 N. Clark St., Andersonville, Chicago, IL 60640; (773) 561-8919; www.swedishbakery.com; Bakery/Swedish; $. It's always crowded at this 1929 fixture, where generations of sweet tooths succumb to Swedish treats. Expect an incomparable collection of cardamom-scented breads, chocolate custard cake rolls, and ganache treasures as well as marzipan-enrobed slices, Bundts, cookies, coffeecakes, and tortes. This cavity-inducing destination is a favorite among brides-to-be.

Tampopo, 5665 N. Lincoln Ave., Rogers Park, Chicago, IL 60659; (773) 561-2277; www.tampopochicago.com; Japanese/Sushi; $$. Sushi and noodles every which way—from udon to ramen and soba—are the hook at this spot named for a Juzo Itami flick. But the lengthy appetizer selection brings the focus back to food. Start with lightly fried oysters or crunchy tempura green beans, keeping in mind that the fried, gingery *agedashi* tofu is a necessity. The generous selection of *maki*—including the avocado-topped Caterpillar with *unagi* and cucumber—is affordably priced.

Thai Pastry, 4925 N. Broadway Ave., Unit E, Uptown, Chicago, IL 60657; (773) 784-5399; www.thaipastry.com; Thai; $$. The desserts beckon diners to this low-key, highlighter-hued storefront, though the expertly prepared Thai classics keep them coming back. Go with the jerky-like seasoned dry beef or fresh spring rolls, followed by sweet pad Thai when playing it safe, or choose curry-sauced frog's legs when an adventurous mood strikes. While you're at it, share the spicy, citrus-y roasted duck salad showered with cilantro and chile, and finish with Thai custard. There's a second location at 7350 W. Lawrence Ave., Harwood Heights, (708) 867-8840.

Trattoria Trullo, 4767 N. Lincoln Ave., Lincoln Square, Chicago, IL 60625; (773) 506-0093; Italian/Deli; $$$. Fans of Puglian fare can't get enough of Giovanni DeNigris's quaint restaurant, where a front deli gives way to a pleasant, airy dining room turning out generous portions of tender, fried calamari; homemade cavatelli with raw, ricotta forte–topped tomato sauce; and assertive, classic chicken Parm. Also, check out sister spot, **Macello,** 1235 W. Lake St., (312) 850-9870.

Tre Kronor, 3258 W. Foster Ave., Albany Park, Chicago, IL 60625; (773) 267-9888; www.trekronorrestaurant.com; Swedish; $$. Scandinavian eats—served in a peculiarly muraled, cafe-like setting—bring high-calorie comfort in the form of Danish cinnamon rolls, a dilled Oslo omelet with smoked salmon and cream cheese, and *falukorv* (veal sausage). You may also be tempted to linger over gravlax; melon salad with Danish blue cheese; Swedish meatballs; and herbaceous fish plated with dilled sun-dried tomato rice and aquavit-pickled cucumber-egg salad.

Tweet, 5020 N. Sheridan Rd., Uptown, Chicago, IL 60640; (773) 728-5576; www.tweet.biz; New American; $$. Not exactly under the radar, this popular eatery is head of its class for breakfast—biscuits and gravy, fluffy pancakes, even fluffier omelets, and a host of breakfast burritos. Salads and sandwiches (especially the Reuben) successfully hold court midday. Don't forget to bring cash, as credit cards are not accepted.

Udupi Palace, 2543 W. Devon Ave., Rogers Park, Chicago, IL 60659; (773) 338-2152; Indian/Vegetarian; $$. Most who dine at this satisfying South Indian vegetarian—believe it or not, many of them carnivores—begin with the oversized *masala dosa,* followed by any number of ubiquitous, hearty lentil dishes and spicy vegetable curries to collective joy.

Uru-Swati, 2629 W. Devon Ave., Rogers Park, Chicago, IL 60659; (773) 262-5280; www.uru-swati.net; Indian/Vegetarian; $$. Set apart by its solid *chaat* (snacks), lively vegetarian curries, and combustible, chile-dotted *uttapam* with veg "soup" for dipping—not to mention its hipper vibe—this vegetarian updates the Devon dining experience. Other items to sample amid its mock-skyline backdrop: doughnut-like, ground vegetable fritters, puffy *pani puri,* and the two-foot-long paper *dosa.* Make it easy on yourself and ask for the translated menu.

Usmania, 2244 W. Devon Ave., Rogers Park, Chicago, IL 60659; (773) 262-1900; usmaniagroupofchicago.com; Indian/Pakistani; $$. A gussied up dining room sets the tone for better-than average fare, be it charcoal-fired *seekh kebab,* tender frontier chicken, or mutton *biryani.* Risk-takers, however, should tackle the *paya,* cow's foot swimming in spicy, complex broth.

Near North

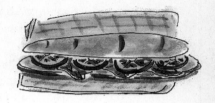

Avondale, Belmont Cragin, Hamlin Park, Hermosa, Irving Park, Lakeview, Logan Square, North Center, Portage Park, Roscoe Village, Wrigleyville

From gustatory go-tos in Lakeview to hyped Logan Square hot-spots and Wrigleyville reliables, Chicago's Near North communities are chock-full of places to chow down.

Go on and suss out sub-Saharan cuisine, entertain an underground dining experience, or get down with a griddle-pressed Cuban—whatever you choose, there's an absurdly good meal worth munching.

A La Turka, 3134 N. Lincoln Ave., Lakeview, Chicago, IL 60657; (773) 935-6101; www.alaturkachicago.com; Middle Eastern/Turkish; $$$. Expect dinner and a show when belly dancers weave their way between tables at this romantic, mid-priced meze maven, which serves a dizzying array of shareable hot and cold plates. Gimmicks notwithstanding, the food is pretty good, namely the zucchini cakes with dilled yogurt dipping sauce; the savory, feta-filled *burek* rolls; and chopped, lemon-dressed salad. Kebabs in many configurations, oregano-accented lamb chops, and classics like moussaka are more substantial, if less memorable.

Andalous, 3307 N. Clark St., Lakeview, Chicago, IL 60657; (773) 281-6885; www.andalous.com; Moroccan; $$$. The tagines stand out at this affordable BYOB. Knowing that, also settle in the intimate, vibrant dining room—a pleasing place for groups—and share lemony carrot-olive salad and herbal *bakoula,* spinach gone glam with oodles of herbs and lemon confit. After a stewy, heady main course, be sure to relax over a pot of aromatic mint tea.

Ann Sather, 909 W. Belmont Ave., Lakeview, Chicago, IL 60657; (773) 348-2378; www.annsather.com; Swedish; $$. Though the original outpost, once a few doors down, is no more, tradition lives on at this Swedish-American eatery, where folks gorge on sticky cinnamon rolls and Swedish pancakes, plus a hearty sampler of lingonberry-glazed roast duck, Swedish meatballs, potato sausage, spaetzle, kraut, and brown beans. There are additional locations on Clark Street, Southport Avenue, and Broadway Street.

The Art of Pizza, 3033 N. Ashland Ave., Lakeview, Chicago, IL 60657; (773) 327-5600; Pizza; $$. Carnivores, when going for broke, must veer toward the sausage, bacon, Italian beef, ground beef, and pepperoni-jammed rendition at this come-as-you-are pie purveyor. Though it's known for its sublimely sauced, deep-dish pizza, the other versions (pan and thin crust, though not particularly thin at all)—plus passable pastas and chicken Parm—are serviceable.

Arun's, 4156 N. Kedzie Ave., Irving Park, Chicago, IL 60618; (773) 539-1909; www.arunsthai.com; Thai; $$$$. Fancy Thai from Arun Sampanthavivat is served via a 12-course, fixed-price tasting menu in a formal, gallery-like setting. Intricate dishes arrive as if they're presents, wrapped in delicate zucchini ribbons or topped with edible, carved roses or lacy butterflies. The ever-changing preparations may include a roll of burdock, shiitake, and carrot-stuffed chicken, gilded with shiso leaf in sweet, caramelized soy sauce, or delicate steamed rice dumplings revealing a minced chicken, shrimp, and jicama interior. But be prepared for the $85 you'll spend per person; if it's an issue, seek out potentially more interesting Thai meals around town.

The Bad Apple, 4300 N. Lincoln Ave., North Center, Chicago, IL 60618; (773) 360-8406; www.badapplebar.com; Burgers; $$. The friendly bar with a "bad" attitude boasts serious, atypically topped burgers made from custom-ground beef. Take as examples the Frenchie, which wears a crown of Brie, truffle, and frizzed fried onion and the Elvis' Last Supper, a strangely appealing peanut butter–slathered version with bacon. Couple them with fancified, house-cut fries, homemade ketchup, and a large craft and import beer and cocktail selection, and it's easy to see why Craig Fass and Mandy Franklin's spot is swamped.

Belly Shack, 1912 N. Western Ave., Logan Square, Chicago, IL 60647; (773) 252-1414; www.bellyshack.com; Pan-Asian/Latin; $$. Melding in harmony two seemingly dissimilar cuisines beneath the Blue Line, this BYOB achieves star status thanks to Bill Kim (also of urbanbelly) and his wife, Yvonne Cadiz-Kim. Don't be put off by the stark, urban space—you'll feel nothing but forgiveness when the tostones arrive, garlicky enough to ward off vampires in their cloak of *chimichurri*. Then, head straight for the *ssam kogi* and refreshing, noodle-y Asian meatball sandwich, saving room for soft-serve christened with Mindy Segal–designed, huckleberry-lime topping. (See recipe from Bill Kim on p. 359.)

Bittersweet Pastry Shop, 1114 W. Belmont Ave., Lakeview, Chicago IL 60657; (773) 929-1100; www.bittersweetpastry.com; Bakery; $. Equally indulgent and inviting, Judy Contino's patisserie is a go-to for brides-in-waiting. It's also destination-worthy for the casual sweet seeker. The cases brim with temptations—oversized, chocolate-dipped cookies, scones, and lemon bars—ideal for pairing with a steaming cup of hot chocolate. Look for light, cafe-style bites as well.

Bobtail Ice Cream. 2951 N. Broadway Ave., Lakeview, Chicago, IL 60657; (773) 880-7372; www.bobtailicecream.com; Ice Cream; $. There's a nostalgic feel to this home-grown soda fountain with house-made ice cream. Signature Sunset—Merlot with dark chocolate chips—and Daley Addiction—vanilla with butter-fudge swirl—are standouts. Even Sox fans may succumb to the Cubby Crunch, vanilla rife with toffee, Oreo chips, and sprinkles. Design-your-own sundaes allow for self-expression, while coffee concoctions provide a cool weather warm-up. Seasonal locations are at Grant Park near Buckingham Fountain, 522 S. Lake Shore Dr., (312) 786-1014; and 1114 Central Ave., Wilmette, (847) 251-0174.

Bleeding Heart Bakery, 1955 W. Belmont Ave., Roscoe Village, Chicago, IL 60657; (773) 327-6934 www.thebleedingheartbakery .com; Bakery; $. What began as a small farmers' market stand grew into a hyped, sustainable punk-rock pastry shop, where Michelle Garcia trots out ginger-mint mojito cupcakes, packed-with-goodness scones, basil–goat cheese croissants, and peanut butter and jelly cheesecake bars. There's also a location at 1010 North Blvd., Oak Park, IL 60301, (708) 358-0559, and plans are in the works for a 1916 W. Chicago Ave. locale.

Bolat African Cuisine, 3346 N. Clark St., Wrigleyville, Chicago, IL 60657; (773) 665-1100; www.bolatchicago.com. African; $$. It'd be easy to overlook this unassuming spot from the owners of Iyanze, located where the Brown and Red Lines converge. Don't, since dishes—when judiciously chosen—surprise. Emphasizing the cuisines of Nigeria and Ghana—as well as sub-Saharan Africa as a whole—the crowded but rarely disappointing dining room serves aromatic, saucy jerk chicken on a bed of cooling coconut rice; flavorful *jollof* rice; starchy *fufu* topped with spinach and scallops; and rousing, if tough, goat pepper stew. A selection of native beers, cocktails, and house-made ginger beer is available.

Bonsoirée, 2728 W. Armitage Ave., Logan Square, Chicago, IL 60647; (773) 486-7511; www.bonsoiree.com. New American; $$$$. Shin Thompson, the chef-owner of this once underground dinner club, does what he wants. The conceptual, highly seasonal cuisine incorporates foraged and other local ingredients, set atop specially chosen dishware amid floral arrangements that play off of what's on plates. Served in four-, seven- and 13-course configurations ($58–$150), the poetic preparations—think rabbit, cooked slow and low with pancetta gnocchi, tomato "intensity," Madeira butter, and sage "silhouette"—give diners stuff to discuss. A go-to dish is the whimsical "duck duck goose," a trio of duck confit, duck breast, and goose *foie gras* alongside fig jam with saffron gastrique. On "no menu Sundays," locally culled produce inspires impromptu menus ($45 for four courses, $75 for seven). The intimate, BYOB, degustation destination also features "underground Saturdays," which are open to a handful of "members."

The Brown Sack, 3581 W. Belden Ave., Logan Square, Chicago, IL 60647; (773) 661-0675; www.thebrownsack.com; Deli; $. Who needs to brown bag it when you've got options like this better-than-ever sandwich shop with a cozy-food bent? Chipotle-warmed tortilla or creamy tomato soups complement a classic sandwich lineup, including a venerable BLT with avocado and shrimp and a many-napkins-required Reuben. Salads are packed with fresh ingredients. Meanwhile, fruit smoothies are available, too. When weather cooperates, snag a seat on the quaint back patio, a thick-churned peanut butter shake in hand.

Browntrout, 4111 N. Lincoln Ave., North Center, Chicago, IL 60618; (773) 472-4111; www.browntroutchicago.com; New American; $$$. Green-minded, sustainable, and communal in approach, this low-key, oft-changing modern American from Sean Sanders and his wife, Nadia, sources ingredients from local, organic, sustainable farms; seafood from natural waters; and grass-fed, free-range meat from nearby producers. The result may be luxurious Illinois pappardelle with Spence Farm Iroquois corn, stinging nettles, and baby carrots christened with Parmesan and herbs from the rooftop garden.

Carnitas El Paisa, 3529 W. Fullerton Ave., Logan Square, Chicago, IL 60647; (773) 278-2062; www.carnitaselpaisa.com; Mexican; $. Saucy *cochinita pibil* is one of those things you can't help but love; here, it—along with *carnitas* and *chicharrones*—is made with the utmost love. For that matter, the steamy *barbacoa* is, too.

Chalkboard, 4343 N. Lincoln Ave., North Center, Chicago IL 60618; (773) 477-7144; www.chalkboardrestaurant.com; New American;

SOMETHING IS BUZZING

Beehives are abuzz on the roof of City Hall and at the Garfield Park Conservatory. They're also humming at the Chicago Cultural Center, where honey is being sold to assist the Gallery 37 Art Center. Lately, though, it seems honey-producing ventures are at every turn, with apiaries providing gainful employment while helping to restore the ecosystem. Those interested in how-tos can find information on classes, events, webinars, and seminars by contacting the **Cook-DuPage Beekeepers' Association** (www.cookdupagebeekeepers.com). You can also score some pretty sweet stuff from these ventures.

Chicago Honey Co-op (www.chicagohoneycoop.com) is an urban beekeeping cooperative with an apiary in the North Lawndale community. It employs sustainable practices, while offering job training for the underemployed. Its products—which include everything from honey to lip balm and candles—are sold at **Green City Market** (see p. 340) and online.

Bron's Bees at Heritage Prairie Farm (630-443-8253; www.hpmfarm.com/brons_bees.html) produces a wide variety of all-natural honeys, selling them at locations such as **Green City Market** (see p. 340) and **Provenance Food & Wine** (see p. 304).

Jinglebees (773-821-6508) is an urban apiary on the South Side of Chicago's Pullman State Historic Site.

HoneyGirl Honey (www.honeygirlhoney.com) produces honey bears, containers of honey, and honey straws in Fullton, IL. Purchase products direct from the company by e-mailing akoch@honeygirlhoney.com.

Belfry Bees & Honey (630-303-3775; www.BelfryBees.com) is a collection of honeybee apiaries scattered throughout Illinois's Fox River Valley. Score the sweet nectar or find out about educational programming online.

$$$. Gilbert Langlois (SushiSamba Rio, Rushmore) is behind this cozy, conversation-friendly storefront with a Victorian vibe and an eponymous, frequently changing menu. Plump mussels, perhaps steamed in toasted curry-coriander-inflected beer, pave the way for interesting mains, from pork tenderloin with apple-potato confit and ancho-corn vinaigrette to whitefish with cauliflower-potato hash, white-bean puree and *aji amarillo* sauce. Come for afternoon tea, or plan to brunch in style (you'll want the duck "Mick" muffin, bolstered by a poached egg and Brie).

Chicago Diner, 3411 N. Halsted St., Lakeview, Chicago, IL 60657; (773) 935-6696; www.veggiediner.com; Vegetarian; $$. Ingredients, like seitan and tofu, masquerade as meat at this come-as-you-are vegetarians' Eden. But those preferring to skip the vegan cheese can find merits, too, such as panko-herb lentil cakes, drizzled with horse-radish tahini or pumpkin ravioli with roasted apple and onion-laced butternut squash sauce. Always a hit: the "Whopping Deluxe," an assert-ively seasoned, black bean–pepper burger with storied sweet-potato fries. Finish with a cookie dough–peanut butter or chocolate-banana-coffee shake.

Chief O'Neill's Pub & Restaurant, 3471 N. Elston Ave., Avondale, Chicago, IL 60618; (773) 583-3066; www.chiefoneillspub .com; Irish; $$. A spacious, flower-filled beer garden is the lure of this Irishman come summer, though Emerald Isle mainstays—

fish-and-chips, bangers and mash, slow-cooked corned beef with braised cabbage—enjoy a year-round fan club. Named for Chief Francis O'Neill, an Irish music archivist and former Chicago chief of police, its handsome wood dining room affords a respite from the cold, especially when rounds of single-malt scotch and suds come into play.

Chilam Balam, 3023 N. Broadway St., Lakeview, Chicago, IL 60657; (773) 296-6901; www.chilambalamchicago.com; Mexican; $$$. There's zero pretension at this sustainable, upscale BYOB. Located below street level, it's where youngster Chuy Valencia (Frontera Grill, Topolobampo, Adobo Grill) decided to go it alone in funky, farm-to-table fashion, his complexly flavored, deeply satisfying creations deserving of praise. The *memelas* (corn masa "pizzas"), filled with inky black-bean puree and goat cheese, are a must, as are the *epazote*-scented, *pipian verde*–braised mushroom empanadas. Peruse the specials, though—it's where Valencia's genius shines and fleeting dishes, such as foraged mushrooms with fennel, tangy chipotle, fresh cheese, and pomegranate or bacon-accented pork loin with black-fig salsa, morita chile, and spaghetti squash, appear. Hit the ATM first because it's cash only.

Cho Sun Oak, 4200 N. Lincoln Ave., North Center; Chicago, IL 60618 (773) 549-5555; www.chosunokrestaurant.com; Korean; $$. An unassuming exterior belies the happenings inside this smoke-scented Korean barbecue, where some of the best things—*bulgogi, kalbi*—are cooked on the tabletop by you. But don't ignore the brow-mopping *yuk gae jang*, a flaming-hot soup teeming with beef, kimchee, sprouts, and egg or the *mul-naeng myun,* cold beef broth with buckwheat noodles, pickled veggies, and hard-boiled egg, just asking for condiments.

Deleece, 4004 N. Southport Ave., Lakeview, Chicago, IL 60613; (773) 325-1710; www.deleece.com; New American; $$. This neighborhood spot is long on charm, in no small part because its eclectic menu is crammed with potstickers, Spanish rice-stuffed poblanos, and short ribs with horseradish-parsnip puree. Its cost-conscious prix fixe is as popular as its brunch. Nearby sibling **Deleece Grill Pub** (3313 N. Clark St., 773-348-3313) serves comfort food and craft brews.

DMK Burger Bar, 2954 N. Sheffield Ave., Lakeview, Chicago, IL 60657; (773) 360-8686; www .dmkburgerbar.com; Burgers; $$. Michael Kornick (mk) and David Morton (Morton's) elevate the humble burger at this wildly popular joint with an order-by-number approach and an impressive grass-fed lamb burger with sheep's milk feta, olive tapenade, Greek salad, and *tzatziki.* Faced with the griddled patty melt with smoked bacon, burnt onions, and Leroy's remoulade, however, choosing poses a challenge. Fried okra and pickles, glam, hand-cut fries, and thick espresso shakes leave its co-ed clientele hankering for more. For fresh catches raw and cooked, visit **Fish Bar** (2956 N. Sheffield Ave., 773-687-8177) next door.

El Cubanito, 2555 N. Pulaski Rd., Logan Square, Chicago, IL 60639; (773) 235-2555; Cuban; $. No-frills and tiny, this simple storefront can hardly keep up with the demand for its exemplary, jam-packed (if pickle-shy) Cuban sandwich. And the steak, guava-cheese number, and *ropa vieja* sandwiches? Goodness, they're tasty, too—not to mention rock-bottom-cheap.

El Rinconcito Cubano, 3238 W. Fullerton Ave., Logan Square, Chicago, IL 60647; (773) 489-4440; Cuban; $. When the *vaca frita*—shredded, fried beef—is available at this friendly Cuban, make it a double. But come with a crew: The ham croquetas and *ropa vieja* are winning, too.

erwin, 2925 N. Halsted St., Lakeview, Chicago, IL 60657; (773) 528-7200; www.erwincafe.com; American; $$. The brainchild of Chef Erwin Drechsler, this unfussy, ingredient-driven restaurant favors a pared down approach. Start with the cornmeal-crusted, fried green tomatoes with bacon and tangy buttermilk dressing or bacon-wrapped, wood-grilled, Gorgonzola-filled dates. Follow with moist, crisp-skinned roast chicken with duck fat potatoes and lemony garlic-rosemary sauce. The burger is good, too—it's topped with horseradish slaw and piquant, house-made pickles.

Frasca Pizzeria & Wine Bar, 3358 N. Paulina St., Lakeview, Chicago, IL 60657; (773) 248-5222; www.frascapizzeria.com; Italian; $$. You'll wind up wishing this laid-back, hip, and family-friendly spot from the D.O.C. Wine Bar crew was in your 'hood. Even if its entrees and pastas are fairly forgettable, the apps, wood-fired pizza, and affordable wine list are of note. Make like the locals and snag wild mushroom risotto fritters and prosciutto-wrapped fontina, drizzled with balsamic vinegar. Then, keep it simple with a classic Margherita pie, or get your roasted fingerling, onion, bacon, and three-cheese 'za adorned with an egg. On Wednesday, pizzas are buy one, get one free. Also, check out siblings **Dunlays on Clark, Dunlays on the Square,** and **Smoke Daddy.**

Fritz Pastry, 1408 W. Diversey Pkwy., Lakeview, Chicago, IL 60614; (773) 857-2989; www.fritzpastry.com; Bakery; $. Excelling at baked creations both savory and sweet, Nathaniel Meads' flaky croissants, buttery brioche, and German *springerle* have tongues wagging. (So does his commitment to creating 100 different *macarons*.) Try the delish chocolate–black pepper cookies and gâteau Breton. Meads— along with partners Elaine Heaney and Jared Nance (both of **Nacional 27**)—specializes in confections not readily found elsewhere.

Glunz Bavarian Haus, 4128 N. Lincoln Ave., North Center, Chicago, IL 60618; (773) 472-4287; www.glunzbavarianhaus.com; German/Austrian; $$. The German repertoire is well represented here thanks to the beer, wine, and spirit-distributing Glunz family (The House of Glunz), who crafted this schnitzel den with Stieglswillers in mind. Cheese and sausage platters are fit for a baron, and sauerbraten or roast pork with bread dumplings, kraut, and caraway jus are so welcoming—and filling. Before throwing in the towel, tack on some Viennese strudel.

Harmony Grill, 3159 N. Southport Ave., Lakeview, Chicago, IL 60657; (773) 525-2508; www.schubas.com; American; $$. The locally sourced, better-than-average bar fare comes courtesy of the Schuba's crew. The star of the show is design-your-own mac and cheese. Upon closer inspection, you'll see attention to details, like house-fried potato chips, brisket that's smoked on site and Maker's Mark–sauced chocolate bread pudding.

HB Home Bistro, 3404 N. Halsted St., Lakeview, Chicago, IL 60657; (773) 661-0299; www.homebistrochicago.com; New American; $$$. Joncarl Lachman's inviting, seasonal BYOB delivers knockout, homespun cuisine to a repeat clientele. Comforting starters, such as almond-stuffed, bacon-wrapped dates and artichoke-Edam fritters set the tone; anise-scented, beer-steeped mussels, pork shank pappardelle, and lamb-shoulder burgoo with butter beans and vinegar slaw follow suit. Also, visit its Netherlands-bent brother, **Vincent** (1475 W. Balmoral Ave., 773-334-7168).

Hearty, 3819 N. Broadway St., Wrigleyville, Chicago, IL 60613; (773) 868-9866; www.heartyboys.com; New American; $$. Updated comfort food and great cocktails benchmark this Steve McDonagh and Dan Smith charmer, offering a solid, reliably satisfying experience time after time. If you can handle something so, well, hearty, start with the corn-battered rabbit sausage with ale syrup, and continue to cornflake-crusted chicken or a coffee-chocolate barbecue-lacquered turkey leg with lemon-pepper fries and zippy slaw. And don't skip dessert—the root beer float cupcakes and lavender peach cobbler can't be denied. (See recipe on p. 348.)

Hot Doug's, 3324 N. California Ave., Avondale, Chicago, IL 60618; (773) 279-9550; www.hotdougs.com; Hot Dogs; $. Yes, you can procure a classic, Chicago-style dog, but (good as it is) don't bother. The real reason to succumb to this serious stand is Doug Sohn's creative sausages, which vary by day. Be wooed by specials—maybe bacon sausage, christened with crème fraîche, caramelized onions, and double-cream Brie—and named-for-celebrity standbys like The Marty Allen, snappy, garnished-as-you-wish Thuringer.

Irish Oak, 3511 N. Clark St., Wrigleyville, Chicago, IL 60657; (773) 935-6669; www.irishoak.com; Irish; $$. Kitted out with an Emerald Isle bar, this near-ballpark pub with a Cubs-loving, backwards-cap clientele exudes authentic charm. Fried food fans frequent the beer-battered pickles and wings, a precursor to standard sandwiches; shepherd's pie, fish-and-chips, and Guinness stew feel more true blue. Pints of beer, whiskey, and Irish-cream-based concoctions contribute to the convivial vibe.

Istanbul, 3613 N. Broadway St., Lakeview, Chicago, IL 60613; (773) 525-0500; Turkish/Middle Eastern; $$. A BYOB policy helps keep prices pocketbook-friendly at this casual eatery, where hipsters dive into meaty, pizza-ish *lahmacun,* tender kebabs with tangy yogurt, crave-worthy *manti* (Turkish-style tortellini), and crisp-outside, crumbly-inside falafel.

Jack's on Halsted, 3201 N. Halsted St., Lakeview, Chicago, IL 60657; (773) 244-9191; www.jacksonhalsted.com; American; $$. Aiming to be all things to most people, this trusty neighborhood bar and restaurant is an American standby serving icy-cold martinis. Pork lovers rejoice in the tasting of Asian barbecue-sauced baby backs, Memphis-style pulled pork, and grilled pork tenderloin with ginger-y pineapple chutney alongside sweet-sour cabbage and maple whipped potatoes. You'll also encounter decent burgers and plenty of shareable plates.

Julius Meinl, 3601 N. Southport Ave., Lakeview, Chicago, IL 60613; (773) 868-1857; www.meinl.com; Austrian; $$. The Viennese pastries—from apple strudel to a flourless chocolate-almond torte and six-layered, fondant-covered hazelnut dacquoise—enjoy a loyal following. They, as well as cafe-type fare, pair with stellar French-press coffee, espresso, and cappuccino. There are additional locations at 4363 N. Lincoln Ave., (773) 868-1876, and 1416 W. Irving Park Rd., (773) 883-1864, though this one is not full-service.

Kit Kat Lounge & Supper Club, 3700 N. Halsted St., Lakeview, Chicago, IL 60613; (773) 525-1111; www.kitkatchicago.com; New American; $$. There's a bawdy vibe: Therein lies the allure of this bachelorette party–populated locale, where cross-dressing divas perform and the updated American comfort food and martini-centric libations play a supporting role. However, its brunch menu, filled with cheekily named dishes, has an audience of its own. (In other words, leave the kiddos at home.)

Kitsch'n on Roscoe, 2005 W. Roscoe St., Roscoe Village, Chicago, IL 60618; (773) 248-7372; www.kitschn.com; Eclectic; $$. The name says a lot at this Naugahyde nook, where the adornments—bubbling lava lamps, vintage action figures, lunchboxes, and Formica-topped tables—meet a modernized menu crammed with comfort fare. Faves include fried chicken and waffles with ancho honey, meatloaf with port gravy, and chicken-fennel potpie. Then again, the mac and cheese—topped with bacon-flecked breadcrumbs—always does the trick. There's barbecue, too, and a not-to-be-missed, Twinkie-fied take on tiramisu. Ask to sit in the tiki garden when it's warm, but expect a wait during brunch.

Kuma's Corner, 2900 W. Belmont Ave., Avondale, Chicago, IL 60618; (773) 604-8769; www.kumascorner.com; Burgers; $$. Burgers get top billing at this lodge-y, wood-trimmed tap. Settling on one is hard, but the namesake, topped with bacon, cheddar, and a fried egg is classic; the Metallica, which drips with buffalo sauce and blue cheese, is hardcore; and the Motorhead, a mess-maker of goat cheese, kalamatas, oregano, onions, and *tzatziki,* proves gut-busting to say the least. Diversions include chorizo-stuffed poppers with jalapeño-raspberry jam and slow-cooked pork on a pretzel roll. A just rough-and-tumble enough staff, pleasant patio, and extensive craft-beer selection are also attributes.

La Oaxaqueña, 3382 N. Milwaukee Ave., Irving Park, Chicago, IL 60641; (773) 545-8585; Mexican; $. This casual, pint-sized Oaxacan taqueria turns out regional, mole-soused chicken and destination-worthy *camarones rellenos;* jam, bacon, and cheese-stuffed shrimp; tender, garlicky squid *al ajillo;* delish *tortas;* and warming *caldo* (soup).

Laschet's Inn, 2119 W. Irving Park Rd., North Center, Chicago, IL 60618; (773) 478-7915; www.laschetsinn.com; German; $$. Great German food and beer at prices that don't send you to the poorhouse—that's what you'll get at this wood-beamed, beer mug-adorned Old-World pub, turning out artery-clogging classics to great success. It turns out, the *rouladen* (beef rolls filled with pickles, bacon, and onions blanketed in gravy), fantastically crisp potato pancakes, and Wiener schnitzel do more than fill a niche. Consider starting with the *hackepeter*—steak tartare with capers and onions on rye—followed by fried chicken, goulash, or sauerbraten, savoring your Hirter and Hoegaarden before the food coma sets in and the apple schnapps, a meal-ending tradition, arrives.

Las Tablas, 2942 N. Lincoln Ave., Lakeview, Chicago, IL 60657, (773) 871-2414; www.lastablas.com; Colombian/Steakhouse; $$. Bring your appetite and prepare to loosen your belt—a meal at this hopping, meat-minded Colombian demands both. Sip a vodka-spiked *limonada* in wait of flaky beef empanadas pocked with hard-boiled egg. Next, turn to gut-busting meat and seafood combinations or *bandeja paisa,* sizzling rib eye piled with crisp pork belly, fried, yolky egg, rice, beans, plantains, and avocado. Alternatively, procure a gluten-free empanada and fair-trade coffee at **Macondo.**

Leo's Coney Island, 3455 N. Southport Ave., Lakeview, Chicago, IL 60657; (773) 281-5367; www.leoschicago.com; Hot Dogs; $. A tough sell in a city that's known for its dogs, this diner sates Motor City imports with its chili, mustard, onion, and cheese-topped red hot as well as Greek-tinged eats, including spinach-cheese pie, lemon-rice soup, and a fabled, fixing-filled salad. Griddled morning mainstays, burgers, and pita sandwiches are among the backups.

Little Bucharest Bistro, 3661 N. Elston Ave., Irving Park, Chicago, IL 60618; (773) 604-8500; www.littlebucharestbistro .com; Eastern European/Romanian; $$. Quite the character, Branko Podrumedic resurrected his longtime eatery, which features stained-glass panels salvaged from a former address. From the kitchen comes vibrant borscht and roasted beet, artichoke, and Spanish onion salad, swathed with creamy garlic dressing. Rib-sticking mains—schnitzel, paprikash, and goulash, not to mention grilled Romanian sausages, which pair nicely with Old-World vinos—more than suffice. What you'll come back for, though, is the sausage-stuffed chicken thighs on a bed of creamy blue-cheese polenta, draped with tomato sauce. Regular live acts enliven the scene.

Los Moles, 3140 N. Lincoln Ave., Lakeview, Chicago, IL 60657; (773) 935-9620; www.losmoles.net; Mexican; $$. The name of this cantina offers insight; it began under the deft hand of mole man Geno Bahena. Seasonal, sustainable ingredients and complex sauces from Oaxaca and beyond inspire, be it a *sopes* sampler with lap-pable red mole chicken or rack of lamb with *mole negro* and creamy, pumpkin seed-based *pollo mole verde*.

Lula Cafe, 2537 N. Kedzie Ave., Logan Square, Chicago, IL 60647; (773) 489-9554; www.lulacafe.com; New American; $$$. This Midwest-leaning, globally inspired neighborhood gem leaves an impression with all-hits, purveyor-driven menu that's long on flavor but (relatively) easy on the wallet. Though dishes are ever-changing, expect to encounter things like celery soup with Seckel pear, black walnut, pumpernickel, and sea-urchin roe, or lime-accented Illinois flank steak with ground cherries and spicy field greens. In the end, the eats are about as offbeat-cool as the crowd that frequents the funky digs.

Mia Francesca, 3311 N. Clark St., Lakeview, Chicago, IL 60657; (773) 281-3310; www.miafrancesca.com; Italian; $$. The flagship

TEAM EFFORT

It's no secret that city-dwellers are short on space. That's where community gardens come in. Thanks to organizations like not-for-profit **GreenNet** (www.greennetchicago.org), greening up the urban landscape is within reach. Currently, the city of Chicago has over 600 active gardens in 50 wards; community gardens are cropping up in the 'burbs, too. Some feature youth programs, while others have a beautification bent. Education is a component, too, as at Irma Ruiz Elementary School, where there's an outdoor class-room with geodesic dome, solar and wind-powered fountain, and a stream.

of the Francesca family, Scott Harris's loud, lively Italian cucina has an inviting, cobbled terrace and crazy-tight tables in a narrow dining room, where everyone eats while packed like sardines. Whether seated inside or out, the Northern Italian fare—carpaccio scattered with capers; pancetta-studded linguine all'Amatriciana; lemony, rosemary-scented roast chicken—is a recipe for success.

Mirabell, 3454 W. Addison St., Irving Park, Chicago, IL 60618; (773) 463-1962; www.mirabellrestaurant.com; German; $$. This hardy German "lodge" is outfitted with the expected trappings (steins, beer signs), while offering a bygone menu of schnitzel preps, chill-abating goulash, smoky Thuringer with kraut, and zesty sauerbraten, accompanied by red cabbage and dumplings. Best of all, you can bust out your lederhosen—no one will bat an eye.

Mixteco Grill, 1601 W. Montrose Ave., Lakeview, Chicago, IL 60613; (773) 868-1601; www.mixtecogrill.com; Mexican; $$. Bring your own libations to this über-busy Mexican, where bespectacled hipsters chow down on mid-priced moles (including a deeply smoky version atop *sopes*) in a deceptively underwhelming setting. And while anything mole-sauced is a best bet, achiote-burnished *cochinita pibil*—topped with pickled onions and flaming habañero salsa—is amazing, too. Also, come for brunch.

Mrs. Murphy & Sons Irish Bistro, 3905 N. Lincoln Ave., North Center, Chicago, IL 60613; (773) 248-3905; www.irishbistro.com; Irish; $$$. Quite the departure in more ways than one, this modern Irishman affords an upscale, if off-kilter, experience in the home of a former funeral parlor. Drawing inspiration from its Emerald Isle roots, boxty-style potato cakes are gussied up with smoked salmon and crème fraîche, and ribs are slathered with whiskey barbecue sauce and arrive with creamy Guinness mac and cheese. The place pays homage to the late, legendary Jim Murphy.

90 Miles Cuban Cafe, 3101 N. Clybourn Ave., Hamlin Park, Chicago, IL 60618; (773) 248-2822; www.90milescubancafe.com;

Cuban; $$. A taste of Cuba in an intimate shack adorned with vintage news clippings and reclaimed barn-wood details, Alberto and Christine Gonzalez's *ropa vieja*-fragranced cafe prepares crackly Cubano, *lechón,* and guava-Swiss sandwiches that are worth seeking out. A second location opened at 2540 W. Armitage Ave., (773) 227-2822.

Penny's Noodle Shop, 3400 N. Sheffield Ave., Lakeview, Chicago, IL 60657; (773) 281-8222; www.pennysnoodleshop.com; Asian; $$. You won't pay a lot but you'll get plenty at this likeable noodle house. Expect all mainstays, including pad Thai, chicken satay, and *lad nar.* However, soups—such as *tom yum,* greens-flecked barbecue pork, udon, and ramen—are its strength. There are multiple locations in the city and suburbs.

The Piggery, 1625 W. Irving Park Rd., Lakeview, Chicago, IL 60613; (773) 281-7447; www.thepiggerychicago.com; Barbecue; $$. Southern-tinged barbecue—and pork, in particular—takes center stage at this sporty smokehouse. (There may be a problem, though, when bacon-wrapped, cream cheese–filled jalapeños potentially steal the show.) From generously doused pork nachos and a pulled-pork salad to ribs and a ham-stuffed burger, the shtick is clear.

pingpong, 3322 N. Broadway St., Lakeview, Chicago, IL 60657; (773) 281-7576; www.pingpongrestaurant.com; Asian; $$. The vibe—right down to the styling staff—is cool. The good news is, the fare—tempura fish tacos, crab Rangoon, curried Singapore noodles—is up to the task. And the salt-and-pepper shrimp? The *bulgogi* and the twice-cooked pork belly? Well, they're good, too. BYO or order from the full bar.

Pitchfork Food and Saloon, 2922 W. Irving Park Rd., Irving Park, Chicago, IL 60618; (773) 866-2010; www.pitchforkchicago .com; Barbecue/American; $. This cost-conscious, honky-tonk saloon sets itself apart with a whiskey selection that's over 50 labels strong and an array of more than 20 scotches. Winning Cordis Brothers ribs are your best bet among eats. Otherwise, expect all the usual suspects, from chili to chicken fingers, burgers to buffalo-chicken sandwiches. Check out the eponymous Pitchfork punch and house-made sangria when getting your buzz on.

Pollo Campero, The Brickyard, 2730 N. Narragansett Ave., Hermosa, Chicago, IL 60639; (773) 622-6657; www.campero.com. Guatemalan; $$. There are things in life—like this Guatemalan fried-chicken chain—you simply have to experience. Visit once, and opine over the moist, crispy-skinned meat with just the right kick. Torn from the bone, tucked into warm corn tortillas, and topped with salsas, cilantro, and onions from the condiment bar, it'll leave you at a loss for words. Throw in sides of bacon-y pinto beans and slaw, and you've got something akin to bliss. There is also an Albany Park location (4830 N. Pulaski Rd., 773-282-1966).

Pork Shoppe, 2755 W. Belmont Ave., Avondale, Chicago, IL 60618; (773) 961-7654; www.porkshoppechicago.com; Barbecue; $$. Organic, local, upscale barbecue from the former Tizi Melloul crew is divvied out amid farm tool decor. And while porcine scents do emanate from a central smoker, the end result—be it rubbed ribs or pulled pork—isn't super-smoky at all. A backup is beef brisket (get it as a taco, topped with cilantro and onions), while sides include mac and cheese and burnt-end beans. Don't forget to wet your whistle with some bourbon and beer.

Resi's Bierstube, 2034 W. Irving Park Rd., North Center, Chicago, IL 60618; (773) 472-1749; German; $$. They don't make them like this brauhaus anymore, which may have something to do with why this holdout is so beloved. But credit also goes to the schnitzel, massive, *weiss*-centric beer list, and inviting *Biergarten,* the perfect place to procure sausages—from liver to knackwurst, beerwurst, and bratwurst—with sides of sauerkraut and lacy potato pancakes.

Sabatino's, 4441 W. Irving Park Rd., Irving Park, Chicago, IL 60641; (773) 283-8331; www.sabatinoschicago.com; Italian/Pizza; $$. Fantastic, affordable Sinatra staples await at this low-lit Italian stalwart, where service is as back-in-the-day as the puttanesca-sauced tagliatelle, **eggplant** Parm, and seafood-packed *zuppa di mari*. And the veal saltimbocca? You'll be back for more, guaranteed. End the evening on a romantic note with a tableside flambé.

Sapori di Napoli, 1406 W. Belmont Ave., Lakeview, Chicago, IL 60657; (773) 935-1212; www.saporedinapoli.net; Pizza; $$. It's one of many Neapolitan-style pizza joints out there, though this BYOB does it better than most. Plus, it serves luxuriously creamy gelato, to boot. These wood-fired lovelies arrive generously topped with quality ingredients—prosciutto, homemade sausage, bright tomato sauce— atop charred crusts. Even the straightforward Margherita is a work of art. There are a handful of antipasti selections, salads, and pastas as well, though no one really seems to notice.

Smoque BBQ, 3800 N. Pulaski Rd., Irving Park, Chicago, IL 60641; (773) 545-7427; www.smoquebbq.com; Barbecue; $$. Roll up your sleeves—this anything but low-key neighborhood BYOB with its own "meat manifesto" will leave you licking your fingers and clamoring for more. Choose between the long-smoked, crisp-edged Texas-style brisket—fantastic in sandwich form—rubbed and sauced spare ribs, or vinegary hunks of pulled pork. (Opt for taste portions if you're wise.) Sides, like creamy mac and cheese and slaw, are good but not the star of the show.

socca, 3301 N. Clark St., Lakeview, Chicago, IL 60657; (773) 248-1155; www.soccachicago.com; French/Italian; $$$. The affordable French- and Italian-inflected fare served here has earned a loyal following. Repeat diners make a beeline for the chickpea-flour crepe dish for which the restaurant is named. Also justifiably popular are the house-made pastas and comfort-minded main courses, perhaps spoon-tender, braised short ribs. Then again, the pizzettes are quite good as well.

Sola, 3868 N. Lincoln Ave., North Center, Chicago, IL 60613; (773) 327-3868; www.sola-restaurant.com; Hawaiian/Asian; $$$. Carol Wallack's Hawaiian-bent spot is one to keep in your back pocket. Take note of the seasonal specials, which feature a themed ingredient—apples, for example. They may yield grilled Wagyu sirloin with apple-onion chutney, braised beans, and fingerlings. From artichoke fritters with soy-lime and white truffle–honey sauces to sturgeon accented by morels, ramps, and bacon brittle, narrowing down options is an exercise in discipline. Come for the short ribs Benedict during brunch.

Sol de Mexico, 3018 N. Cicero Ave., Belmont Cragin, Chicago, IL 60641; (773) 282-4119; www.soldemexicochicago.com; Mexican; $$$. A bit off the beaten track, this impressive destination from Carlos Tello (brother-in-law of mole master Geno Bahena) has Clementina Flores (Bahena's mom) in the kitchen. There, she preserves the art of authentic, regional Mexican cooking using the freshest of ingredients. The flawless, complex moles— whether elevating ostrich or mussels, sea bass or scallops—are a revelation. Also celebratory: the sweet-savory *chile en nogada*, poblanos brimming with fruit-flecked pork picadillo, sprinkled with pomegranate seeds and finished in silky walnut sauce.

Southport Grocery, 3552 N. Southport Ave., Lakeview, Chicago, IL 60657; (773) 665-0100; www.southportgrocery .com; New American; $$. The stroller set loves this close-quarters storefront, though dining at this pint-sized grocer and cafe is not always the pleasantest of experiences. However, the insanely good eats—a house-made, grown-up Pop Tart bursting with berry preserves and mascarpone cheese; scones that don't resemble a hockey puck; and moist cupcakes are a good reward for surviving close confines. Sandwiches, such as grilled Brie or house-made pastrami, are appealing at midday. Packaged goods—oils, sauces, cheeses, and pastas—are tempting at any hour.

Sticky Rice, 4018 N. Western Ave., North Center, Chicago, IL 60618; (773) 588-0120; www.stickyricethai.com; Thai; $$. Seriously, skip the pad Thai. This vibrant, welcoming haunt serves some of—if not the—best Thai citywide. (Ask for the translated Thai-language menu.) Then, go with the brow-moppingly hot, house-made sausage; tart-spicy *nam prik num* sauce with veggies and sticky rice; Thai *larb*, a commingling of ground pork and intestines; and tongue-singeing banana-blossom salad. Daring diners may also procure a handful of insect-based dishes.

Sura Thai Bistro, 3124 N. Broadway St., Lakeview, Chicago, IL 60657; (773) 248-7872; www.surachicago.com; Thai; $$. This space-age den with orb-like seating comes courtesy of the owners of Peep, Spice, and Sea in New York. Cost-conscious small plates sport a fusion of Asian flavors, including flash-fried ginger calamari with toasted chile, coconut, and jalapeño; duck confit with fried egg, pickled carrot, and plum sauce; and tuna with olive fried rice and spinach tempura. On the Japanese side, look to kooky *maki* and sashimi platters fit for a crowd.

TAC Quick, 3930 N. Sheridan Rd., Wrigleyville, Chicago, IL 60613; (773) 327-5253; www.tacquick.net; Thai; $$. Trim and stylish, locals look to this approachable spot for authentic Thai, namely items on its (translated) "secret" menu. Once it's in hand, order the bracing papaya salad with blue crab and Isaan-style pork and rice sausage, pronto. Follow with the fried chicken with scorching tamarind sauce—it'll haunt your dreams.

Tango Sur, 3763 N. Southport Ave., Lakeview, Chicago, IL 60613; (773) 477-5466; Argentine/Steakhouse; $$. Carnivores—at least the ones patient enough to wait—descend on this lively BYOB, known for its empanadas, generously cut steak with *chimichurri* sauce, and slick, sweet flan—all of which benefit from a backing of live Latin guitar. **Folklore,** its similarly minded Argentine sib, is in Wicker Park at 2100 W. Division St., (773) 292-1600.

Taqueria Ricardo, 4429 W. Diversey Ave., Hermosa, Chicago, IL 60639; (773) 292-0400; Mexican; $. Hidden in a nondescript *supermercado* is this bright, jerry-built hole-in-the-wall, a pitch-perfect place for *tacos al pastor* (slightly charred and carved from a spit behind the counter) as well as juicy, wood-grilled chicken. Also solid is anything—including tacos and tortas—with grilled steak. Fantastic salsa verde brightens dishes, which arrive with grilled knob onions and jalapeños.

Terragusto, 1851 W. Addison St., Roscoe Village, Chicago, IL 60614; (773) 248-2777; www.terragustocafe.com; Italian; $$$. Chef-owner Theo Gilbert's frequently changing pastas emphasize what's local and organic. Settle on simply sauced tortelli, black noodles topped with plump shrimp, or meat-filled agnolotti, with affordable Italian vinos offering the perfect foil. There's another location at 340 W. Armitage Ave., (773) 281-7200, and an outpost in Glencoe is in the works. Pasta-making classes are offered on an ongoing basis.

Thai Classic, 3332 N. Clark St., Lakeview, Chicago, IL 60657; (773) 404-2000; www.thaiclassicrestaurant.com; Thai; $$. Solid renditions of familiar Thai dishes and an extensive, rock-bottom weekend brunch featuring more than two-dozen dishes have earned a reputation for this reliable, casual institution. All the basics are covered and done well, from the *tom yum* soup and refreshing papaya and beef salads to the spicy, saucy drunken noodles.

Tropi Cuba, 3000 W. Lyndale St., Logan Square, Chicago, IL 60647; (773) 252-0230; www.tropicubachicago.com; Cuban; $. A classic case of don't judge a book by its cover, this bitty bastion of Cuban flavors serves superb sandwiches, though its bar-stool seating is nestled into the back of a no-frills grocery store. If the black beans and rice don't tug at your heartstrings, odds are the guava and cheese *pastelito* or *lechón* will.

Turquoise, 2147 W. Roscoe St., Roscoe Village, Chicago, IL 60618; (773) 549-3523; www.turquoisedining.com; Mediterranean/Turkish; $$$. Turkish cuisine, served in a wood-trimmed, white-tablecloth setting, gets a boost the moment a basket of warm, house-made bread arrives. Is it a bit spendy? Yes. But the expertly prepared, almost elegant *sogurme*—a creamy, garlicky mélange of smoked eggplant, yogurt, brown butter, and toasted walnuts—homemade *lahmacun* (meat-topped flatbread), and salt-crusted fish justify the mini-splurge.

Uncommon Ground, 3800 N. Clark St., Wrigleyville, Chicago, IL 60613; (773) 929-3680; www.uncommonground.com; Eclectic; $$$. Come as you are—this green-minded, kid-friendly coffeehouse welcomes it. Then, dig into dishes constructed from locally sourced ingredients. Generally, the feel-good chopped salad and grownup Butterkäse grilled cheese are enough to appease the carbon-offset crowd, though the roster of regular entertainment goes a long way to keep things interesting. The Edgewater location is at 1401 W. Devon Ave., (773) 465-9801, complete with certified organic rooftop garden.

urbanbelly, 3053 N. California Ave., Avondale, Chicago, IL 60618; (773) 583-0500; www.urbanbellychicago.com; Pan Asian; $$. Gluttons flock to Bill Kim's tearfully good noodle shop, where the communal wood seating is ever-packed. It's understandable, since the *pho*-scented duck dumplings; chewy rice cake–chicken noodle bowl specked with mango; and uncommonly good short rib–scallion rice will leave you longing for seconds, thirds, and a visit the following day. Get sides of pungent kimchee and blistered green beans for full-on bliss. Best of all, you can afford it since the BYOB policy keeps prices down. (See recipe on p. 359.)

Victory's Banner, 2100 W. Roscoe St., Roscoe Village, Chicago, IL 60618; (773) 665-0227; www.victorysbanner.com; Vegetarian; $$. The eggs here are ethereal, and the French toast with real maple syrup is worth every calorie—just as the sari-wearing servers suggest. While taking in the spiritual vibe, order perfectly presentable cinnamon apple–topped oatmeal, or try the Indian *uppama*—a hot, cream of wheat–like porridge, dotted with peas, onions, and tomatoes alongside coconut chutney and tangy yogurt accompaniments. The fresh, light lunch fare—from wraps to sandwiches and salads—is good, though it never trumps the served-all-day a.m. eats.

Volo, 2008 W. Roscoe St., Roscoe Village, Chicago, IL 60618; (773) 348-4600; www.volorestaurant.com; American/Wine Bar; $$$. Wine enthusiasts unite at this small plates gem with a picturesque garden patio. Although the selections alter by season, its artisan cheeses, luxurious bone-marrow starter, and brined, slow-simmered duck confit certainly are welcome finds. Add that to the fact that halibut—perhaps with English peas, asparagus and artichokes—and sweet-pea flatbread with cipollini and pea shoots are just as fresh as can be.

Mid City

Bucktown, Gold Coast, Humboldt Park, Lincoln Park, Noble Square, Old Town, Streeterville, Ukrainian Village, Wicker Park

Chicago is a city of distinct neighborhoods. Following its midsection from the lake outward, this is evidenced by Lincoln Park's tree-trimmed, brownstone-lined streets, artistically rich Old Town, and funky Ukie Village digs, all offset by multicultural, working-class Humboldt Park and the buzzing tract of Bucktown and Wicker Park.

For food enthusiasts, that means everything from molecular gastronomy to seasonally minded scenes and mom-and-pop shops. When craving swanky vegetarian fare or desperate for hangover correctives, look no further to fill the bill.

Adobo Grill, 1610 N. Wells St., Old Town, Chicago, IL 60614; (312) 266-7999; www.adobogrill.com; Mexican; $$. Tableside-prepped guac and 'ritas shaken before your eyes promise a festive experience at this tightly packed, upscale Mexican whose kitchen has been graced with many notable chefs. It's hard to find fault with gooey, chorizo-studded queso, which arrives in an earthenware dish, though the lengthy list of starters—a hit with the after work crowd—hosts plenty of other musts; try, for example, the achiote chicken salbutes, topped with pickled red onions. Oaxacan black mole, which sauces pork tenderloin, is rounded in flavor, while the simple-but-luxurious *cochinita pibil* is made for tucking in to warm tortillas.

Alinea, 1723 N. Halsted St., Lincoln Park, Chicago, IL 60614; (312) 867-0110; www.alinea-restaurant.com; New American; $$$$. Dining is a theatrical experience at this stunner from Grant Achatz, whose artful plates confound, demand instruction, and fool by way of deceptively simple menu descriptors. Nothing is what it appears to be—rather, the menu is a composite of ingredients, revealing little about the magic on plate. The set-price, sticker-shock adventure ($195) consists of a single, seasonal, constantly evolving 20-plus-course arrangement, served by a polished (some would say stoic) waitstaff. This is special-occasion dining in its truest, most destination-worthy form. But romantic it is not. Instead, it's legendary and gastronomic, and you may be left scratching your head. The extensive wine list is top shelf. Achatz has two additional projects under way: **Next,** a by-ticket-only restaurant that must be paid for in advance, and **Aviary,** a molecular cocktail lounge—reimagined, of course.

Aloha Eats, 2534 N. Clark St., Lincoln Park, Chicago, IL 60614; (773) 935-6828; www.alohaeats.com; Hawaiian; $. Enter beneath the surfboard sign and be transported to a balmier place, one where island eats—crisp, panko-breaded *katsu,* tender Kahlua pork with crunchy cabbage, and Spam *musubi*—promote a beachy state of mind. Alternately, slurp your way through noodle-packed *saimin,* punched up with kimchee, knowing you'll be left with pocket change. Mix plates are key for indecisive types.

a tavola, 2148 W. Chicago Ave., Ukrainian Village, Chicago IL 60622; (773) 276-7567; www.atavolachicago.com; Italian; $$$. Though petite, this neighborhood charmer executes its rustic, handily sauced Northern Italian classics with might. Start with the lightly dressed, grilled duo of portobello and oyster mushrooms; bank on being wowed by the slow-simmered Bolognese and celestial, brown butter–kissed gnocchi; and never rule out the specials, perhaps spoon-tender short ribs beneath a confetti of gremolata. Cooking classes, which require advance reservations, are offered on select Monday evenings.

Bagel on Damen, 1252 N. Damen Ave., Wicker Park, Chicago, IL 60622; (773) 772-2243. Deli; $$. The bagels, hailing from legendary **New York Bagel & Bialy** in Lincolnwood, are the reason to come here. Cash-only and backed by Dion Antic, its sandwiches—

served on the aforementioned wonders—unleash a string of (positively used) expletives of adoration. The Breakfast II is a hangover godsend, its four-napkin contents of egg, bacon, cream cheese, and avocado hardly contained by its mish-mosh bagel foundation. At the same time, avoiding muffaletta-inspired The Moof—salami slathered with onion relish and roasted-jalapeño cream cheese—would be an exercise in willpower. Join the legions in ordering a cup of Stumptown coffee alongside. There is also a location at 4639 N. Damen Ave., (773) 878-8523.

Balsan, Elysian, 11 E. Walton St., Gold Coast, Chicago, IL 60611; (312) 646-1400; www.balsanrestaurant.com; New American; $$$$. Head to the third floor of this tony hotel and be bowled over by what you encounter: a sleekly casual, seasonally informed respite that has quickly found its groove. House-cured charcuterie is a must; start with the off-the-charts rabbit terrine and torchon of *foie gras*. Do yourself a solid and get some briny oysters from the raw bar, too. Both the small and large plates continue the refined-yet-casual approach, be it airy, brown-butter ricotta *gnudi* or veal heart with pear and Parmesan. Desserts end on a high note.

Big Bowl, 6 E. Cedar St., Gold Coast, Chicago, IL 60611; (312) 640-8888; www.bigbowl.com; Chinese/Thai; $$. Bountiful, if standard, Asian faves comprise the menu at this Lettuce Entertain You eatery. House-made ginger ale helps cool mouths fired up by wrinkled Szechuan green beans—for some, it doesn't take much. Familiar, sweet-tart orange chicken and pad Thai are safe bets, though many prefer to design their own stir-fry creations. Other locations are at 60 E. Ohio, (312) 951-1888; 1950 E. Higgins Rd., Schaumburg, (847) 517-8881; and 215 Parkway Dr., Lincolnshire, (847) 808-8880.

Big Star, 1531 N. Damen Ave., Wicker Park, Chicago, IL 60622; (773) 235-4039; www.bigstarchicago.com; Mexican; $$. At his taco bar with a mock dive-bar mentality, Paul Kahan crafts one amazing, carved-from-the-spit taco *al pastor;* studded with smoky pineapple bits and garnished with grilled onions and cilantro, it takes a rightful position this side of heaven. Diversions include grilled, salted jalapeño toreados and a bacon-wrapped Sonoran hot dog. Wash everything down with shot-ready whiskies and tequilas, and don't leave without getting a *dulce de leche* milkshake. Upping the cool factor, honky-tonk tunes are curated by Danny's Tavern DJs and the folks at Reckless Records.

bin wine cafe, 1559 N. Milwaukee Ave., Wicker Park, Chicago, IL 60622; (773) 486-2233; www .binwinecafe.com; New American/Wine Bar; $$. John Caputo's eclectic small plates are reason to go beyond the (admittedly awesome) cheese selection at this neighborhood-y **Bin 36** sib. Start with the crunchy tempura green beans, dunking them in citrus aioli, following with

the piquant, giardiniera-topped burger or a wood oven–fired pizza. Wine pairings make choosing accompanying vino a cinch, including during its popular brunch.

Birchwood Kitchen, 2211 W. North Ave., Bucktown, Chicago, IL 60647; (773) 276-2100; www.birchwoodkitchen.com; Cafe; $$. When it's warm, hang out in the courtyard of this local food-centric, counter-service sandwich shop; when it's not, get cozy within the exposed brick storefront, which is perfumed with house-roasted meat. Other efforts that show in the final product include seasonal, house-made chutneys, jams, and pickles, which are used as garnishes. Try the turkey meatloaf with house-made mozzarella and tangy-sweet tomato jam or the Spanish tuna melt with roasted tomato and Gruyère—or, maybe, the baguette stuffed with goat cheese, pickled beets, and walnut pesto. A notable brunch breaks the mold to include bacon bread pudding and the like.

Bistronomic, 840 N. Wabash Ave., Gold Coast, Chicago, IL 60610; www.bistronomic.net; French; $$. Martial Noguier is behind this seasonal, rustic eatery, where artisanal charcuterie and cheeses; small, medium, and large plates; and cans and jars of olives to sardines find fans. A classy setting, complete with looming, architectural lighting and grey banquettes, lends a romantic edge.

Bistro 110, 110 E. Pearson St., Gold Coast, Chicago, IL 60611; (312) 266-3110; www.bistro 110restaurant.com; French; $$$. Everything a bistro is supposed to be—convivial, crowded, classic—this favored Frenchie does the standards and does them right. So, quit counting carbs and indulge in slices of warm baguette, slathered with roasted garlic. The French onion soup is deserving of accolades, its bubbly, cheesy canopy revealing rich, beefy stock once punctured. Also of note: Julia Child's peerless duck à l'orange; homey, herbaceous wood-roasted chicken; and rustic, deeply flavorful cassoulet. Finish with Tahitian vanilla bean crème brûlée or profiteroles.

Bistrot Zinc, 1131 N. State St., Gold Coast, Chicago, IL 60610; (312) 337-1131; www.bistrotzinc.com; French; $$. An authentic Left Bank feel permeates every nook of this neighborhood constant with State Street views. Although it dishes up both the familiar— plump *moules frites* redolent of shallots and fines herbes—and con- temporary, stick with the former. Steak frites, topped with requisite maître d'hôtel butter, for example, will not let you down. Finish with decadent chocolate-espresso pot de crème.

Black Dog Gelato, 859 N. Damen Ave., Wicker Park, Chicago, IL 60622; (773) 235-3116; www.blackdogchicago.com; Gelato; $. Dessert darling Jessica Oloroso, who earned chops as the pastry chef at Stephanie Izard's Scylla, started supplying her atypical, amazing gelato to the city's best restaurants. These days, her hot pink storefront also dispenses the inventive, ever-changing flavors. Not to be denied is the allure of zippy, goat cheese-caramel-cashew and salty peanut flavors. A good case can be made for the smoky, creamy, bacon-dipped whisky gelato bar, too. Creative sodas and gelato cookie sandwiches are also available.

BOKA, 1729 N. Halsted St., Lincoln Park, Chicago, IL 60614; (312) 337-6070; www.bokachicago.com; New American; $$$. As sexy as they come, this Kevin Boehm and Rob Katz-owned venture is a force to be reckoned with, thanks to Giuseppe Tentori's grownup, Mediterranean-inflected cuisine. You'd be wise to go with one of the tasting menus, available as four-, six-, and nine-courses. Ordering a la carte proves rewarding as well. Begin, perhaps, with a refined, light starter of raw, citrus *tobiko*-kissed hamachi, graced with pomelo, pickled fennel, and parsnip sauce. By the time fragrant *vadouvan* spice-crusted halibut arrives with its grilled bok choy, eggplant, and coconut-prawn couscous, you'll be ready to make a follow-up reservation on the spot. (See recipe on p. 344.)

Bon Bon Vietnamese Sandwiches, My Gourmet Kitchen, 2333 W. North Ave., Wicker Park, Chicago, IL 60647; (773) 278-5800; www.bonbonsandwiches.com; Vietnamese; $. Sharing space with My Gourmet Kitchen, this approachable, stylish *banh mi* counter is a prime pit stop, one that's worlds away from (admittedly more authentic) Argyle Street. Pair its *char siu* pork sandwich, dressed with fresh carrot-daikon slaw, with some spring rolls or Japanese potato croquettes and passion-fruit bubble tea.

Bongo Room, 1470 N. Milwaukee Ave., Wicker Park, Chicago, IL 60622; (773) 489-0690; www.thebongoroom.com; American; $$. A hit with the brunch bunch, this casual hangover helper turns the greasy spoon on end with dessertlike red-velvet pancakes beneath cream-cheesy sauce; a breakfast burrito stuffed with eggs and taco accoutrements; and funky riffs on French toast. Numerous creative salads and sandwiches carry through the lunch hour. There's a sister in the South Loop, 1152 S. Wabash Ave., (312) 291-0100.

Borinquen Restaurant, 1720 N. California Ave., Humboldt Park, Chicago, IL 60647; (773) 227-6038; Puerto Rican; $. Inspired by a sandwich he read about in a Latin paper, Juan Figueroa created the city's first *jibarito*—a garlicky, crisp, smashed plantain–encased sandwich that's now a quintessential Chicago eat. Choose your meat—the roast pork and steak are superior—and enjoy it zapped with mayo, melted American cheese, onion, lettuce, and tomato. Get *arroz con gandales,* rice studded with pigeon peas, on the side. Figueroa family members own restaurants at 3811 N. Western Ave., 773-442-8001, and 3020 Central Ave., (773) 622-8570.

The Bristol, 2152 N. Damen Ave., Bucktown, Chicago, IL 60647; (773) 862-5555; www.thebristolchicago.com; New American; $$$. Locavores converge at Chris Pandel's sustainably minded, exposed brick Midwestern, featuring a shareable daily menu and hipster clientele. Take in the indie tunes while inhaling porky Scotch olives, crunchy duck-fat fries, and tweaked panzanella, with pumpkin bread, speck, smoked mozzarella, and pear. Cheese boards, which arrive with Marcona almonds, semolina cookies, and house-made jam, are every bit as savvy as the larger plates. If the braised pork shank with house-made kraut and white beans is available, give it a shot. Also worthy is the otherworldly raviolo; when popped, its silky egg-yolk interior melds into a pool of nutty brown-butter sauce. At meal's end, wrangle up the Basque cake with apple sabayon. (See recipe on p. 353.)

Cafe Absinthe, 1954 W. North Ave., Wicker Park, Chicago, IL 60622; (773) 278-4488; www.absinthechicago.com; French; $$$. Make your way to the alley entrance of this neighborhood Frenchie, popular for its seasonal cuisine. Check out the generously sized, bacon-accented ostrich wing starter or earthy, creamy mushroom risotto with mascarpone. And anytime crisp-skinned duck breast is available, do indulge. Also, check out the prix-fixe menu on Sunday and Tuesday—at $35 it's a pretty good deal.

Cafe Ba-Ba-Reeba!, 2024 N. Halsted St., Lincoln Park, Chicago, IL 60614; (773) 935-5000; www.cafebabareeba.com; Spanish/ Tapas; $$. This Lettuce Entertain You joint helped make tapas a local household name. Happy-hour enticements—a pintxos menu with short rib–stuffed piquillo, for example—draw crowds. But anything on the menu tastes extra-enticing when you're passing the hours on the enclosed patio. Veer toward the small plates—the paella is just so-so—such as chorizo-wrapped, Manchego dates, beef tenderloin brochettes with caramelized onions, or meatballs in sherry-accented tomato sauce. Come for brunch, when the bleary-eyed sip rounds of deceptively fruity sangria.

Cafe Bernard, 2100 N. Halsted St., Lincoln Park, Chicago, IL 60614; (773) 871-2100; www.cafebernard.com; French; $$$. Unassuming, quiet and extremely inviting, this bistro is the stuff of first dates. Traditional French fare reigns, and it's done the way doctrine ordains. Whether you start with the oozy baked Brie *en croûte* or entertain an order of escargots, move onward to bouillabaisse, cassoulet, or steak au poivre. Then it's time for the ultimate reward: luxe white chocolate mousse. For a budget-friendly, casual experience, visit its sister wine bar, **Red Rooster,** in back (see p. 271).

Cafe des Architectes, Sofitel Chicago Water Tower, 20 E. Chestnut St., Gold Coast, Chicago, IL 60611; (312) 324-4063; www.cafedesarchitectes.com; French; $$$$. Martial Noguier got food folks excited about this Sofitel-centered brasserie, designed by Pierre-Yves Rochon. He has since moved on, and it remains in apt hands. Greg Biggers (Morimoto in Philadelphia, Fulton's on the River, Tru) is in the house, shaking things up with dishes that include seared Hudson Valley *foie gras* with black pepper financier, violet mustard-blackberry jam, and braised pear. Also, set price and degustation menus are available daily.

Cafe Laguardia, 2111 W. Armitage Ave., Bucktown, Chicago, IL 60647; (773) 862-5996; www.cafelaguardia.com; Cuban; $$. There's no pretension at this family-run Cuban, its solid selections backdropped by animal-print details and its fame cemented after a visit from Rachael Ray. Come hungry and start with the sampler platter, complete with ham croquettes. Among entrees, the crisp, fried pork chops are head and shoulders above all else, though it's rare to encounter a dud. Great mojitos and live music ratchet up the volume—but also heighten the fun factor.

Cafe Spiaggia, 980 N. Michigan Ave., Level Two, Gold Coast, Chicago, IL 60611; (312) 280-2750; www.spiaggiarestaurant.com; Italian; $$$. The (somewhat) more affordable sister to Tony Mantuano's nearby Spiaggia features rustic-chic, frescoed confines and intoxicating Italian eats. Nibble on crostini with ruby trout, parsley, and fried capers; young goat's cheese with fresh clover honey; or barely there gnocchi with rich wild-boar *ragù*. Craving porchetta? This version, hit with Calabrian peppers, will ruin you for the rest.

Cape Cod Room, The Drake Hotel, 140 E. Walton Pl., Gold Coast, Chicago, IL 60611; (312) 787-2200; www.thedrakehotel.com; Seafood; $$$. Not as stodgy as its address would suggest, this circa-1933 blast from the past—decked in nautical trappings— keeps its menu true to form and its fabled, carved-wood bar intact. You'll want to get the Dover sole, prepared tableside, and lobster thermidor (if money allows). There are more contemporary options, too, like salt-roasted prawns with dry aged, pork–studded collards, mascarpone grits, and lemon vinaigrette.

Carmine's, 1043 N. Rush St., Gold Coast, Chicago, IL 60611; (312) 988-7676; www.rosebudrestaurants.com; Italian; $$$. This Rush and Division mainstay, a member of the Rosebud family of restaurants, has a dark, clubby, and convivial feel and loyal, if aging, following. The bi-level dining room turns out Soprano-esque staples, from fried calamari, bruschetta, and clams baked in garlic butter to a hand-rolled meatball salad. There are requisites, like chicken Parm and Milanese, in sandwich form, plus handmade noodles swathed in marinara—all generally satisfying if it's your thing.

Cemitas Puebla, 3619 W. North Ave., Humboldt Park, Chicago, IL 60647; (773) 772-8435; www.cemitaspuebla.com; Mexican; $. The foods of Puebla take center stage at this neighborhood joint with a cultlike following. Its namesake sandwich is an unequivocal must, its sesame-studded roll stocked with avocado, house-marinated chipotles, a sprinkle of Oaxacan cheese, *papalo* (seasonally), and a choice of meat. The *carne asada* and gut-busting *Atomica*— Milanesa, guajillo pork enchilada, and ham—are masterpieces.

Charlie Trotter's, 816 W. Armitage Ave., Lincoln Park, Chicago, IL 60614; (773) 248-6228; www.charlietrotters.com; New American; $$$$. The epitome of haute dining, Charlie Trotter's eponymous dining room will set you back a serious sum, particularly if you sit at the kitchen table, which has its own extravagant preparations. The sedate dining room serves two additional, seasonal menus daily: a grand and a vegetable degustation. Both are lavish and ever-changing arrays, with plates such as Bobwhite quail breast, plated with toasted farro and red Russian kale, or Tasmanian ocean trout graced with grapefruit and fennel blossom. The wine list is extensive, sophisticated and, not surprisingly, spendy. For a more down-to-earth taste, try **Trotter's To Go** (1337 W. Fullerton Ave., 773-868-6510).

Chickpea, 2018 W. Chicago Ave., Ukrainian Village, Chicago, IL 60622; (773) 384-9930; www.chickpeaonthego.com; Middle Eastern; $. Jerry Suqi (Narcisse, Sugar, La Pomme Rouge) switched gears for this family affair; his mother turns out expertly prepared *kibbeh,* tender, lemony *malfoof* (rice and lamb-filled cabbage rolls), and a tangy dip of homemade yogurt, zucchini, and mint to hipsters amid walls hung with import movie posters.

C-House, Affinia Chicago, 166 E. Superior St., Streeterville, Chicago, IL 60611; (312) 523-0923; www.c-houserestaurant.com; Seafood; $$$. Celeb chef Marcus Samuelsson's stylish seafooder skips the underwater hues in favor of a sepia-toned dining room, hung with copper orbs of light. The briny deep gets its nod in raw bar preparations—*hiramasa* with Asian pear, hearts of palm, and sunflower seeds—and comforting small and large plates that incorporate Midwestern ingredients. But it's Nicole Pederson (Lula, Gramercy Tavern) who deserves most of the kitchen cred. Look to her handmade valcasotto cheese and winter squash ravioli in sage-brown butter; whole, bacon-wrapped trout with homemade kraut, lentils, spinach, and beer mustard; and scallops with crab-apple butter, golden raisins, and smoked almonds for evidence. After seasonal finales, head to **C-View,** a swanky indoor-outdoor rooftop lounge with panoramic city views. (See recipe on p. 355.)

Cipollina, 1543 N. Damen Ave., Wicker Park, Chicago, IL 60622; (773) 227-6300; www.cipollinadeli.com; Deli; $$. Milk & Honey's Carol Watson is behind the enticing array of Italian preparations at this quaint, cool-kid carryout where panini are given the porchetta treatment. A palate-perking Italian sub—layered with wisps of imported meat and daubed with house-made giardiniera—is the standout hand-held, along with a number donning prosciutto, Parmesan-truffle butter, Calabrian peppers, and arugula. Seasonal orange-lavender sandwich cookies and almond croissants address the sweeter side.

Coast Sushi, 2045 N. Damen Ave., Bucktown, Chicago, IL 60647; (773) 235-5775; www.coastsushibar.com; Japanese; $$$. Downright sexy, this low-lit sashimi slinger is BYOB. Signature rolls like the White Dragon—spicy-sauced shrimp tempura, wasabi *tobiko,* cream cheese, and scallion with tempura crunch—may turn off purists, but that's beside the point. The kitchen also sees success with fiery orange-tamarind duck breast, its skin glistening and crisp. A South Loop counterpart is at 1700 S. Michigan Ave., (312) 662-1700.

Coco Pazzo Cafe, 636 N. St. Clair St., Streeterville, Chicago, IL 60611; (312) 664-2777; www.cocopazzocafe.com; Italian; $$. The casual Coco Pazzo cousin is equally ingredient-driven, though more straightforward in its execution. Start with antipasti, perhaps house-cured salmon with fennel and orange, pan-fried Marsala chicken livers with polenta, or white bean–black truffle bruschetta. Then, choose appetizer portions of pasta—perhaps penne with sage-scented veal sauce or butternut squash cappellacci with crumbles of amaretti—saving room for incredibly tender, braised lamb shank, topped with frizzles of leek. Dine alfresco when weather allows.

Crust, 2056 W. Division St., Wicker Park, Chicago, IL 60622; (773) 235-5511; www.crustorganic.com; Pizza; $$. Michael Altenberg's minimalist, organic eatery maintains a fan base for unpredictable pizzas, which embrace sustainable ingredients from Chicago's surrounds. Settle in for the *Flammkuchen*—a béchamel-slathered, caraway seed–studded number with nubs of bacon, caramelized onions, and Parmigiano-Reggiano—or the cilantro-sprinkled Mexicali Blues, a mixture of cheeses, roasted shrimp, pico de gallo, and a spurt of lime. Sit on the pretty back patio when possible.

Cumin, 1414 N. Milwaukee Ave., Wicker Park, Chicago, IL 60622; (773) 342-1414; www.cumin-chicago.com; Nepalese/Indian; $$.

Rocking out aromatic dishes in a contemporary setting, this hip haunt has your standards: samosas, biryani, and chicken tikka masala. But it's the Nepalese dishes—like chicken momo, steamed dumplings filled with herbaceous, minced chicken—you'll pine for. Don't pass go without ordering the *palungo ko saag,* wilted spinach, spruced up with mustard, cumin, and fenugreek seeds, plus roasted garlic, and fiery chiles.

deca Restaurant + Bar, Ritz-Carlton Chicago, 160 E. Pearson St., Gold Coast, Chicago, IL 60611; (312) 573-5160; www.decarestaurant .com; French; $$$. Located on the 12th floor of the luxury Ritz-Carlton hotel, this casual, mid-priced brasserie appeals to modern-day diners with casual eats from Mark Payne. A highlight of the menu is the glorious seafood tower, chock-full of oysters and crab legs, plump shrimp and periwinkles. Other options range from duck rillettes with celery-root remoulade to pan-seared skate with golden raisins, fennel confit, and piquillo peppers.

Del Seoul, 2568 N. Clark St., Lincoln Park, Chicago, IL 60614; (773) 248-4227; www.delseoul.com; Korean; $. Drawing inspiration from Kogi trucks, this updated Korean tackles *banh mi* (*soju*-marinated *bulgogi,* smoky *gochujang* pork), *kalbi* tacos, bibimbap, and barbecue plates with sautéed onions, house kimchee, and baby bok choy—all on the cheap.

Duchamp, 2118 N. Damen Ave., Bucktown, Chicago, IL 60647; (773) 235-6434; www.duchamp-chicago.com; New American; $$. After parting ways with Michael Taus, this French-tinged American from the Lumen crew forges on, maintaining its crowd-pleasing menu of large and small plates, served on the popular, seasonal patio. Creative tipples are ideal companions to braised short ribs with mashed lavender sweet potatoes and grilled rosemary swordfish with polenta.

Enoteca Roma, 2146 W. Division St., Ukrainian Village, Chicago, IL 60622; (773) 342-1011; www.enotecaroma.com; Italian; $$. This rustic Italian wine bar—an offshoot of Letizia's Natural Bakery—has a not-so-secret weapon: a picturesque garden patio in back, where couples converse over mix-and-match bruschetta, antipasti, and cheese and salumi platters. Baked terrines, pastas, and pizzas offer something more substantial. A large vino and beer list is thrown in for good measure.

Feast, 25 E. Delaware Pl., Gold Coast, Chicago, IL 60611; (312) 337-4001; www.feastrestaurant.com; New American; $$. There's no denying the attraction of this haunt, a breakfast and brunch darling that dives into comforting global flavors—bourbon-soy-glazed short ribs, blackened fish tacos with red onion marmalade—from lunchtime on. There's also an outpost at 1616 N. Damen Ave., (773) 772-7100.

Feed, 2803 W. Chicago Ave., Humboldt Park, Chicago, IL 60622; (773) 489-4600; www.feedrestaurantchicago.com; American; $$. Check pretension at the door—this Southern-tinged eatery won't have it. Instead, you'll be met with winning rotisserie chicken, fried okra, and sides of mac and cheese and corn pudding. Grab cash in advance.

Franks 'N' Dawgs, 1863 N. Clybourn Ave., Lincoln Park, Chicago, IL 60614; (312) 281-5187; www.franksndawgs.com; Hot Dogs; $. Aussie Alexander Brunacci is behind this ramped-up stand with Joe Doren (Blackbird, Sixteen) in the kitchen. He, like Hot Doug's Doug Sohn, has a formula that works. Some of the encased meats are made in house; the artisanal ingredients are stuffed into French-style *pain de mie* buns; and local chefs are enlisted to create signature, gourmet sausages. Try the "mystery" corn dog coated in Anson Mills polenta batter—you'll never go state fair again. Whether you settle on a German-style brat topped with Waldorf salad or knockwurst garnished with grilled eggplant, goat cheese, and salsa verde, be sure to order the truffle fries. Incidentally, Brunacci's brother, Frank, is Sixteen's executive chef.

Geja's Cafe, 340 W. Armitage Ave., Lincoln Park, Chicago IL 60614; (773) 281-9101; www.gejascafe.com; Fondue; $$$. Romance is in the air at this intimate subterranean den, an anniversary-appropriate fondue destination. Plunk pumpernickel into a cauldron of melty, kirsch-infused Gruyère; place beef tenderloin, lobster, and shrimp in bubbling oil, dunking the results in an array of sauces once cooked; and finish with a flaming chocolate finale. A large wine list and live flamenco guitar are added appeals.

Gemini Bistro, 2075 N. Lincoln Ave., Lincoln Park, Chicago, IL 60614; (773) 525-2522; www.geminibistrochicago.com; American; $$$. Jason Paskewitz is on to something at this inviting, contemporary bistro with a roster of comforting, by-the-books small, medium, and large plates built from familiar ingredients. Robust, creamless tomato soup with grilled cheese and a filler-light jumbo lump crab cake with Tabasco aioli are strengths. But the prime burger—served on a pretzel roll that barely contains the juices—is nothing to sniff at.

Gibsons Bar & Steakhouse, 1028 N. Rush St, Gold Coast, Chicago, IL 60611; (312) 266-8999; www.gibsonssteakhouse.com; Steakhouse; $$$. A gold standard steakhouse, this joint serves expense account steaks, chops, and sweet, football-sized lobster tail in the heart of the so-called Viagra Triangle. Start with the fantastic shrimp cocktail, served on a bed of ice with nose-clearing cocktail sauce. Or, grab some jumbo crab claws with Dijon dipping sauce and slurp an oversized, ice-cold martini. Clear room for the nicely marbled Chicago cut (a bone-in rib eye) with a brittle pepper crust. Sides—like the double-baked potato—and ridiculously large desserts are meant to be shared. Additional locations are at 5464

N. River Rd., Rosemont, (847) 928-9900; and 2105 S. Spring Rd., Oak Brook, (630) 954-0000.

Green Zebra, 1460 W. Chicago Ave., Noble Square, Chicago, IL 60642; (312) 243-7100; www.greenzebrachicago.com; Vegetarian; $$$. Shawn McClain mans this dazzler with a deceptively straightforward menu of unique, largely vegetarian small plates. Things that are the stuff of dreams: chilled sweet corn and summer squash soup; artfully plated burrata with tempura peaches, cashews, arugula, and melon granita; and ginger-accented lemon spaetzle with local pea shoots and baby carrots. The five-course tasting menu with wine or nonalcoholic, house-made soda pairings is worth considering.

Honey 1 BBQ, 2241 N. Western Ave., Bucktown, Chicago, IL 60647; (773) 227-5130; www.honey1bbq.com; Barbecue; $$. Roll up your sleeves and prepare to pig out—pitmaster Robert Adams's wood-smoked barbecue is the real deal. Chewy, full-flavored rib tips, spicy, spurting hot links, and sauced sparerib racks—all worthy of a detour—team with addictive, fried, sauce-free wings just begging to be dunked in house-made sauce.

HotChocolate, 1747 N. Damen Ave., Bucktown, Chicago, IL 60647; (773) 489-1747; www.hotchocolatechicago.com; American; $$. At Mindy Segal's solid, market-driven restaurant, it's true that the desserts shine. However, the pastry chef's savory side conjures up "oohs" and "ahhs," too. Get your cheese on with a house-made, beer-poached pretzel with Taleggio fondue, followed by creamily sauced mac and cheese. But don't feel bad coming for the over-the-top finales alone. The "Thoughts on a Peanut Butter Cup"—a composition of peanut butter mousse and peanut butter cup with milk chocolate hot fudge, Concord grape syrup, and a peanut butter–cookie dough truffle—is worth the trip.

Hugo's Frog Bar & Fish House, 1024 N. Rush St., Gold Coast, Chicago, IL 60611; (312) 640-0999; www.hugosfrogbar.com; Seafood; $$$$. This clubby adjunct to Gibsons Bar & Steakhouse shares a kitchen and offers the same superior steaks, while empha-sizing super-fresh catches and its namesake amphibian in garlic butter. Great beginnings include the shrimp cocktail, king crab fingers, and lump crab cake. From there, it's on to Alaskan halibut en papillote, pan-seared scallops with truffle butter, or lobster tail with lemon butter. Desserts are sized for sharing—with a crowd. There's also a location at 55 S. Main St., Naperville, (630) 548-3764.

Irazu, 1865 N. Milwaukee Ave., Bucktown, Chicago, IL 60647; (773) 252-5687; www.irazuchicago.com; Costa Rican; $$. Providing a reliable entry point for those unfamiliar with the food of Central America, this welcoming, cash-only eatery kicks things off with fried plantains topped with roasted garlic oil. Another dish you'll be smitten with is the *casado,* rib eye with rice, beans, plantains, and an over-easy egg alongside cabbage salad. And don't miss the *pepito* sandwich, steak with onions and cheese, as well as the oatmeal shake.

Jam, 937 N. Damen Ave., Ukrainian Village, Chicago, IL 60622; (773) 489-0302; www.jamrestaurant.com; American; $$. Jerry Suqi (Chickpea, La Pomme Rouge) and chef and co-owner Jeffrey Mauro (Charlie Trotter's, North Pond) are behind this cash-only, BYOB joint, where a.m. eats take a turn for the best. Whether you come for malted custard French toast with macerated rhubarb, pink peppercorn and lime-leaf cream or an egg sandwich stuffed with pork cheek, green-apple ketchup, and ricotta fillings, return later for sophisticated *foie gras* tortellini with melted onions and English-pea puree—even when your wallet is slim. Jam is opening a Logan Square location at 937 N. Damen Ave., (773) 489-0302.

John's Place, 1200 W. Webster Ave., Lincoln Park, Chicago, IL 60614; (773) 525-6670; www.johnsplace.com; American; $$. Diners take stock in knowing what's in store: comfort food and lots of it, served in homey, wood-trimmed, exposed-brick surrounds. From chili to loaded nachos, chopped salad, burgers, and meatloaf, this catchall has something to suit everyone. There is a spin-off at 2132 W. Roscoe St., (773) 244-6430.

Kith & Kin, 1119 W. Webster Ave., Lincoln Park, Chicago, IL 60614; (773) 472-7070; www.knkchicago.com; New American; $$. It's neighborhood-y, affordable, and inventive—all qualities that up the likability factor of this high-end-casual New American, where pimiento cheese spread meets offerings such as duck rillettes with pickled prunes; house-made tagliatelle topped with braised-rabbit *ragù*; buttermilk-fried chicken thighs; and seared scallops with cauliflower "couscous," curry pudding, and grilled tomato soup.

Landmark Grill + Lounge, 1633 N. Halsted St, Lincoln Park, Chicago, IL 60614; (312) 587-1600; www.landmarkgrill.net; New American; $$$. Thank the BOKA boys (also of Perennial Virant and Girl & the Goat) for this hub, a short-lister among theatergoers and bottle service–seeking, late-night loungers. And while the flattering glow cast upon the two-floor space—a one-time candle factory—furthers its cause, the Giuseppe Tentori–designed menu fares way better than most. Communal dishes may include pickled jalapeño-studded deviled eggs, black-pepper polenta fries, or latkes topped with smoked salmon and  fennel applesauce. But Thanksgiving-y roasted butternut squash soup with chestnut-squash *ragù* and a barbecue-lacquered heirloom pork chop with bacon spaetzle and sweet-onion marmalade may help ground you when rounds of craft cocktails come into play.

La Pasadita, 1141 N. Ashland Ave., Ukrainian Village, Chicago, IL 60622; (773) 278-0384; www.pasadita.com; Mexican; $. Keep your eyes peeled, and enter the original—the one with sun-yellow façade. Dive-y and longstanding, the taqueria's cilantro and onion-topped *carne asada* tacos—set ablaze with *salsa verde*—spawned two counter-service siblings within the same block. However, there's nothing like procuring them from the storied source. But be forewarned: late at night, lines snake out the door.

Las Palmas, 1835 W. North Ave., Wicker Park, Chicago, IL 60622; (773) 289-4991; www.laspalmaschicago.com; Mexican; $$. This vibrant, artsy neighborhood gem—a creative, Frida Kahlo-hung off-shoot of the same-named mini-chain—has it going on. The menu takes a turn for the inventive, with ahi with jalapeño chimichurri and roast duck atop parsnip puree with prickly pear-habañero salsa. Don't miss the creative cocktails, such as a refreshing cucumber margarita, but do grab a perch on the secluded patio when weather allows.

Le Bouchon, 1958 N. Damen Ave., Bucktown, Chicago, IL 60647; (773) 862-6600; www.lebouchonofchicago.com; French; $$$. Petite, loud, and pleasing, Le Sardine's sibling serves a similar spread. Make a meal of steamed mussels and an onion tart, or begin with house-made pâté, followed by robust grilled hanger steak with red-wine sauce; slow-simmered beef Bourguignon; or roast duck à l'orange. Ubiquitous as it may be, the silky crème brûlée is a must.

Les Nomades, 222 E. Ontario St., Streeterville, Chicago, IL 60611; (312) 649-9010; www.lesnomades.net; French; $$$$. Harking back to another time and place, this sophisticate with an elegant, tucked away townhouse setting, winning wine list, and haute French fare is as special occasion—and solid—as ever. Pedigreed cuisinier Chris

Nugent (Tru, Grace, Zealous, et al.) quietly, skillfully crafts what few in the city do anymore: *très chic,* technique-driven French cuisine. The intricate preparations are not mere throwbacks, though. So sit pretty over crispy poached egg, crawfish, Maitake mushroom, *rouge vif d'etampes,* and Iberico ham or roasted venison loin with sage-braised root vegetables, prune confit, and Armagnac *aigre-doux.* Or skip the guesswork, and opt for the tasting menu ($115–$130).

Lillie's Q, 1856 W. North Ave., Wicker Park, Chicago, IL 60622; (773) 772-5500; www.lilliesq.com; Barbecue; $$. This self-proclaimed bastion of "urban barbecue"—an industrial-sleek spot with a smoker manned by Charlie McKenna (Tru, Avenues)—is generally delish. Then again, it should be: It's a family-run follow-up to the Destin, Fla., original and a byproduct of a Memphis in May–winning pork-shoulder recipe. You can't come without getting the lean, supple tri-tip; competition-sauced ribs; fab beer-battered pickles and pimiento cheese; and spiky, meringue-topped banana pudding. Moonshine-based cocktails, served in Ball jars, add a touch of Southern kitsch.

Lovely: A Bake Shop, 1130 N. Milwaukee Ave., Noble Square, Chicago, IL 60622; (773) 572-4766; www.lovelybakeshop.com; Bakery; $. Cute as a button, seasonal mini-pies, chewy coconut macaroons, airy *pain au chocolat:* they're worth every calorie. Thank French Pastry School–trained partners Brooke Dailey and Gina Howie (also of Bakin' & Eggs) for that. Sweets aside, don't overlook the house-made soups (apple-fennel, red pepper, minted split pea) and grainy mustard–smeared salami sandwich, which you can enjoy in full amid a collection of vintage aprons and kitchen accessories.

L20, Belden-Stratford Hotel, 2300 N. Lincoln Park West, Lincoln Park, Chicago, IL 60614; (773) 868-0002; www.l2orestaurant .com; Seafood; $$$$. Everything about this Lettuce Entertain You marvel—the austere, spa-y setting, masterful tasting and prix-fixe menus, the carefully curated wine list—flies in the face of the prevailing, modern-day sentiment: that dining should be accessible, affordable, and local. But this superlative seafooder does what it wants and does so with swagger. About all that's heard in response is a collective "ooooh." From start to finish, dining here is a rarefied experience, one in which flavor pairings—tofu, pickles, tomato sorbet, and spicy parsley vinegar or smoked *kinmedai* with apricot oil, for example— transport and transform those who splurge.

LuxBar, 18 E. Bellevue Pl., Gold Coast, Chicago, IL 60611; (312) 642-3400; www.luxbar.com; American; $$$. Set amid a sea of pricier picks, this wood-paneled place is refreshing. Serving savory staples—tomato soup, sliders, buttermilk fried chicken—to all manner of diners, it also serves the big brother Gibsons' steaks, only at a less frenetic pace. Come on Friday and Saturday nights for prime rib, or tumble out of bed for weekend brunch.

MANA Food Bar, 1742 W. Division St., Wicker Park, Chicago, IL 60622; (773) 342-1742; www.manafoodbar.com; Vegetarian; $$. One of the most exciting vegetarian places to open in years comes from veterans of sushi wabi and de cero. The multiculti results— served in a trim, minimalist setting—range from *wakame*-cucumber salad with daikon sprouts in lemon-sesame dressing to tofu *bulgogi* with shiitake and a blue-cheese tart with caramelized onions. Stay and sip sake cocktails, or grab grub from the pickup window on Division when dining (oh-so-virtuously) on the fly.

Margie's Candies, 1960 N. Western Ave., Bucktown, Chicago, IL 60647; (773) 384-1035; www.margiescandies.com; Ice Cream; $. This vintage soda fountain, which opened its doors in 1921, is a place where nostalgia meets a new generation of sundae slicker. Spiked with wafer cookies, the candy-colored creations arrive in clamshell-like bowls with hot fudge on the side, and they're churned out until quite late. Signature chocolate confections (and rather forgettable sandwiches) may be procured here and at its Ravenswood offshoot (1813 W. Montrose Ave., 773-348-0400).

Markethouse, Doubletree Magnificent Mile, 611 N. Fairbanks Ct., Streeterville, Chicago, IL 60611; (312) 224-2200; www.market housechicago.com; New American; $$$. Though a hidden, corporate-feeling setting leaves this dining room frequently overlooked, blaze your own trails. Executive Chef Scott Walton is at the helm, and he utilizes a cache of fresh produce—much grown on the rooftop in season. The benefits are clear in dishes like honey-thyme-glazed pork belly with fava beans, morels, and truffles or smoked Muscovy duck breast with salsify and artichoke barigoule.

M Burger, 161 E. Huron St., Streeterville, Chicago, IL 60611; (312) 254-8500; www.mburgerchicago.com; Burgers; $. This Rich Melman–backed, secret-sauced-burger and shake shack presents an affordable choice amid a backdrop of Mag Mile excess. There's a second installment at 5 W. Ontario St., (312) 428-3548.

The Meatloaf Bakery, 2464 N. Clark St., Lincoln Park, Chicago, IL 60614; (773) 698-6667; www.themeatloafbakery.com; American; $$. In the event Mom's rock-hard meatloaf left its mark, head to this "fakery," where the innocuous cupcakes, tarts, and pies aren't what they seem. Take A Wing and a Prayer, for example; it's actually a blue-cheesy, wing-sauce-seasoned ground-chicken cupcake with a buttery blue-cheese crust.

Mike Ditka's, The Tremont Hotel, 100 E. Chestnut St., Gold Coast, Chicago, IL 60611; (312) 587-8989; www.mikeditkaschicago.com; Steakhouse; $$$$. Da coach's quintessential Chicago steakhouse serves a mighty juicy pork chop, noteworthy half-pound burger, and self-professed, "kick-ass" 30-ounce paddle steak, as well as sustainable seafood. Par for the course, it all takes place in a manly, memorabilia-filled setting. There is also a location at 2 Mid America Plaza, Oakbrook Terrace, (630) 572-2200.

Milk & Honey Cafe, 1920 W. Division St., Wicker Park, Chicago, IL 60622; (773) 395-9434; www.milkandhoneycafe.com; Cafe; $. The masses descend on weekends, but it's understandable given this cheery storefront serves reputable, brunch-y bites, like orange brioche French toast and trademark granola. During calmer times, sandwiches—from a smoked turkey Reuben to a BLT with thick slabs of bacon—suffice. When seating is at a premium, consider stopping by its counterpart, Italian-style deli **Cipollina.**

Mirai Sushi, 2020 W. Division St., Wicker Park, Chicago, IL 60622; (773) 862-8500; www.miraisushi.com; Sushi/Japanese; $$$. Oozing style—sans airs—Miae Lim's upscale, bi-level sushi and sake bar strikes a balance between classic and global-leaning flavors. Take the *sakana* carpaccio—tuna, salmon, and whitefish with cilantro, capers, and sesame oil—as an example. When dining here, get the *bin cho,* citrus-dressed baby tuna with arugula, too, and the spicy *mono,* octopus topped with spicy tuna and sweet *unagi* sauce.

Mon Ami Gabi, Belden-Stratford Hotel, 2300 N. Lincoln Park West, Lincoln Park, Chicago, IL 60614; (773) 348-8886; www .monamigabi.com; French; $$$. Consistency reigns at this Lettuce Entertain You bistro, where the steak frites—sauced with maître d'hôtel butter or prepared au poivre style—and lemony chicken paillard win every time. Then again, the skate wing shellacked with caper-brown butter doesn't exactly falter. Grab a seat on the patio when it's warm. There's also a location at 260 Oakbrook Center, Oak Brook, (630) 472-1900.

More Cupcakes, 1 E. Delaware Pl., Gold Coast, Chicago, IL 60611; (312) 951-0001; www.morecupcakes.com; Bakery; $$. Excelling at both sweet and savory cupcakes, Patty Rothman's creations range from obvious (milk chocolate–frosted vanilla, red velvet with cream-cheese topping) to kooky (maple-bacon) and just plain indulgent (salted caramel). The bottom line is these moist, crumby numbers are plain good. They're also available by mobile truck.

Morton's The Steakhouse, 1050 N. State St., Gold Coast, Chicago, IL 60610; (312) 266-4820; www.mortons.com; Steakhouse; $$$$. This original outpost—which spawned a national chain—exudes clubby charm with service, complete with tableside presentation, to match. Prime steaks (especially the bone-in rib eye) are really the way to go, though its lobster tail, crab cakes, and chocolate cake appease its suited-up clientele as well. There are numerous area locations.

North Pond, 2610 N. Cannon Dr., Lincoln Park, Chicago, IL 60614; (773) 477-5845; www.northpondrestaurant.com; New American; $$$$. Bruce Sherman's arts and crafts–style dining room—set so picturesquely within Lincoln Park proper—takes a farm-to-table to approach to dishes, be it prawns à la plancha, offset by eggplant-raisin agnolotti, minted yogurt sauce, and almonds or pork belly confit with carrot-coconut milk broth, Manila clams, and carrot-lime escabeche. Provided everyone concurs (it's a full-table affair), the tasting menu is a wise choice.

Orange, 2413 N. Clark St., Lincoln Park, Chicago, IL 60614; (773) 549-7833; www.orangerestaurantchicago.com; New American; $$. Earning fame for fruishi—fruit sushi—and creative pancake flights, brunch lovers wait endlessly for a table at this trusty joint. Coconut-infused French toast skewers and pesto green eggs and ham further clarify why. There are additional locations in the River West, River North, and Roscoe Village neighborhoods as well as in suburban Glenview.

The Original Gino's East Pizza, 162 E. Superior St., Gold Coast, Chicago, IL 60611; (312) 266-3337; www.ginoseast.com; Pizza; $. Tourists (and enough locals) don't mind waiting for seats at this legend, famous for it brightly sauced, cornmeal-crusted deep-dish delights. Sausage is a safe bet, though many a hardcore carnivore gorges on the "meaty legend," a gut-expander loaded with bacon, Canadian bacon, pepperoni, and sausage. There are numerous city and suburban locations.

Pane Caldo, 72 E. Walton St., Gold Coast, Chicago, IL 60611; (312) 649-0055; www.pane-caldo.com; Italian; $$$$. Tucked just off of the energetic Magnificent Mile, this upscale, Northern Italian vet is a respite for weary shoppers and a gem of a find for daters seeking an intimate, quality meal. A large, savvy wine list complements offerings like grilled polenta with shiitake and oyster mushrooms and Gorgonzola. There's also house-made shrimp and avocado–filled ravioli cloaked in saffron-fennel sauce or a *mille foglie* of roast chicken, layered with prosciutto, spinach, mozzarella, and haricots verts in wild-mushroom sauce.

Pelago Ristorante, Rafaello Hotel, 201 E. Delaware Pl., Gold Coast, Chicago, IL 60611; (312) 280-0700; www.pelagorestaurant.com; Italian; $$$. Mauro Mafrici serves three squares daily at this serene spot in a boutique hotel, where riffs on routine Italian entice. Perfect veal ravioli get a boost from pistachio sauce, while pesto-sauced *trofie* lounges with string beans and potatoes. Meanwhile, gremolata-showered monkfish takes an osso-buco approach and rolled, duck-filled pork arrives redolent of marjoram. Desserts—like lemon cake with grapefruit salad and orange sorbet—sweeten the pot.

Perennial Virant, 1800 N. Lincoln Ave., Lincoln Park, Chicago, IL 60614; (312) 981-7070; www.perennialchicago.com; New American; $$$. BOKA's Rob Katz and Kevin Boehm are behind this inviting, sustainably minded American bistro with a fab patio; rustic-chic, wood-trimmed dining room punctuated by hot pink; and Vie's Paul Virant in the kitchen, whipping up stuff inspired by nearby Green City Market. Expect dishes that make the most of the season's bounty (and, no doubt, the bounty preserved).

Podhalanka, 1549 W. Division St., Wicker Park, Chicago, IL 60622; (773) 486-6655; Polish; $. There's no vibe to speak of at this dank, old-school gem, where cold-weather Polish comforts—tangy white borscht with sausage, pierogi generously topped with sour cream, stuffed cabbage—fortify. Bar stools are the seat of choice, but it's fruity *kompot*—rather than booze—that's dispensed.

The Purple Pig, 500 N. Michigan Ave., Gold Coast, Chicago, IL 60611; (312) 464-1744; www.thepurplepigchicago .com; Small Plates; $$$. It's all about the swine and wine at this buzzing Scott Harris, Jimmy Bannos Sr., Tony Mantuano, and Chef Jimmy Bannos Jr. collaboration, which quickly rose to acclaim for its pig ear with crispy kale, piquant cherry peppers, and fried egg. Cured meat, schmears, and heftier plates— including meltingly tender, milk-braised pork shoulder—attract an after-hours crowd, a fact that's furthered by the affordable import wine list. (See recipe on p. 373.)

Ria, Elysian, 11 E. Walton St., Gold Coast, Chicago, IL 60611; (312) 880-4400; www .riarestaurantchicago.com; New American; $$$. This haute, fine-dining destination in the tony Elysian hotel presents a concise menu of aesthetically pleasing, artful plates. A quiet counterpart to Balsan across the way, it has rapidly topped the short list of food enthusiasts, who indulge in shaved *foie gras* with pumpernickel, preserved plum, and tatsoi whenever the mood strikes.

Riva, Navy Pier, 700 E. Grand Ave., Streeterville, Chicago, IL 60611; (312) 644-7482; www.rivanavypier .com; Seafood; $$$. Phil Stefani's stylish catch—a getaway for the tourist-weary traveler—has an amazing Lake Michigan view, coupled with pristine seafood-centric eats. Indulge in the platter of oysters, chilled shrimp, jumbo lump crab, and tuna tartare or rich lobster bisque, followed by Pacific halibut with sweet-corn essence. Plan ahead and dine when there's a fireworks display.

Sabor Saveur, 2013 W. Division St., Ukrainian Village, Chicago, IL 60622; (773) 235-7310; www.saborsaveur.com; Mexican/French; $$. A stark, minimalist dining room sets the tone for a culinary journey, one in which gordita-like *bocoles*—accented by saffron butter and cilantro oil—brim with lobster and shrimp; *chicharrones* fill tortellini; and sea bass gets the *al pastor* treatment. A BYOB policy goes a long way to smooth potential rough edges.

Sayat Nova, 157 E. Ohio St., Streeterville, Chicago, IL 60611; (312) 644-9159; www.sayatnovachicago.com; Armenian; $$. Lanterns cast a moody, low glow at this quiet, all-but-hidden Armenian surprise just off of the Mag Mile. It's a pleasant pit stop for kebabs, broiled lamb chops, and tangy *labneh*. No meal is complete without a finisher of *mahalabiya,* comforting milk pudding topped with walnuts.

Schwa, 1466 N. Ashland Ave., Wicker Park, Chicago, IL 60622; (773) 252-1466; www.schwarestaurant.com; New American; $$$$.

Michael Carlson's casual-haute BYOB defies categorization—but, really, that's the point. Dining at the restaurant, located along a dreary stretch of Ashland, is an experience, one where chefs themselves serve intricate, fantastical tasting menus to those who are privileged enough to have reservations, left on the notoriously full voice mail, confirmed. Provided you can see through the foams (and don't mind dining to the not-so-occasional hip-hop beat), Carlson's wizardry—honed alongside Grant Achatz—shines bright.

Seasons, Four Seasons Hotel Chicago, 120 E. Delaware Pl., Gold Coast, Chicago, IL 60611; (312) 649-2349; www.fourseasons.com/chicagofs; New American; $$$$. This swanky, wood-paneled hotel dining room, located on the seventh floor of the Four Seasons, could easily be dismissed as crusty. However, Executive Chef Kevin Hickey's ever-changing, fancy-pants dishes, served while framed by gracious Lake Michigan views, deserve recognition. So, slip on those Ferragamos and get down with the best of them, reveling in Ewe's blue-cheese soufflé with truffle honey–glazed black mission figs and lamb's lettuce or crispy veal sweetbreads with Michigan cherry crème fraîche.

Signature Room at the 95th, John Hancock Center, 875 N. Michigan Ave., Streeterville, Chicago, IL 60611; (312) 787-9596; www.signatureroom.com; American; $$$$. Admittedly, this panoramic dining room, with its 96th-floor companion lounge, is known foremost for its pretty face. However, Patrick Sheerin (Crofton on Wells, Everest, Naha) challenges diners to tear their eyes from the view. The reward for doing so is produce-driven dishes, such as bacon-wrapped Berkshire pork tenderloin with white beans, yuzu-apple relish, and miso butterscotch or butter-poached South African lobster tails with roasted salsify, wilted greens, and fragrant curry-carrot puree. While taking in the glittery skyline, take time to peruse the extensive, global wine list.

Simply It, 2269 N. Lincoln Ave., Lincoln Park, Chicago, IL 60614; (773) 248-0884; www.simplyitrestaurant.com; Vietnamese; $$. Affordable and stylish, Tuan Nguyen's BYOB storefront puts fresh flavors at the forefront. More mainstream than its Argyle street counterparts, this menu provides an entry point to Vietnamese cuisine by way of lemongrass beef with rice-paper wrappers, Saigonese crepes, and sticky rice cakes wrapped in banana leaves and stuffed with chicken, mung beans, and shiitakes. Clay-pot and noodle dishes are among the entrees, though coconut-mango beef—showily served in a coconut shell—is too appealing to pass by.

The Smoke Daddy, 1804 W. Division St., Wicker Park, Chicago, IL 60622; (773) 772-6656; www.thesmokedaddy.com; Barbecue; $$. A retro feel pervades this down-home 'cue shack, ignited with smoked-until-pink ribs, brisket, and pulled pork. Sides, including delish sweet-potato fries, and finales—fried apple pie, a skillet cookie—aren't just afterthoughts. Live music, typically of the blues and jazz persuasion, ups the lively vibe.

Sono Wood Fired, 1582 N. Clybourn Ave., Lincoln Park, Chicago, IL 60642; (312) 255-1122; www.sonowoodfired.com; Pizza; $$. Daters dig this Lincoln Park pizzeria, next door to fellow Urban Burger Bar. The thrust of the menu is creatively topped, red or white, wood-fired pies. Try the one donning spicy soppressata, buffalo mozzarella, tomatoes, and charred onions with basil. Bruschetta, salads, and pastas are among the added options.

Spiaggia, 980 N. Michigan Ave., Gold Coast, Chicago, IL 60611; (312) 280-2750; www.spiaggiarestaurant.com; Italian; $$$$. Tony Mantuano's staggering, ostentatiously adorned (and priced), multi-level dining room is as special occasion as the buzz suggests. From the jaw-dropping cheeses—kept in a climate-controlled cave—to pastas that bring diners to their knees, this is mind-blowing dining at its best. For something more down to earth, try the regional Italian at casual-chic **Cafe Spiaggia,** or head to **Terzo Piano,** located in the Modern Wing of the Art Institute.

Sprout, 1417 W. Fullerton Ave., Lincoln Park, Chicago, IL 60614; (773) 348-0706; www.sproutrestaurant.com; New American/French; $$$. Chicagoans were crushed by Dale Levitski's *Top Chef* misfire, though there's little but praise for the inventive, enchanting, haute cuisine he's crafting at this offbeat, DePaul area eatery. Among the comeback kid's most memorable dishes—if you're going a la carte, that is—are the starter of *foie gras* with cashew and golden beet components and earthy, truffle-y short ribs. However, opting for the prix fixe is *de rigueur*.

Sweets & Savories, 1534 W. Fullerton Ave., Lincoln Park, Chicago IL 60614; (773) 281-6778; www .sweetsandsavoriesrestaurant.com; French; $$. It's French—presented without 'tude or high prices—making it an unpretentious dater's dream. David Richards's Kobe burger is a sight to behold, what with its smear of *foie gras* pâté and truffle mayo. Other hits include chilled vichys-soise christened with a butter-poached lobster claw, lavender-roasted chicken with walnut-parsley pesto sauce, and decadent beef-tallow pommes frites. After making short work of said plates, proceed to Seville orange cheese-cake with chocolate ganache sauce or apple tart tatin dolloped with soft cream.

TABLE fifty-two, 52 W. Elm St., Gold Coast, Chicago, IL 60610; (312) 573-4000; www.tablefifty-two.com; Regional American; $$$. Art Smith, Oprah's personal chef, had tongues wagging from the moment he opened these doors. However, it's safe to say his food is what earned adherents (the Obamas included). Join the fan club in enjoying well-wrought Southern classics, such as fried green tomatoes with hot-sauce aioli and tomato jam or cornmeal-crusted catfish with cheesy grits and bacon-braised collards. Don't leave without some goat-cheese biscuits—or the coconut-y pineapple hummingbird cake at meal's end.

Takashi, 1962 N. Damen Ave., Bucktown, Chicago, IL 60647; (773) 772-6170; www.takashichicago.com; Asian/French; $$$. Star chef Takashi Yagihashi (Ambria) crafts brilliant fare in an elegant, Zen-like space. Combining his French training with Japanese-accented, American ingredients, Yagihashi turns out a striking trio of pâté and terrine; practically meltable, caramelized pork belly steamed buns offset by pickled daikon; and grilled Bob White quail with roasted apples and quince, sauced with port-balsamic reduction. Order the *omakase* (chef's tasting), and see what he really can do. Also consider visiting fast-serve **Noodles by Takashi,** located in Macy's on State Street.

Toast, 746 W. Webster Ave., Lincoln Park, Chicago, IL 60614; (773) 935-5600; www.toast-chicago.com; American; $$. Crowds swell from this petite, contemporary spot, its solid, affordable brunch accruing waits. From classic and tweaked Benedict preparations, scrambles, and omelets to a hyped French toast "orgy"—a trio stuffed with fresh strawberries, Mexican chocolate, and mascarpone—the bevy of bites delights. Later, come for sandwiches, buffalo sliders, or a croque Monsieur. There's also a location at 2046 N. Damen Ave., (773) 772-5600.

Tocco, 1266 N. Milwaukee Ave., Wicker Park, Chicago, IL 60622; (773) 687-8895; www.toccochicago.com; Italian; $$. Owner Bruno

Abate is the kind of consummate host you can't help but feel an affinity toward; the same is true of the space-age boîte he oversees alongside his wife, Melissa. It churns out crackly pizzas and calzones from a wood-burning oven and antipasti and salads brimming with fresh, honest ingredients. Pair them with smoky carbonara and *scottata con rucola,* seared, thinly sliced strip steak topped with arugula and shards of nutty Parmesan. There's an affordable wine list to match.

Trader Vic's, 1030 N. State St., Gold Coast, Chicago, IL 60610; (312) 642-6500; www.tradervicschicago.com; Hawaiian; $$$. If you're into pupu platters and tiki trappings, escape to this Palmer House transplant, resurrected in a dimly lit den, filled with Polynesian kitsch and anchored by a Chinese oven. Claiming to have invented the mai tai back in 1944, it remains a good place for boozy cocktails and private colloquies, even if the food isn't always up to snuff.

Tru, 676 N. St. Clair St., Streeterville, Chicago, IL 60611; (312) 202-0001; www.trurestaurant.com; French; $$$$. Break out the suit and tie (it's a must) at this luxe, expense-account restaurant, serving caviar on crystal steps and ever-changing tastings—a.k.a. "collections"—that are almost too artsy to eat. Although Rick Tramonto has since departed for New Orleans and Executive Pastry Chef Gale Gand isn't involved in the day-to-day, Executive Chef

Anthony Martin (Joël Robuchon) keeps its reputation intact. Inspired desserts, available as a three-course tasting as well as a la carte, continue to devastate diners in the very best way. The wine list is, as one would expect, superior; the gallery-like dining room is a sight for sore eyes.

Twin Anchors, 1655 N. Sedgwick St., Old Town, Chicago, IL 60614; (312) 266-1616; (312) 266-1616; www.twinanchorsribs.com; Barbecue; $$. Chicagoans either love or are ambivalent toward this barbecue joint. Those in the former camp tout the old-school tavern's zestily sauced, fall-apart baby backs and porky beans, served where *Return to Me* and a scene from *The Dark Knight* was filmed. The pretension-free setting—much the same as it ever was with checked floors, leather books, and Sinatra on the juke—is half the charm.

Volare, 201 E. Grand Ave., Streeterville Chicago, IL 60611; (312) 410-9900; www.volarerestaurant.com; Italian; $$. This perpetually packed, carb-heavy Venetian presents bruschetta and carpaccio, minestrone and veal Milanese, in high-decibel surroundings. Fans of its vodka sauce may find the suburban ristorante (1919 S. Meyers Rd., Oakbrook Terrace; 630-495-0200) more conversation-friendly.

WAVE, W Hotel-Lakeshore, 644 N. Lake Shore Dr., Streeterville, Chicago, IL 60611; (312) 255-4460; www.waverestaurant.com; Mediterranean; $$. Kristine Subido's small plates stand out despite glittering Lake Michigan views from within the hip W Hotel. Expect noshes like feta-flecked watermelon and spiced-beef salad; phyllo-

wrapped shrimp with cinnamon-infused coffee sauce; and lamb shawarma with Jerusalem salad and *harissa*. The global-chic cocktails may have something to do with the happy hour and hangover-soothing brunch scene. (See recipe on p. 357.)

West Town Tavern, 1329 W. Chicago Ave., Noble Square, Chicago, IL 60642; (312) 666-6175; www.westtowntavern.com; American; $$$. Susan Goss makes a marvelous mess of an open-faced, Southwestern-style steak sandwich on Wednesday—a rival to her beloved Monday-only fried chicken dinner. Heaped with avocado and buttermilk-battered with chipotle-lime vinaigrette, it gives credence to a weekly visit. Among the other regularly available hits: tavern beer cheese with toasts, fall-apart pot roast with Pennsylvania Dutch black vinegar sauce, and comforting banana cream pie.

The Wieners Circle, 2622 N. Clark St., Lincoln Park, Chicago, IL 60614; (773) 477-7444; Hot Dogs; $. The off-color banter is half the charm of this Chicago-style dog stand, an institution where char-dogs are forked out with insults on the side. Expect a rowdy (read: drunk) late-night crowd that spews plenty of f-bombs. In other words, keep the kiddos at home as the evening wears on.

Near South

East Village, Fulton River District, Garfield Park, Greektown, Loop, Near West Side, River North, River West, West Loop, West Town

Heavily trafficked with a plentiful pedestrian population, you'll find navigation downright nightmarish around these parts; however, there is a palpable pulse only these 'hoods provide. Home to the European-inspired **Chicago French Market** (see p. 288), restaurants, and lounges with panoramic views and spots from lauded chefs, these stomping grounds are a sight for sore eyes—and hungry bellies.

Ai Sushi Lounge, 358 Ontario St., River North, Chicago, IL 60610; (312) 335-9888; www.aichicago.us; Japanese/Sushi; $$$. Thank the folks behind Ringo and Tsuki for this trendy, lounge-like spot, where the contemporary menu encourages grazing, the results occasionally surprise, and meals most often deliver. Among the rolls that stand out is the volcano; full of contrasts, it melds crunch (cucumber, soft-shell crab, and tempura) with buttery avocado and spicy mayo. But watch out when ordering *maki*—like the tempura-fried habañero lobster with spicy caper-inflected seviche—because tabs quickly add up. Competent dishes from the kitchen make meals pleasing, even for the sushi-shy.

aja, dana hotel and spa, 660 N. State St., River North, Chicago, IL 60657; (312) 202-6050; www.ajachicago.com; Pan-Asian; $$$. Having shifted its concept from Kobe to more affordable, share-able plates and sushi, this splashy, hotel-centered scenester takes a seasonal, market-driven approach. The star on the menu—no joke—is the mountainous, herbaceous, soy and rice wine–dressed 18-vegetable salad; it's the kind of thing you could eat every day. Korean fried chicken, tempura rock shrimp, and five-spice duck—customizable, thanks to house-made sauces on tables—create interactive appeal. Just be careful climbing (or descending) the sweeping staircase after a couple of those fruity cocktails.

aria, Fairmont Chicago, 200 N. Columbus Dr., Loop, Chicago, IL 60601; (312) 444-9494; Pan-Asian/Eclectic; $$$. Custom iPads describe dishes and ingredients while providing info on wineries at this hotel haunt, where the menu defies tradition with atypical uses for farmers' market ingredients. Classic examples include the refreshing heirloom tomato gazpacho with cucumber kimchee and a swirl of licorice-y Thai basil oil or tempura rock shrimp with pickled mango, miso blue cheese, and micro celery. Short rib *pad see ew*; grilled Wagyu with tomato-horseradish vinaigrette, and wok-fried long beans; and Peking duck breast with coconut, Anson

Mills polenta, yu choy, and mango-chile jam further the theme. Conversation-friendly and curtain-swathed with low lighting, this is a smart choice for a tête-à-tête.

Artopolis Bakery, Cafe & Agora, 306 S. Halsted St., Greektown, Chicago, IL 60661; (312) 559-9000; www.artopolischicago.com; Greek/Mediterranean; $$. Affordable Mediterranean fare—*artopitas,* puff pastries stuffed with *kasseri,* feta, and mint; lemony avgolemono; wood-fired pizzas; sandwiches on hearth-baked bread—lend this popular Greektown spot plenty of charm. Roasted leg of lamb—heady with scents of oregano and rosemary—and specials, such as pastitsio, are offset by European-style bakery creations. The agora (market) brims with tempting imports, from jam and honey to olive oil and Greek wine.

Athena, 212 S. Halsted St., Greektown, Chicago, IL 60661; (312) 655-0000; www.athenarestaurantchicago.com; Greek/Mediterranean; $$. There are few better places to hang out on a summer evening than this garden patio, even if the cozy, date-appropriate dining room is welcoming in its own right. It's not just the setting that will grab you, however: spicy *tirokafteri* (feta spread), savory feta-stuffed, roasted red peppers, and charbroiled *loukaniko* sausage seal the deal. Hearty, traditional dishes, such as roast leg of lamb and moussaka, also are attention-getters.

Atwood Cafe, Hotel Burnham, 1 W. Washington St., Loop, Chicago, IL 60602; (312) 368-1900; www.atwoodcafe.com; New American; $$$. Nestled quite comfortably in a historic building along bustling State Street, this intimate, Art Deco dining room received a proverbial shot in the arm when Derek Simcik graced its kitchen, bringing with him a world of tasty travels and plenty of pastry cred. Count yourself lucky if the following appear on the menu: seemingly weightless crab soufflé with fried green tomato, freeze-dried corn, and pureed arugula accompaniments; a spruced up "pot roast" of Wagyu beef cheeks; and rummy, charred cherry bread pudding with *dulce de leche* ice cream.

avec, 615 W. Randolph St., West Loop, Chicago, IL 60606; (312) 377-2002; Mediterranean/Small Plates/ Wine Bar; $$. Koren Grieveson puts a Vulcan stove to good use at Paul Kahan's beloved eatery, a Mediterranean mob scene adjacent to **Blackbird.** Make a meal of selections from the cheese cave or *brandade* and chorizo-stuffed dates with piquillo-tomato sauce, or turn to the pissaladière topped with caramelized onions, niçoise olives, anchovies, and thyme as well as porcini-black pepper pappardelle, sauced with a feta- and mint-infused, braised lamb neck *sugo*. On the sweeter side, expect closers like corn-semolina cake, layered with ricotta and whipped cream alongside apple, fig, and raisin compote. The notable wine list highlights boutique labels from Portugal, Italy, France, and Spain.

Avenues, The Peninsula Chicago, 108 E. Superior St., River North, Chicago, IL 60611; (312) 337-2888; www.peninsula.com/Chicago; New American; $$$$. Come with an expense account and an open mind—the progressive cuisine of Curtis Duffy (Alinea, Trio, Charlie Trotter's) requires both. Then, perch within a buttoned-up dining room, where you'll taste your way through fixed-price or a la carte dining experience (go for the former). Throughout, refined dishes—built from prized and organic ingredients—are provocative and artfully arranged.

Benny's Chop House, 444 N. Wabash St., River North, Chicago, IL 60611; (312) 626-2444; www.bennyschophouse.com; Steak/Seafood; $$$$. Any cues to the recession are checked at the door of this modern throwback, where the steaks are cooked to order, the oysters are way fresh, and there's enough dark wood details to take out a small forest. (Naturally, there's a Champagne cart, too.) Beyond prime, dry-aged steaks, turn to the Kurobuta pork chop, red wine–braised short ribs, or Maine lobster, either broiled or Southern-fried.

Ben Pao, 52 W. Illinois St., River North, Chicago, IL 60610; (312) 222-1888; www.benpao.com; Chinese; $$. Well-prepared regional Chinese dishes of the Hunan, Szechuan, Cantonese, and Mandarin persuasion are the benchmark of this elevated Lettuce Entertain You pleaser, where the sticky "cherry bomb" shrimp; caramelized, crisp sesame chicken; and star anise–scented, shredded pork buns deliver exactly what's expected.

The Berghoff, 17 W. Adams St., Loop, Chicago, IL 60603; (312) 427-3170; www.theberghoff.com; German; $$. An institution with wood-paneled walls, checkered floors and a bar that fills with business types and tourists ten deep, its hefty menu holds formulaic dishes, like crisp Wiener schnitzel, tangy sauerbraten, and creamed spinach. Everything benefits from a round of house brews or Berghoff-label root beer.

Berry Chill, Ogilvie Transportation Center, 500 W. Madison St., West Loop, Chicago, IL 60686; (312) 993-9644; www.berrychill.com; Ice Cream; $. A holdout from the fat-free fro-yo trend, this health-conscious hub features tart "original" and a rotating selection of flavors, such as passion fruit. And while it's all—okay, mostly—about the 'scream, the kaleidoscope of toppings (Fruity Pebbles, anyone?) often negates the holistic bent. Check out the local sprinkles, from Milk & Honey granola to Hoosier Mama Pie Company crumbles and bits of Carol's Cookies. A handful of locations are around town.

Billy Goat Tavern, 430 N. Michigan Ave., Lower Level, River North, Chicago, IL 60611; (312) 222-1525; www.billygoattavern.com; Pub; $. This subterranean tavern—made famous by the SNL "cheezborger" skit—pays homage to reporters past, while luring the average working man and tourist for a quick, cheap meal. Are its burgers the best in the city? Not by a long shot, but traditions run deep. Just remember: no Coke, Pepsi. There are several other area locations.

Bin 36, 339 N. Dearborn St., River North, Chicago, IL 60654; (312) 755-9463; www.bin36.com; New American/Wine Bar; $$$. With more than a decade under its belt, this deservedly popular wine bar and bistro from Dan Sachs, executive chef John Caputo, and wine director Brian Duncan thrives. Start with a basket of plush gougères and serious, house-label wine, moving on to the extensive artisan cheese and salumi selections. A holdover from its early days, pepper-crusted swordfish with Bordelaise still enchants. Suggested pairings—even for gooey-good grilled cheese with truffle oil and caramelized onions—keep the approachable vibe alive. Snag a bottle or two from the wine shop on the way out for a rainy day. (See recipe on p. 350.)

Blackbird, 619 W. Randolph St., West Loop. Chicago, IL 60611; (312) 715-0708; www.blackbirdrestaurant.com; New American; $$$$. Paul Kahan is behind this hot-spot, its eco-friendly, mini-malist dining room still among the hippest in town. With CIA-trained Alinea vet David Posey at his side, Kahan continues to craft brilliant, surprising dishes from local products: silky, coffee-scented fluke tartare with lemon, cucumber, saffron, and bread sauce; rich, grilled Wagyu tri-tip with sprouting granola, figs, and cassia bud accents; crisp walleye with wal-nuts, brightened by green papaya, dande-lion greens, and charred beef vinaigrette. Finales, whether a cheese course or fried polenta with Mick Klug Farms blueberries, lemon verbena, and smoked brown-sugar ice cream, also deliver. Kahan also owns adjacent wine bar, **avec;** rustic, beer- and pork-bent **The Publican;** and budget-friendly taqueria **Big Star.** He also has a butcher shop in the works. (See recipe on p. 364.)

Blue 13, 416 W. Ontario St., River North, Chicago, IL 60610; (312) 787-1400; www.blue13chicago.com; New American; $$$. Creative but also unpretentious in spirit, this collaboration between executive chef Chris Curren and partner Dan Marunowski announces its edginess with Sailor Jerry artwork, mock-snakeskin banquettes, and a modern rock playlist. But there's a bit of 'tude on the plate as well. Look to sweetbreads with sauerkraut puree, caramelized apples, Dijon aioli, and juniper bubbles or tender lamb glazed with Asian flavors and served alongside cilantro-flecked lime rice with soy-glazed haricots verts and onion confit. Also, consider attending the steal of a family-style meal on Sundays.

Bombon Cafe, 36 S. Ashland Ave., West Loop, Chicago, IL 60607; (312) 733-8717; www.chicagobestcakes.com; Mexican/Bakery; $$. Sweet and savory collide at this sunny cafe from husband and wife team Laura Cid-Perea and Luis Perea, which popped up after its Pilsen location suffered a fire. The authentic Mexican *tortas* are a specialty, and they're loaded with big, bold flavors—no surprise since Rick Bayless is Cid-Perea's former boss. This is true whether you opt for the Sonora—layered with marinated skirt steak, caramelized onions, roasted peppers, jalapeños, and avocado—or the Toluca with spicy chorizo, avocado, pickled red onions, Oaxaca cheese, and a slather of beans. Save room for the sweets, especially the sinful tres leches. Nearby, **La Lagartija** turns out Mexican and Tex-Mex dishes, while **Bombon Cake Gallery** tempts commuters ever-so-sweetly from the second floor of Ogilvie Transportation Center.

Branch 27, 1371 W. Chicago Ave., West Town, Chicago, IL 60642; (312) 850-2700; www.branch27.com; New American; $$$. Located in a former branch of the Chicago Public Library with coveted atrium seating, this rustic American bistro dispenses classic steak tartare studded with capers; fried Great Lakes smelt with crispy lemons and spicy remoulade; and rich, red wine-braised short ribs with garlicky kale and black olive polenta.

Cafe Iberico, 737 N. La Salle St., River North, Chicago, IL 60610; (312) 573-1510; www.cafeiberico.com; Spanish/Tapas; $$. Start with sangria at this tapas veteran, a deafening outpost with a crowd-minded—okay, cattle-call—feel. Then, nosh on marinated olives, ubiquitous *tortilla española,* and spicy-sauced *patatas bravas*. There's a large wine list and decent sangria—sip some while you wait for a table.

Carnivale, 702 W. Fulton Market, West Loop, Chicago, IL 60661; (312) 850-5005; www.carnivalechicago.com; Nuevo Latino; $$$. Jerry Kleiner's boisterous, kaleidoscopic modern Latin hot-spot has

a menu that's as showy as its setting. Standouts are the starters, including a seviche sampler that includes lime-y *hiramasa* with Scotch bonnet puree and flecks of cilantro, mint, and basil. Another winning dish is the tender, flavorful *ropa vieja,* perfect with a mojito or two.

Carson's Ribs, 612 N. Wells St., River North, Chicago, IL 60612; (312) 280-9200; www.ribs.com; Barbecue; $$. Barbecue is a hotly contested category in Chicago—especially these days—yet this dimly lit tourist trap marches on, serving its signature, sweetly sauced racks with mounds of slaw and au gratin potatoes. Boneless, center-cut pork chops are a decent alternative. There's also a location at 200 N. Waukegan Rd., Deerfield, (847) 374-8500.

Chicago Chop House, 60 W. Ontario St., River North, Chicago, IL 60654; (312) 787-7100; www.chicagochophouse.com; Steakhouse; $$$$. Located in a picturesque Victorian brownstone, this classic chophouse—adorned with vintage Chicago photos—baits carnivores with classic cuts. A 20-ounce, bone-in strip and prime rib, served traditionally or charred, hold court with a Frenched, bone-in veal chop, swordfish with sherry butter, and beer-battered shrimp. Signature potato pancakes with applesauce and sour cream and American fries are go-to, a la carte sides. A piano player performs nightly.

cibo matto, theWit, 201 N. State St., Loop, Chicago, IL 60601; (312) 239-9500; www.eatcibomatto.com; Italian; $$$. When Todd

Stein packed his knives, a hush fell upon this hyped hotel haunt. Evan Percoco (Bokx 109 American Prime, near Boston), has since stepped in, switching things up with tender, tangy grilled octopus with citrus vinaigrette and endive; vibrant burrata-beet salad plated with prosciutto and chestnut vinaigrette; and sweet and savory rabbit raviolo, with pumpkin seed, amaretti, and Parmesan accents. However, the stylish, second-floor dining room—with its high-backed booths and conversation-worthy, muraled ceiling—remains the same.

Coalfire, 1321 W. Grand Ave., West Town, Chicago, IL 60622; (312) 226-2625; www.coalfirechicago.com; Pizza; $$. Crackly, blazing-coal-fired Neapolitan pies have telltale charred crusts and come in versions both classic (Margherita) and creative (ricotta-topped pesto with black olives). A handful of salads—such as Caesar and caprese—provide a counterpart to the creations, which also may be customized. Expect a wait during peak times, as the oven can't always keep up with demand.

Coco Pazzo, 300 W. Hubbard St., River North, Chicago, IL 60654; (312) 836-0900; www.cocopazzochicago.com; Italian; $$$. Still plating some of the best Tuscan cuisine in the city, this loft-like, house-made pasta purveyor has earned its cred. Incorporating seasonal ingredients with a contemporary eye, CIA-trained Chris Macchia's cuisine is spirited, whether it's a tangle of chestnut tagliatelle with pumpkin, mushrooms, and speck or pappardelle with slow-simmered wild-boar *ragù*. The unfussy, expertly prepared entrees—braised rabbit with lush, creamy polenta; crisp pork Milanese; whole, wood-roasted sea bass—are equally prized.

Crepe Bistro, 186 N. Wells St., Loop, Chicago, IL 60606; (312) 269-0300; www.crepebistro.net; French; $$. This quiet, candlelit dining room and martini bar—popular with the pre-theater set—encases eclectic, savory, and sweet fillings within paper-thin crepes. The coq au vin features Mornay-licked chicken and mushrooms; the Tahiti sports ham, cheese, and hunks of pineapple; and the Kathmandu—cheesy, chicken and mushroom curry with mango chutney—provides a departure from the norm. Dessert crepes, including one oozing Nutella, sate sweet tooths.

Crofton on Wells, 535 N. Wells St., River North, Chicago, IL 60610; (312) 755-1790; www.croftononwells.com; New American; $$$. Named for its proprietor, Suzy Crofton, this pricy River Norther serves refined, sensible seasonal plates using local ingredients when possible. Turn with confidence to dishes such as swanky lobster corn chowder with Green Zebra tomato gelée, house-cured bacon, and a lobster corn fritter; sweetbreads with cucumber-watermelon relish, caramelized garlic-lemon-caper vinaigrette, and a *pata negra jamón* crisp; and cornmeal-crusted Great Lakes walleye with kohlrabi slaw and malt-vinegar syrup. Also noteworthy are the vegetarian dishes.

Cyrano's Bistrot & Wine Bar, 546 N. Wells St., River North, Chicago, IL 60654; (312) 467-0546; www.cyranosbistrot.com; French; $$. A master of traditional French fare, Didier Durand—the restaurant's ever-present chef-owner—quietly crafts authentic French onion soup, escargots, and coq au vin, serving it to canoodling couples. Below, Parisian cabaret **Cafe Simone**—named for Durand's daughter—dishes up smaller plates to the tune of occasional live acts.

David Burke's Prime Steakhouse, The James, 616 N. Rush St., River North, Chicago, IL 60611; (312) 660-6000; www.david burkesprimehouse.com; Steakhouse; $$$$. Manned by Exec Chef Rick Gresh, this meatery dry-ages its beef on site in a room flanked by Himalayan salt and has a penchant for using locally sourced, seasonal ingredients. Start with the Wagyu beef sashimi with earthy mushroom chips and truffle mayo, or the rich, silky lobster bisque, punched up with green-apple essence. Splurge on the marbled, 55-day rib eye, a bone-in masterpiece. When dining with a crowd, sample the difference between 40- and 75-day aged cuts. For something funky and fun, check out its brunch-in-a-box offerings on weekends.

de cero, 814 W. Randolph St., West Loop, Chicago, IL 60607; (312) 455-8114; www.decerotaqueria.com; Latin; $$. Nestled along

Restaurant Row, this modern taqueria promotes sharing with snacks and customizable taco platters—beer-battered shrimp, grilled tuna with chile mangoes and habañero, and chorizo-potato with cilantro versions among them. But odds are, you won't want to share the duck confit nachos at all.

Elate, 111 W. Huron St., River North, Chicago, IL 60654; (312) 202-9900; www.elatechicago.com; New American; $$$. At this LEED-certified hot-spot next to the Hotel Felix—now manned by Blue 13's Chris Curren—scene-seekers converge over Kobe beef tartare, fresh oysters, and composed, creative small and large plates. From halibut served atop pancetta-brown butter with cast-iron cornbread, honeycomb, and pickled okra to brussels sprouts lounging with black-trumpet mushrooms, pink grapefruit, almonds, and hollandaise, there are plenty of appealing options to entertain. Tweaked classic cocktails are also a draw.

Epic, 112 W. Hubbard St., River North, Chicago, IL 60654; (312) 222-4940; www.epicrestaurantchicago.com; American; $$$. All things to well-heeled people, this expense account–worthy, River North restau-lounge—its rooftop patio perched above Hubbard—attracts its share of the food-enthused. Michael Shrader's sophisticated cuisine ranges from duck breast prosciutto with persimmon, hazelnuts, lavender honey, and thyme to roasted king crab legs with herbed chile butter. The soaring, two-floor industrial space—not to mention impressive desserts—are further fineries.

Everest, 440 S. LaSalle St., 40th Fl., Loop, Chicago, IL 60605; (312) 663-8920; www.everestrestaurant.com; French; $$$$. Hovering 40 floors above street level with staggering skyline views, this Chicago Stock Exchange–housed, gallery-like gem—a Lettuce Entertain You venture with Jean Joho—remains at the top of its game. Though you may order a la carte—Michigan pea soup with crispy veal sweetbreads lends credence—it's preferable to go the degustation route. It yields incentives, such as chilled *foie gras* with rosehips, marinated melon, and nectarine gelée.

Flo, 1434 W. Chicago Ave., West Town, Chicago, IL 60642; (312) 243-0477; www.eatatflo.com; Regional American; $$. Southwestern comfort is the name of the game at this cozy cafe, which gets its chiles from Hatch, N.M. From grilled shrimp and grits with roasted poblano sauce to chicken-fried steak with creamy, roasted garlic–chipotle gravy and Frito pie, the guilty pleasures abound. But be forewarned: the crowds are crazy during breakfast—especially weekend brunch.

The Florentine, JW Marriott, 151 W. Adams St., Loop, Chicago, IL 60603; (312) 660-8866; www.the-florentine.net; Italian; $$$. Located in a Daniel Burnham-designed building, this second-floor door dining room has a corporate, mock-library feel, albeit one with gauzy curtains and endless wood details. More attention-grabbing is the get-anything menu of modern Italian fare, executed by Todd Stein (ex-cibo matto). A lemony, shaved brussels sprout salad dappled with Marcona almonds, currants, and Pecorino could easily have anti-cabbage converts. Ditto the not-as-sweet-as-it-sounds butternut squash caramelle, bathed in brown butter with candied walnuts, sage, and amaretti crumbles. However, you must order two of the beloved bucatini carbonara, arriving loaded with cracked black pepper, chunky, caramelized nubs of pancetta, and a raw duck egg on top. Tossed, it melds into a silky, chewy, salty dish you'll want seconds of. Come to think of it, it's doubtful you'll want to share the pillow-y bomboloni with caramel, vanilla cream, and berry sauces either.

Fogo de Chão, 611 N. LaSalle Blvd., River North, Chicago, IL 60654; (312) 932-9330; www.fogodechao.com; Brazilian/ Steakhouse; $$$. Come hungry, leave stuffed—that's the mantra at

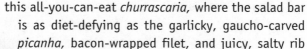

this all-you-can-eat *churrascaria,* where the salad bar is as diet-defying as the garlicky, gaucho-carved *picanha,* bacon-wrapped filet, and juicy, salty rib eye. Starchy sides, including warm cheese bread and caramelized bananas, are included. However, desserts—including papaya cream—will set you back extra cash.

Frontera Grill, 445 N. Clark St., River North, Chicago, IL 60654; (312) 661-1434; www.rickbayless.com; Mexican; $$$. Rick Bayless's wildly popular, casual counterpart to Topolobampo lives up to the hype. The sustainable seviche and seasonal, revelatory creations—served in a folk art–adorned dining room—change often but may include a sashimi-grade yellowfin cocktail with avocado-tomatillo guac and mango-grapefruit salsa; poblano gazpacho, garnished with Alaskan king crab, hardboiled egg, and croutons; or a *cazuela* of lamb-pork meatballs dressed in bright, chile-tomato sauce with fingerlings and dry jack cheese. If the sour orange–marinated *poc chuc* is available, make it your main meal. When in the mood for a sandwich and soup, however, head to Bayless's ultra-tasty **XOCO.** (See recipe on p. 351.)

The Gage, 24 S. Michigan Ave., Loop, Chicago, IL 60603; (312) 372-4243; www.thegagechicago.com; Gastropub; $$$. Located across from Millennium Park, this noisy, fancified tavern with Dirk Flanigan at the helm is a must for hearty fare. Dive in with the Scotch egg with spicy mustard; *poutine* topped with elk *ragù* and cheese curds; or duck confit with white asparagus and orange caramel. Plenty come for the fish-and-chips but end up ordering the prime burger, topped with local Camembert and melted onion marmalade, instead. See how he handles French fare at refined follow-up, **Henri,** 18 S. Michigan Ave., (312) 578-0763.

Giordano's, 135 E. Lake St., Loop, Chicago, IL 60601; (312) 616-1200; www.giordanos.com; Pizza; $$. This now-national, deep-dish destination, a Chicago original, has been serving pies alongside red-sauce standbys since the '70s. There are many locations scattered throughout Chicagoland.

Girl & the Goat, 809 W. Randolph St., West Loop, Chicago, IL 60607; (312) 492-6262; www.girlandthegoat.com; New American; $$$. Topping the list of good things in life is Stephanie Izard's inventive, modern American—the epitome of the Chicago dining aesthetic. Izard, a *Top Chef* winner, crafts risky, hyper-local small plates, and she clearly has a way with surf and turf. The menu changes often, but you can expect turn-tos like *hiramasa* crudo with crisp pork belly, caperberries, and *aji* aioli or grilled baby octopus with guanciale and lemon-pistachio vinaigrette. Her bravado is also apparent in vegetable dishes, like roasted, minted cauliflower with pickled peppers and pine nuts. Izard—and her fans—also dig animals' forgotten parts, so check out the "pig face," bedecked with a sunny side egg. Soon, she plans to open follow-up **The Little Goat,** a three-meal diner with a classic aesthetic. (See recipe on p. 380.)

Gold Coast Dogs, 159 N. Wabash Ave., Loop, Chicago, IL 60601; (312) 917-1677; www.goldcoastdogs.net; Hot Dogs; $. This Chicago stalwart made its name with a signature char dog—a singed, split beef frank, tucked into a poppy seed bun topped with mustard, relish, onions, sport peppers, celery salt, tomato, and a pickle. There are several outposts, including at both Midway and O'Hare airports.

graham elliot, 217 W. Huron St., River North, Chicago, IL 60610; (312) 624-9975; www.grahamelliot.com; New American; $$$$. On the short list of Chicago chefs who spark dissenting opinions: Graham Elliot. His "bistronomic" eatery, having a penchant for cranked-up tunes and a middle-finger-to-convention mentality, is as much about the experience as it is about the chef's science-project cooking techniques. Good luck denying the appeal of his Parmesan-truffle popcorn, though. As for the tangy, creamy cheddar risotto, jabbed with Cheez-Its? It's as fanciful as it is fantastic. Although purportedly accessible, the staff has 'tude; service feels rushed; and tabs—especially for tastings—are sky-high.

grahamwich, 615 N. State St., River North, Chicago, IL 60654; (312) 624-9188; www.grahamwich.com; Deli; $$. Celebrity chef Graham Elliot (also of an eponymous restaurant nearby) is another luminary to roll out a casual concept, this one focusing on $10, globally inspired sandwiches, house-made sodas, signature truffle popcorn, and soft serve in flavors like cinnamon stick with roasted apple, salted caramel, and pie crust. Top billing goes to the grilled cheese with Wisconsin cheddar, cheese curds, wisps of prosciutto, and tomato marmalade. Lines can be long, and the setting isn't among the most comfortable around.

Greek Islands, 200 S. Halsted St., Greektown, Chicago, IL 60661; (312) 782-9855; www.greekislands.net; Greek/Mediterranean; $$. Always festive and packed to the rafters, this veteran churns out venerable Greek dishes (flaming *saganaki, tzatziki,* and tender, char-broiled baby octopus). The lengthy menu, filled with *dolmades,* gyros, and chicken *riganati,* includes a family-style component that begs for Sunday suppers or festive, late-night feasts. There is a suburban counterpart at 300 E. 22nd St., Lombard, (630) 932-4545.

Habana Libre, 1440 W. Chicago Ave., West Town, Chicago, IL 60642; (312) 243-3303; www.habanalibrerestaurant.com; Cuban; $$. There's much to love about this cheery neighborhood Cuban: the flaky, guava-cheese empanadas, the garlic-laden *tostones,* the really good *ropa vieja,* and the even better *pollo frito.* And the *jibarito*? It'll leave you wanting another. There's the BYOB policy, which keeps the cost factor down.

Hannah's Bretzel, 180 W. Washington Blvd., Loop, (312) 621-1111; www.hannahsbretzel.com; Cafe; $$. The organic bread, baked on site, has everything to do with the success of this sandwich spot. Make short work of the Serrano-Manchego sammie with fig chutney and shards of fennel. The vegetarian options are noteworthy, too; try one with Brie, apples, caramelized onions, and apple-thyme yogurt tucked in a whole-grain baguette. There are additional locations at 233 N. Michigan Ave. and 131 S. Dearborn St.

Harry Caray's, 33 W. Kinzie St., River North, Chicago, IL 60654; (312) 828-0966; www.harrycarays.com; Steakhouse/Italian; $$$$. This nod to the legendary late announcer serves one of the biggest and best shrimp cocktails in town. The memorabilia-laden confines may have something to do with the allure, though the Vesuvio-style prime steaks and standard pasta preparations have accrued a justified fan base. There are outposts and offshoots in the city and suburbs.

Heaven on Seven, 111 N. Wabash Ave., 7th Fl., Loop, Chicago, IL 60602; (312) 263-6443; www.heavenonseven.com; Cajun/ Creole; $$. Spice-seekers flock to Jimmy Bannos's cash-only lunchbreakers' Eden, where the gumbo, po' boys, and andouille with jalapeño-cheddar corn muffins are tops. A wall of hot sauce allows for customization. There are follow-ups at 600 N. Michigan Ave., 2nd Fl., (312) 280-7774; and 224 S. Main St., Naperville, (630) 717-0777.

Henri, 18 S. Michigan Ave., Loop, Chicago, IL 60603; (312) 578-0763; www.henrichicago.com; French/New American; $$$$. This hushed expense accounter, kin to **The Gage,** is heavy on indulgent classics, though atypical options are in the mix. Whether you start with the *pissaladière* with market tomatoes, Raclette, and Virginia ham or head straight for the slow-roasted Illinois lamb for two, save room for the *mille-feuille,* a napoleon layered with vanilla crème. And do peruse the biodynamic wine and wine-based cocktail lists.

Hubbard Inn, 110 W. Hubbard St., River North, Chicago, IL 60654; (312) 222-1331; www.hubbardinn.com; Gastropub; $$. A worldly collection of artifacts sets the tone at this communal, bi-level boîte serving sensible-but-stylish bar snacks, flatbreads, sandwiches, and small plates from Bob Zrenner (North Pond). Nibbles range from deviled eggs to a standout crock of pickled, seasonal vegetables and perfectly pink filet and quail eggs atop red wine-truffle reduction. Also solid are the fall-apart-tender braised short ribs and grilled prawns on a bed of mushroom conserve with garlic-potato puree and sun-dried tomato vinaigrette.

HUB 51, 51 W. Hubbard St., River North, Chicago, IL 60654; (312) 828-0051; www.hub51chicago.com; New American; $$. Rich Melman's boys, R.J. and Jerrod Melman, are behind this trendy pleasure den. The all-encompassing menu hosts everything from *maki* to tacos, house-made jerky, and oversized sandwiches, with plenty of shareable plates—dry-rubbed ribs, pulled-chicken nachos—for tipplers.

Ina's, 1235 W. Randolph St., West Loop, Chicago, IL 60607; (312) 226-8227; www.breakfastqueen.com; American; $$. Ina Pinkney's breakfast institution is adorned with iconic, off-the-wall salt and pepper shakers, and it's all about the morning eats. Faves include scrapple—a commingling of eggs, cornmeal, black beans, and cheddar—and "heavenly hots," thin pancakes with peach, raspberry, and blueberry compote. Linger through lunch and find curried chicken salad, chicken potpie, and house-made meatloaf.

India House, 59 W. Grand Ave., River North, Chicago, IL 60654; (312) 645-9500; www.indiahousechicago.com; Indian; $$. The consistent, moderately priced Indian fare—served in sedate, exposed-brick environs—leaves spice-lovers smitten. Though there is a large selection of vegetarian dishes, from aromatic lentils to delish *palak paneer,* it's the royally sauced lamb and chicken creations that provide a true palate-perk. *Gulab jamun* and refreshing mango *kulfi* are finales of note. Its original location is in Schaumburg; other outposts are in Oak Brook, Rockford, Hoffman Estates, and Buffalo Grove.

The Italian Village, 71 W. Monroe St., Loop, Chicago, IL 60603; (312) 332-7005; www.italianvillage-chicago.com; Italian; $$. A contrary commingling of romantics and suits patronize this old-school, upper-level spot with intimate, semiprivate booths. Serving

CHEW ON THIS

Fans of licorice and ginger chews must visit the Loop location of **Merz Apothecary** in the Palmer House Hilton (17 E. Monroe St., Loop, Chicago, IL 60603, 312-781-6900). You'll find everything from cat-shaped licorice drops and floral violet pastilles from Germany to salty, *salmiak*-filled licorice from Holland and spicy apple-ginger candies from California-based The Ginger People.

fare from the boot without fanfare inside the family-run Italian Village complex, its frequented dishes include grilled calamari, many classic chicken and veal preparations, and lasagna.

Japonais, 600 W. Chicago Ave., River North, Chicago, IL 60610; (312) 822-9600; www.japonaischicago.com; Japanese; $$$. Pretty people are an extension of this sultry hot-spot, which spans contemporary and classic Japanese cuisines and is all-but-built for mavens. You'll want to head downstairs to the romantic riverside lounge, but first fuel up on ginger-soy-glazed Wagyu carpaccio, lobster spring rolls with mango relish, and blood-orange vinaigrette, and Tokyo "drums."

Joe's Seafood, Prime Steak & Stone Crab, 60 E. Grand Ave., River North, Chicago, IL 60611; (312) 379-5637; www.joes.net; Seafood/Steakhouse; $$$$. People come to this pricey seafooder, a Miami original that partnered with Lettuce Entertain You, for solid renditions of its namesakes. Begin with as much of the chilled stone crab as you can afford, later opting for Dover sole, served tableside Tuesday through Thursday. The bone-in steaks—rib eye, strip, filet—are a decadent, artery-clogging alternative. Finish with pie: the Key lime and banana cream are noteworthy.

Kan Zaman, 617 N. Wells St., River North, Chicago, IL 60610; (312) 751-9600; Lebanese; $$. Settle in at low-slung, pillow-strewn tables, and seek solace in hearty lentil soup, silky hummus, and tender dolma. On weekends, watch belly dancers while munching on rotisserie-cooked shawarma and moist, charbroiled kebabs, leaving you well fed—with bucks to burn.

Karyn's Cooked, 738 N. Wells St., River North, Chicago, IL 60614; (312) 587-1050; www.karynraw.com; Vegetarian/Vegan; $$$. Karyn Calabrese, a raw foodist, has created a mini-empire (Karyn's Fresh Corner, Karyn's on Green), catering to veg loyalists with an upscale take on adventurous cuisine. However, it's doubtful stand-ins, from grilled seitan to ground-soy tacos, fool most carnivores.

Keefer's Restaurant, 20 W. Kinzie St., River North, Chicago, IL 60654; (312) 467-9525; www.keefersrestaurant.com; Steakhouse; $$$. Chef John Hogan fashions fine steakhouse variants in a sweeping dining room. Sure, you'll find the classics—crab cakes, lobster bisque, steak, and more steak—but you'll also encounter French-inflected favorites, including steak Diane, Dover sole meunière, and duck liver terrine accompanied by fruit compote, brioche, toast points, and some sauterne.

Kiki's Bistro, 900 N. Franklin St., River North, Chicago, IL 60610; (312) 335-5454; www.kikisbistro.com; French; $$$. Located just enough off the beaten path to feel secret, this longtime, intimate bistro belonging to its eponymous owner is Francophiles' regular haunt. Tucking into the *magret de canard*—duck breast and leg confit with braised red cabbage, wild rice, and green-peppercorn sauce—it's easy to see why. Contemplate ordering the *plat du jour,* be it skate wing in caper–brown butter sauce or steak frites.

Kinzie Chophouse, 400 N. Wells St., River North, Chicago, IL 60654; (312) 822-0191; www.kinziechophouse.com; Steakhouse; $$. One of the most understated steakhouses around, this handsome spot near the Merchandise Mart is popular with suits and out-of-towners, who converge over hefty salads, competent prime rib, or wild-mushroom risotto and a large array of steaks and chops.

La Madia, 59 W. Grand Ave., River North, Chicago, IL 60654; (312) 329-0400; www.dinelamadia.com; Italian/Pizza; $$. Thin, crackly crust 'zas, topped with local and artisanal ingredients, are popular with a midday and late-night crowd. Warm, foil-wrapped olives and Marsala-glazed wild mushroom bruschetta are good for grazing. Whenever you dine, plan on keeping the white-sauced Taleggio and slow-roasted grape pie to yourself. A late-night prix fixe includes salad, a pizza, and indulgent Wisconsin electric cookies for two—and wine, to boot. There's an interactive chef's table where cooking classes regularly take place.

La Sardine, 111 N. Carpenter St., West Loop, Chicago, IL 60607; (312) 421-2800; www.lasardine.com; French; $$$. This prototypical bistro, Le Bouchon's bro, executes the classics—codfish *brandade,* salade Lyonnaise, beef Bourguignon—with panache. As for Jean Claude Poilevey's seafood-stocked bouillabaisse, it's simply the best. Linger over a cheese plate and a gravity-defying chocolate soufflé, too.

La Scarola, 721 W. Grand Ave., River West, Chicago, IL 60610; (312) 243-1740; www.lascarola.com; Italian; $$. People can't get enough of this joint's Italian-American classics, served in an unassuming storefront setting. Though nothing—from the spaghetti to the meat lasagna—charts new territory, the commonplace preparations suit ever-present diners just fine.

Lawry's the Prime Rib, 100 E. Ontario St., River North, Chicago, IL 60611; (312) 787-5000; www.lawrysonline.com; Steakhouse; $$$$. Silver carts, wafting with the scent of prime rib, rove through this dramatic, multiroom Italian Renaissance–style mansion, which houses this Beverly Hills–based standby. Carved tableside—after its signature "spinning" salad bowl is served—the beef isn't something to balk at.

Leopold, 1450 W. Chicago Ave., West Town, Chicago, IL 60622; (312) 348-1028; www.leopoldchicago.com; Belgian; $$$. Come to this Belgian-bent tavern for hearty across-the-pond riffs: steak tartare (with rye toast), *poutine* (accompanied by lamb sausage gravy), and *moules frites*—one version scented with Madras curry. Chef Jeffrey Hedin, who worked with Shawn McClain at Spring and Green Zebra, is the man with the plan. The beverage program, overseen by Josh Kaplan (mk, restaurants at theWit) is top-shelf.

Lockwood, Palmer House Hilton, 17 E. Monroe St., Loop, Chicago, IL 60603; (312) 726-7500; www.lockwoodrestaurant.com; New American; $$$$. Situated off the lobby of the soaring, historic Palmer House Hilton hotel, this class act attracts guests and tourists alike with mildly esoteric American fare from Greg Elliot (one sixtyblue), served in a swanky, contemporary setting. A standout, when available, is the flaky sablefish and pork belly, resting upon pleasantly bitter, grilled broccolini and lappable Meyer lemon broth.

Lou Malnati's, 439 N. Wells St., River North, Chicago, IL 60654; (312) 828-9800; www.loumalnatis.com; Pizza; $$. The flagship Lincolnwood location, which opened in 1971, spawned spin-offs throughout Chicagoland. These days, its deep-dish wonders may be shipped nationwide. Does it live up to the hype? Let's just say these cheese-laden, butter-crusted pies aren't just for tourists. There's thin-crust, too, but it—and the rest of the menu—are by no means in a starring role. There are additional area locations.

Lou Mitchell's, 565 W. Jackson Blvd., West Loop, Chicago, IL 60661; (312) 939-3111; www.loumitchellsrestaurant.com; American; $$. This charming breakfast institution began serving consistent, perfectly fluffy omelets, crisp 'browns and thick, buttered Greek toast in 1923, and it's still going strong. Though you may have to wait for a table—the malted Belgium waffles are worth it—freebie doughnut holes and Milk Duds, doled out to patrons by the friendly staff, keep hunger pangs at bay until your time arrives.

Mac & Min's, 1045 W. Madison St., West Loop, Chicago, IL 60607; (312) 563-1008; www.macandmins.com; Cajun/ Creole; $$. Jerry's Sandwiches morphed into this New Orleans–inspired BYOB, serving Bayou requisites— from meat-layered muffuletta to seafood-stuffed gumbo and traditional and funky-fresh, custom- izable po' boys and salads. Naturally, there's chicory coffee as well.

Mastro's Steakhouse, 520 N. Dearborn St., River North, Chicago, IL 60654; (312) 521-5100; www .mastrosrestaurants.com; Steakhouse; $$$$. This posh chain joins the city's long list of steak joints, proffering design- your-own seafood towers; large, spendy steaks and chops; fresh seafood; and a lengthy lineup of familiar sides. Butter cake is a best bet for dessert.

Mercadito, 108 W. Kinzie St., River North, Chicago, IL 60610; (312) 329-9555; www.mercaditorestaurants.com; Latin; $$$. This causally cool New York import attracts limelighters with seviche, tacos, and *botanas,* served into the wee hours. Creative cocktails and an extensive tequila selection are a great team. Instead of calling it a night post-nosh, descend to thwump-thwumping Double A, an intimate lounge where an A-list crowd scores libations, pre- pared tableside. Cure your hangover on weekends, when *huevos* goes haute.

Mexique, 1529 W. Chicago Ave., West Town, Chicago, IL 60642; (312) 850-0288; www.mexiquechicago.com; Mexican/French; $$$. Speaking the language of two quite different cuisines—Mexican and French—Executive Chef Carlos Gaytan's off-the-beaten-path eatery is quite the wild ride. Just hop aboard, deciding between duck-leg confit and chipotle-temple tarmarind-glazed duck breast with chard and a corn-cranberry tamal. Another temptation: cocoa nib–adorned, roasted pork tenderloin with mole Teloloapan, spicy-sweet potato puree, and ratatouille.

mk, 868 N. Franklin St., River North, Chicago, IL 60610; (312) 482-9179; www.mkchicago.com; New American; $$$$. Michael Kornick's bricked-out, two-tiered restaurant presents some of the best plates in town. Farm-driven tastings and a la carte offerings—prosciutto with melon, purslane, and peppermint Banyuls vinaigrette, or wood-fired, Chinese mustard-glazed salmon with bok choy, shiitake, and ginger-soy—show both restraint and swagger. Remember, though, that the whimsical desserts—as in a composition of brown sugar–crusted Red Haven peach pie; Maker's Mark ice cream with blackberry custard; and a house-made sarsaparilla soda shooter—are integral to the experience.

Moon's Sandwich Shop, 16 S. Western Ave., Near West Side, Chicago, IL 60612; (312) 226-5094; American; $. This bare-bones institution is a showstopper for homespun sandwiches, like mounded, mustard-slathered corned beef (also available in dinner form) or tomato, mayo, and lettuce-topped meatloaf served on rye. Almost as endearing, though, is the way in which servers present— with flourish—grits and eggs, chopped steak, and roast pork to a roster of regulars.

Moto, 945 W. Fulton Market, West Loop, Chicago, IL 60607; (312) 491-0058; www.motorestaurant.com; New American; $$$$. This is the kind of bait-and-switch experience people either dig or detest. Mad scientist Homaro Cantu's den of molecular gastronomy turns out strange, theatrical tastings that rarely resemble food as we know it. But if an edible menu housing Cracker Jack–coated quail is your thing, Cantu—who starred in Planet Green's *Future Food*—is your man. Moto has a less tricked-out West Loop sibling, **iNG** (951 W. Fulton Market, 855-834-6464).

Mr. Beef, 666 N. Orleans St., River North, Chicago, IL 60610; (312) 337-8500; American; $. About the only reason to come to this quintessential stand—and a good reason it is—is to procure shards of Italian beef, stuffed into a jus-dipped roll piled with crunchy, spicy giardiniera. But the combo—Italian beef with the addition of snappy Italian sausage—is a work of art, too. To the joy of ex-pats (and chagrin of locals), a branch opened on California's Venice Beach boardwalk.

Naha, 500 N. Clark St., River North, Chicago, IL 60654; (312) 321-6242; www.naha-chicago.com; New American; $$$$. Carrie

Nahabedian's elegantly unfussy ode to seasonal cuisine reinvents its menu often. However, expect inspiration from her Armenian roots and a West Coast sensibility to inform what appears. A recent stunner included a tartare of Hawaiian yellowfin tuna, citrus-cured char, and golden whitefish caviar with hard-cooked quail egg, a mosaic of niçoise, aigrelette sauce, and toasted brioche. From there, it's on to roasted quail, crisp Kurobuta pork belly, and a coddled duck egg, swathed in prosciutto with scallion jam, kale, and duck fat–fried Rose Finn potatoes. Both the dessert menu and sophisticated wine list play a supporting role.

Nia Mediterranean Tapas, 803 W. Randolph St., West Loop, Chicago, IL 60607; (312) 226-3110; www.niarestaurant.com; Mediterranean/Small Plates; $$. A chill alternative to neighboring hot-spots, this joint turns out lively French, Turkish, and Greek-influenced, tapas-style plates amid Restaurant Row. From the fairly large (and somewhat hit-or-miss) menu, zero in on the lamb-feta meatballs, chorizo with shrimp cremini in white-wine sauce, and the bacon-wrapped dates with buttery red pepper sauce. Cocktail specials, offered throughout the week, are an added incentive.

9 Muses, 315 N. Halsted St., Greektown, Chicago, IL 60661; (312) 902-9922; www.9museschicago.com; Greek/Mediterranean; $$. A bit of a secret—if there is such a thing—along the Halsted strip, this clublike haunt is favored by Mediterranean imports, who come to gobble up broiled, feta-stuffed florina peppers, feta-topped fries showered with oregano, and generously piled gyros.

N9NE Steakhouse, 440 W. Randolph St., West Loop, Chicago, IL 60606; (312) 575-9900; www.n9negroup.com; Steakhouse; $$$. Sceney and meat-minded with a contemporary edge, this popular steakhouse with a Vegas offshoot is the kind out-of-towners read about in glossies. But, fortunately, the crispy rock shrimp; fried calamari with shards of hot peppers and Tabasco aioli; and béarnaise-sauced filet with sweet, tender, and excessive-to-the-extreme lobster tail live up to the hype.

one sixtyblue, 1400 W. Randolph St., West Loop, Chicago, IL 60607; (312) 850-0303; www.onesixtyblue.com; New American; $$$$. It's true that athletes have an affinity for this place (after all Michael Jordan's part owner). However, Michael McDonald's creative, sophisticated cuisine—served in a posh pad near the United-Center—feels worlds away from what its address and clientle would suggest. Braised beef cheek with cauliflower mushrooms, red wine–pickled cauliflower, and cauliflower puree as well as Berkshire pork tenderloin with house-made sauerkraut, smoked ham hock, grilled kielbasa, and crispy pig tail alongside ricotta dumplings are reasons why. Ingredients from the on-site garden appear seasonally. (See recipe on p. 377.)

Osteria Via Stato, 620 N. State St., River North; Chicago, IL 60654; (312) 642-8450; www.osteriaviastato.com; Italian/Pizza; $$$. Affordable shared plates, served family-style, are the main attraction at this Lettuce Entertain You osteria. When opting to dine this way, with an array of antipasti, two pastas, and a main course (perhaps whitefish with pancetta, corn, and cipollini onions), diners most definitely leave full. There are a la carte options as well. **Pizzeria Via Stato,** located within, turns out artisanal, Roman-style pizzas and offers a selection of 300 Italian wines.

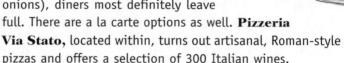

Paramount Room, 415 N. Milwaukee Ave., River West, Chicago, IL 60654; (312) 829-6300; www.paramountroom.com; American; $$. Jon Young (Kitsch'n) and Chef-Partner Stephen Dunne (Volo) are behind this late-night gastro-lounge with a great Belgian and craft beer selection and noshes that tend to go above and beyond. Raves go to the tempura-fried green beans, served with spicy lime-chile dipping sauce, the juicy Kobe burger, and the black and tan float with Guinness ice cream. The bi-level, vintage speakeasy setting is likeable, too.

Paris Club, 59 W. Hubbard St., River North, Chicago, IL 60654; (312) 595-0800; www.parisclubchicago.com; French; $$. R.J. and Jerrod Melman (HUB 51), Jean Joho (Everest), and Tim Graham (Tru) usher in a new era of affordable French dining at this happening hot-spot. Focusing on shareable plates, options include French onion fondue and duck cracklings with spicy vinaigrette as well as vegetable cassoulet, pig's feet bonbons, and charcuterie boards with house-made pâtés and terrines. Pair them with house tap wines and some caviar, served by the ounce.

Park Grill, 11 N. Michigan Ave., Loop, Chicago, IL 60602, (312) 521-7275; www.parkgrillchicago.com; New American; $$$. At this Millennium Park eatery, it's about location, location, location—that and views of the skaters when weather permits. Thankfully, the food is decent as well. Score cornmeal-crusted calamari with pickled tomatoes and spicy scallion remoulade or a peppercorn-crusted Kobe burger with balsamic grilled onions on a grain mustard–smeared pretzel bun. Afterward, ogle "the Bean," a gleaming public sculpture nearby.

The Parthenon, 314 S. Halsted St., Greektown, Chicago, IL 60661; (312) 726-2407; www.theparthenon.com; Greek/Mediterranean; $$. Claiming to have invented *saganaki,* The Parthenon sure does serve a mean block of gooey, flamed cheese. Spit-roasted gyros, pork souvlaki skewers, and many lamb preparations are among the generously sized main courses, though a satisfying meal can be had from appetizers alone.

Pegasus Restaurant & Taverna, 130 S. Halsted St., Greektown, Chicago, IL 60661; (312) 226-3377; www.pegasuschicago.com; Greek/Mediterranean; $$. Take a trip to the Mediterranean seashore at this mainstay, its pitch-perfect, rooftop patio framed by expansive skyline views. There, a meze-style menu—garlicky *skordalia* with marinated beets, tomato-sauced meatballs, baked baby eggplant—encourages sharing. But you'll find plenty of people-pleasers on the main menu, be it spanakopita, moussaka, or pastitsio—including in family-style form.

Perry's Deli, 174 N. Franklin St., Loop, Chicago, IL 60606; (312) 372-7557; www.perrysdeli.com; Deli; $. It's a feeding frenzy in the truest sense at this Financial District sandwich slinger, where triple deckers—layer upon layer of corned beef and spicy salami, stuffed into mustard and mayo-slicked rye bread, for example—meet classics, like a sugar-cured bacon BLT and corned beef–pastrami blend smeared with Russian dressing. Not surprisingly, it's a mob scene during lunch.

Petterino's, 150 N. Dearborn St., Loop, Chicago, IL 60601; (312) 422-0150; www.petterinos.com; Italian; $$. Here's why you should head to Rich Melman's 1940s throwback: the garlicky "rack" of shrimp de Jonghe. The Goodman Theatre–bound crowd flocks to the caricature-adorned dining room for other dishes, too, such as skirt steak topped with melted maitre d' butter and frosty martinis, enjoying them while perched upon rich rouge banquettes.

Piccolo Sogno, 464 N. Halsted St., West Loop, Chicago, IL 60642; (312) 421-0077; www.piccolosognorestaurant.com; Italian; $$$. Home to one of the loveliest patios in town, this inviting trattoria from Tony Priolo and wine guy Ciro Longobardo serves rustic, regional Italian dishes with consistently tasty results. When in need of comfort, twice-cooked bread and vegetable soup can't be beat. That is, until you bite into the selection of antipasti and pleasantly chewy pasta dishes, including striking, string-cut black spaghetti tangled with shrimp, zucchini, and chile-inflected San Marzano tomatoes.

Pizzeria Uno, 29 E. Ohio St., River North, Chicago, IL 60611; (312) 321-1000; www.unos.com; Pizza; $$. Laying claim to Chicago's original deep-dish pizza, this small, tourist-riddled eatery can handle some overflow at roomier **Pizzeria Due,** 619 N. Wabash Ave., nearby. Nothing here is going to knock locals' socks off, but for a hefty slice of Windy City history, this pizza purveyor won't be outdone. There are numerous, less jammed locations in the city and suburbs.

Prairie Fire, 215 N. Clinton St., West Loop, Chicago, IL 60661; (312) 382-8300; www.prairiefirechicago.com; New American; $$$. Sarah Stegner and George Bumbaris (Prairie Grass Cafe) took their act downtown, opening a second, similarly spirited outpost. Midwestern ingredients—plus notable carryovers, like the blue cheese–topped burger—pepper the menu. Baked feta with spicy banana peppers and tomatoes, a citrus-marinated beet salad with toasted hazelnuts and goat cheese, and slow-braised Tallgrass beef brisket with creamy potatoes aim to please. Definitely finish with pie, namely the banana cream when available. (See recipe on p. 368.)

Prosecco, 710 N. Wells St., River North, Chicago, IL 60654; (312) 951-9500; www.ristoranteprosecco.com; Italian; $$$. When in need of a romantic rendezvous, this polished Italian eatery delivers. Serving dishes both rustic and refined—all with an eye toward its noteworthy wine list—meals may begin with slivers of bresaola topped with arugula and Parmesan shards or grilled radicchio, fennel, and endive, followed by orecchiette with wild mushroom and sun-dried tomato-dotted black truffle cream sauce.

Province, 161 N. Jefferson St., West Loop, Chicago, IL 60661; (312) 669-9900; www.provincerestaurant.com; New American; $$$. Rooted in from-the-farm, American cuisine, Randy Zweiban (ex-Nacional 27) nods to Latin flavors at his LEED-certified, fuchsia-hued spot. A small, simple plate of serrano hamachi sashimi is about quality over quantity. Local apple salad with jicama, candied olives, and cider vinaigrette exudes the punchy flavors he's known for. Among small, big, and bigger plates, the red wine–braised oxtail carbonara—tingling from chipotles and served atop house-made pasta—stands out, as does melty goat-cheese fondue. Seats on the patio are coveted when warm weather arrives.

The Publican, 837 W. Fulton Market, West Loop, Chicago, IL 60607; (312) 733-9555; www.thepublicanrestaurant.com; New American/Pub; $$$. Modeled after a beer hall, Paul Kahan's rustic ode to Belgian brews, heirloom pork, and sustainable seafood kicks things off with a dazzling selection of oysters, varying in profile from brackish to crisp. Do order the spicy pork rinds (in fact, make it a double). From less common parts (duck hearts with squash agro-dolce, pecans, and Gem lettuce) to plates of aged ham with goat butter; black bass with baby artichoke barigoule and Jupiter grapes; or porchetta with cabbage and figs, ingredients themselves prove so fundamental.

Rhapsody, 65 E. Adams St., Loop, Chicago, IL 60603; (312) 786-9911; www.rhapsodychicago.com; New American; $$$. When Dean Zanella (312 Chicago) set foot in the kitchen, this pre-theater hub got a much-needed boost. Now, its menu is devoted to farm-to-plate Italian cuisine (think grilled, prosciutto-wrapped shrimp with Calabrian peppers and mint atop chickpea puree). The antipasti holds the utmost interest, whether it's simply prepared salad of local apples, lettuce, and toasted hazelnut or Taleggio arancini resting on a sweet, saba-inflected grape salad. But to be fair, sweet-savory wild boar pappardelle and prime sirloin with salsa verde aren't afterthoughts.

Rockit Bar & Grill, 22 W. Hubbard St., River North; Chicago, IL 60654; (312) 645-6000; www.rockitbarandgrill.com; American; $$. Contemporary bar food served in a Nate Berkus–designed, wood beam dining room—what's not to like? But blame the tuna tartare, the Kobe burger topped with melted Brie, and the truffle fries for why it's always packed to the gills. Head upstairs for a late-night scene, and consider coming for weekend brunch. There's also a location at 3700 N. Clark St., Wrigleyville, (773) 645-4400. (See recipe on p. 383.)

Roditys, 222 S. Halsted St., Greektown, Chicago, IL 60661; (312) 454-0800; www.roditys.com; Greek/Mediterranean; $$. There's a celebratory air to this Halsted Street staple, and comfort in knowing what to expect: friendly, genuine service, heaping portions, and a convivial, cheery feel. Whether you start with *saganaki* dotted with shrimp or go for *dolmades,* one of the many lamb configurations, herbaceous Greek chicken, or comforting pastitsio, it's rare to leave disappointed.

Roti Mediterranean Grill, 10 S. Riverside Plz., Loop, Chicago, IL 60606; (312) 775-7000; www.roti.com; Mediterranean; $. The Mediterranean answer to chipotle, this health-conscious quick-serve allows diners to design their own creations with a vast array of fresh, flavorful ingredients. Get a wrap (it holds more of the good stuff), loading it with assertively seasoned chicken, pearls of Israeli couscous, tangy cucumber-tomato salad, and feta, all dabbed with spicy hot sauce and baba ghannouj. Just thank your lucky stars if lines don't stretch down the block, a common sight at its most frequented area locations.

Russian Tea Time, 77 E. Adams St., Loop, Chicago, IL 60603; (312) 360-0000; www.russianteatime.com; Russian; $$$. Symphony-goers appreciate the Old-World ambience of this czar-worthy affair, a landmark for heavy Russian and Eastern European cuisine, including rich, creamy beef stroganoff, potato-filled dumplings, and caviar-topped blini. Many get tipsy on flights of house-infused vodka.

Sable Kitchen & Bar, Hotel Palomar, 505 N. State St., River North, Chicago, IL 60654; (312) 755-9704; www.sablechicago.com; New American; $$$. There's more than meets the eye at this stylish Kimpton gastro-lounge with Heather Terhune (Atwood Cafe, 312 Chicago) in the kitchen; updated, classic cocktails from Mike Ryan (The Violet Hour); and master sommelier Emily Wines tending to the vino. A simple bowl of warm olives, house-made jerky, and crisp-tender pork belly BLTs aren't over the top, but they're plain tasty. Many plates, poised for sharing, are available in two sizes, though it's hard to do anything but keep the root beer–glazed bison sliders to oneself. (See recipe on p. 379.)

Santorini, 800 W. Adams St., Greektown, Chicago, IL 60607; (312) 829-8820; www.santorinichicago.com; Greek/Mediterannean; $$. Seafood is the specialty at this hopping Greektown lair, so have your way with the fire-grilled calamari and octopus, whole sea bass, and red snapper. Thankfully, the dubious will also find every-thing from the village salad to the citrus-kissed dandelion greens super-fresh. Daily specials expand on the classics, so partake while basking in the comfort of the rustic, hearth-lit dining room.

Sepia, 123 N. Jefferson St., West Loop, Chicago, IL 60661; (312) 441-1920; www.sepiachicago.com; New American; $$$. Eats from Andrew Zimmerman (ex-NoMI), coupled with standout cocktails and a comfortably sultry setting, make this mid-priced, rustic-contemporary Obama fave an all around hit. Logical riffs on American classics range from the cocktail-friendly (pulled barbecue duck with pickled strawberry and rhubarb and a side of duck fat–fried potatoes) to sophisticated (steelhead trout with summer ratatouille and salsa rossa). Swanky box lunches and too-cool desserts—chamomile-lemon ice cream with gingersnaps and agave-glazed stone fruits, for example—complete the package.

Shanghai Terrace, Peninsula Chicago, 108 E. Superior St., River North, Chicago, IL 60611; (312) 573-6744; www.peninsula .com; Chinese; $$$. Come with an expense account—you'll need it. This elevated dim sum experience, set in a regal, Asian supper club–inspired space overlooking the historic Water Tower, features duck prominently. It appears with satay-soused egg noodles or crisped with orange peel. Meanwhile, a multicourse splurge of crisp, lacquered Peking duck proves delicious, with the bird carved and served with Mandarin pancakes, turned into elegant salad, and as an inclusion in hot-sour soup. Alternatives include Shanghai-style halibut in Asian melon-green mustard sauce; red miso and star anise–accented pork belly; and *foie gras* dumplings.

Shaw's Crab House, 21 E. Hubbard St., River North, Chicago, IL 60611; (312) 527-2722; www.shawscrabhouse.com; Seafood; $$$$. Seasonal and sustainable seafood is the bait at this clubby, Art Deco–style dining room, where showstoppers include plump king crab "bites" and briny, shucked-to-order bivalves. From the shellfish platters—popular in its adjacent, casual oyster bar—to the superb sushi, lobster, and prime steaks, there's plenty to choose from. Since the bounty comes with a cost, many frequent this Lettuce Entertain You venture come happy hour, when specials woo. And the seafood-heavy brunch? It's oyster-filled-amazing. There's another location at 1900 E. Higgins Rd., Schaumburg, (847) 517-2722.

Sixteen, Trump International Hotel & Tower, 401 N. Wabash Ave, 16th Fl., River North, Chicago, IL 60611; (312) 588-8000; www.trumpchicagohotel.com; New American; $$$$. Suits with big budgets divert to The Donald's sweeping, window-walled dining room, situated on the 16th floor of the hotel with a spacious, seasonal patio. Executive Chef Frank Brunacci crafts cuisine that competes with—if not outshines—the Swarovski chandelier–lit space. Dishes, which change often, may include beef cheek–potato roulade or a trio of veal with confit potato, creamed corn, andouille sausage, and veal jus ravioli. Many an oenophile has been smitten with the glass-enclosed wine gallery, stocked with stratospherically priced, special sips. (See recipe on p. 367.)

South Water Kitchen, Hotel Monaco, 225 N. Wabash Ave., Loop, Chicago, IL 60601; (312) 236-9300; www.southwaterkitchen.com; American; $$. Familiar comfort food—pot roast with whipped celery root, spicy lamb sausage, and shoulder with sunchoke—define this casual, centrally located standby. It has an interesting tavern menu, too—a fact that's enough to bait tipplers during happy hour.

State & Lake, theWit, 201 N. State St., Loop, Chicago, IL 60601; (312) 239-9400; www.stateandlakechicago.com; New American; $$. This hopping first-floor restaurant—an all-day destination—features a sleek, bottle-lined bar that begs to be bellied up to. Whether you eat there or in the comfy-chic dining room, you've got to try the buffalo fries and gooey truffled mac and cheese, supported by a cast of classic entrees, such as a center-cut, brandy-apricot sauced pork chop with sweet potato mash.

Steve's Deli, 354 W. Hubbard St., River North, Chicago, IL 60654; (312) 467-6868; www.stevesdeli.com; Deli; $$. Overall, this Michigan import delivers on the deli experience, even if the sandwiches themselves are not deserving of top billing. However, the matzoh-ball soup is as comforting as all get-out; the meat-filled knish is memorable; and the flaky, soothing chicken pot pie is as good as gold. Likewise, the generously portioned, beef-stuffed cabbage on a pool of tomato sauce is impossible to ignore.

Sunda, 110 W. Illinois St., River North, Chicago, IL 60654; (312) 644-0500; www.sundachicago.com; Asian; $$$. Billy Dec, Brad Young, and Arturo Gomez back this New Asian hot-spot, with a name that nods to Southeast Asia's Sunda Shelf. Its menu, designed by Rodelio Aglibot (BLT Restaurant Group), who remains the consulting chef, is rife with home runs. Sweet-spicy  brussels sprout salad; crisped-rice sushi, topped with spicy tuna and jalapeño; and fiery, wok-tossed soft-shell crab set ablaze with dried chiles are just a few you can't miss. Throw in a few of the expertly prepared cocktails, too.

SushiSamba Rio, 504 N. Wells St., River North, Chicago, IL 60610; (312) 595-2300; www.sushisamba.com; Japanese/South American; $$$. A sweeping, theatrical dining room and prime rooftop patio are the eye candy; flavor-packed Japanese, Peruvian, and Brazilian eats that the pretty people adore are the hook. The shareable noshes—spicy, salty shishito, yellowtail taquitos with garlic ponzu, and tuna seviche with coconut, lime, and serranos—are most always on point. There's Kobe beef, raw bar selections, and sushi as well, but customizable churrasco platters—simple and non-convoluted—stand out. For dessert, the churros with hot chocolate are pretty sweet.

sushi wabi, 842 W. Randolph St., West Loop, Chicago, IL 60607; (312) 563-1224; www.sushiwabi.com; Japanese; $$$. Perpetually packed, this scene-driven sushi purveyor pulls it all off—from the clubby, boisterous setting to the atypical preparations. Orange-sesame shrimp atop green-tea soba noodles and fried butterfish with uni butter are noteworthy starters, right alongside crunchy Godzilla maki, crammed with umpteen ingredients. Add the grilled salmon with house-made plum sauce and seared, bitter Mizuna greens, and you've got a fine affair.

Tavern at the Park, 130 E. Randolph St., Loop, Chicago, IL 60601; (312) 552-0070; www.tavernatthepark.com; New American; $$. Sometimes location is everything, but thankfully the food at this Millennium Park adjacent is beyond average as well. Settle in the handsome, wood-trimmed dining room for crunchy Parmesan-coated meatballs with vinegar peppers; pulled chicken, roasted garlic, and fontina fondue; or a loaded, chopped salad. When prime rib is available, get it; alternately, the lobster mac and cheese, peppered with applewood bacon, is prime.

Terzo Piano, Modern Wing, The Art Institute of Chicago, 159 E. Monroe St., Loop; Chicago, IL 60603; (312) 443-8650; www.terzopianochicago.com; Italian; $$$. Sit on the spacious patio overlooking Millennium Park or in the stark, white, sunlit dining room filled with mod bucket seats. Either way, you'll be wooed by Tony Mantuano's modern Italian eats. Fortify with a smear of smoked trout spread with pickled ramps, and sip a balanced Cantaloupe e Bianco cocktail with Death's Door white whiskey and cantaloupe puree. Then, pick from the likes of handcrafted, chile-flecked spaghetti with spaghetti squash, hazelnuts, and burrata or a La Quercia prosciutto and truffle-pistachio pesto flatbread with Big Ed's cow's milk cheese and arugula. Yes, the seasonal dishes cost a mint, but you get what you pay for. This museum adjunct only serves lunch, with the exception of Thursday evenings.

Texas de Brazil, 51 E. Ohio St., River North, Chicago, IL 60611; (312) 670-1006; www.texasdebrazil.com; Brazilian/Steakhouse; $$$. As with any fixed price *churrascaria,* the table is set for a meat overload experience. Here, though, an aerial steward fetches bottles from a two-story wine cellar. Before the gauchos begin their onslaught, hit the positively luxurious salad bar, which swells with Manchego, hearts of palm, and shrimp salad. (It's also where you'll want to grab vinaigrette and *chimichurri* to garnish the main event.) Meats, which arrive in endless procession until you flip your disk from green to red, include snappy-skinned sausages, garlicky sirloin, and flank steak. Garlic mashed potatoes and caramelized bananas come with; dessert costs extra.

312 Chicago, Hotel Allegro, 136 N. LaSalle St., Loop, Chicago, IL 60602; (312) 696-2420; www.312chicago.com; Italian; $$. Padova, Italy native Luca Corazzina (Prosecco) plates rustic, regional dishes with a green-market sensibility in a softly lit, wood-heavy dining room outfitted with an exhibition kitchen. Start with some antipasti, perhaps grilled baby octopus and shrimp with cannellini, escarole, and cherry tomatoes popping with juicy goodness. Savor house-made butternut squash tortellini with brown butter and sage, or warm up to the roasted pork chop with black kale, guanciale, and a potato cake in a pool of brandy-infused pan sauce. The large, but thoughtful, wine list is loaded with affordable pairings.

Topolobampo, 445 N. Clark St., River North, Chicago, IL 60654; (312) 661-1434; www.rickbayless.com; Mexican; $$$$. As popular as it ever was, Rick Bayless's world-class, fine dining destination represents his commitment to sustainable, small-farm ingredients—some custom-grown and produced. The artwork-adorned dining room features ever-changing upscale, inventive takes on regional Mexican dishes. Swagger appears in the form of poblano-warmed sunchoke with young coconut, puffed-rice, and lime-pickled turnip, or pan-roasted Maine lobster and sea scallops, finished with a silky sauce of roasted tomatillos. For dessert: devil's food cake, layered with red peanut "mole" buttercream, alongside spiced Mexican chocolate ice cream and candied ancho. Is it really as good as the buzz suggests? You bet. But for a more affordable, casual—though no less eye-popping—experience, try counterparts **Frontera Grill** or **XOCO**. Also meriting consideration on that front are **Frontera Fresco** in Macy's on State Street and **Tortas Frontera** at O'Hare Airport. (See recipe on p. 351.)

Trattoria No. 10, 10 N. Dearborn St., Loop, Chicago, IL 60602; (312) 984-1718; www.trattoriaten.com; Italian; $$$. The raison d'etre of this tucked away subterranean Italian—convenient, near-theater address aside—is its house-made ravioli. The arrabbiatasauced, spicy sausage–stuffed version is plain delicious. Still, you'll also be satisfied by the beef carpaccio with Gorgonzola dolce, the fresh as can be caprese, and the duck confit farfalle studded with pine nuts.

Veerasway, 844 W. Randolph St., West Loop, Chicago, IL 60607; (312) 491-0844; www.veerasway.com; Indian; $$. In addition to Indian greatest hits (lamb *rogan josh,* chicken *tikka masala*), you'll find street food–inspired small plates at Angela Hepler-Lee's hip, contemporary joint along Restaurant Row. A bit of advice: get the crisp okra *chaat* with matchsticks of tomatoes and onions, the Bollywood lollipops with dilled *riata* (chicken wings by any other name), herb-flecked naan, and shrimp curry with just enough sweet heat. The fun, flirty cocktails are a deserving foil.

Venus Greek-Cypriot Cuisine, 820 W. Jackson Blvd., Greektown, Chicago, IL 60607; (312) 714-1001; www.venuschicago.com; Greek/Mediterranean; $$. Taking a refreshingly different tack, this spacious, upscale spot speaks to the island of Cyprus, with minty, yogurt-based *talatouri* dip—a regional take on *tzatziki*—salty, baked *halloumi,* and coriander-marinated pork with *pourgouri* (cracked wheat). Sip selections from the Greek wine list while awaiting your individually baked *tsoukas,* noodle-based pastitsio topped with bubbly, browned béchamel.

Vermilion, 10 W. Hubbard St., River North, Chicago, IL 60654; (312) 527-4060; www.thevermilionrestaurant.com; Indian/Latin American; $$$. What seems like a dissimilar marriage—boldly flavored, contemporary Indian and Latin cuisines—works well, when it works. Small plates and *"dhaba* fare" (street truck eats) generally are the way to go here because they allow for more tastes. However, the tender, spiced tandoori skirt steak and sticky chili-tamarind ribs with avocado *pakoras* are worthwhile mains. The cocktails, while very creative, sometimes are plain strange.

Viand Bar & Kitchen, Marriott Courtyard, 155 E. Ontario St., River North, Chicago, IL 60611; (312) 255-8505; www.viandchicago.com; New American; $$$. Steve Chiappetti (Mango, Rhapsody, et al.) keeps his contemporary comfort food approachable at this handsome, hotel-adjacent space, which serves three squares daily. Design your own meat preparation, choosing between rib eye and lamb t-bone, skirt steak and a pork chop, with accompanying sauces. But do this after having the tomato-garlic soup. Beyond, ubiquitous dishes—cedar-planked salmon, roast chicken—meet more surprising alternatives, such as turducken.

Vivere, 71 W. Monroe St., Loop, Chicago, IL 60603; (312) 332-4040; vivere-chicago.com; Italian; $$$. The finest of the Italian Village eateries is also popular with the CSO and theater-bound set, its dramatic, Jordan Mozer–designed dining room an ideal place to enjoy pheasant-filled agnolotti and semolina gnocchi with hen-of-the-woods 'shrooms and selections from the winning wine list. Going well beyond the red-sauce repertoire, there's also a Wagyu rib eye with whipped Parmesan potatoes and truffle-infused, poached eggs of note.

Weber Grill, Hilton Garden Inn, 539 N. State St., River North, Chicago, IL 60654; (312) 467-9696; www.webergrillrestaurant.com; American; $$$. There's no way to keep the crowds at bay—the signature kettle-cooked creations have what it takes. So, get with the program and sneak peeks of the grilling action. Meanwhile, munch on decent steaks, burgers, and grill-fired pizzas. The mound of onion straws is a perfect match for beer-can chicken, brisket, and barbecue ribs. And the warm Dutch apple pie with Maker's Mark caramel sauce? It's kind of worth the wait. There are additional locations at 2331 Fountain Sq., Lombard, (630) 953-8880; and 1010 N. Meacham Rd., Schaumburg, (847) 413-0800.

Wildfire, 159 W. Erie St., River North, Chicago, IL 60654; (312) 787-9000; www.wildfirerestaurant.com; American; $$$. This haunt proves Rich Melman has the Midas touch. A throwback for steak, chops, and seafood, it's a preferred place to pony up for chopped salads, enjoyable Romanian skirt steak, and passable fillets. There are locations in Schaumburg, Oak Brook, Lincolnshire, and Glenview as well.

Wishbone, 1001 W. Washington Blvd., West Loop, Chicago, IL 60607; (312) 850-2663; www.wishbonechicago.com; Regional  American; $$. Delivering Southern comfort—especially during breakfast and brunch—this casual kitchen causes cravings for creamy, bacon-flecked shrimp and grits, blackened tilapia, and red beans and rice. Sibs are at 3300 N. Lincoln Ave., (773) 549-2663; and 6611 W. Roosevelt Rd., Berwyn, (708) 749-1295.

XOCO, 449 N. Clark St., River North, Chicago, IL 60654; (312) 334-3688; www.rickbayless.com; Mexican; $$. While you'd think the lines, awkward configuration, and uncomfortable seating of Rick Bayless's street food–inspired, counter-service Mexican would prove disconcerting, the wood-burning oven-warmed *pibil torta*—stuffed with meltingly tender, achiote suckling pig, black beans, and pickled onion with a side of brow-mopping habañero salsa—knows only forgiveness. Caldos, served after 3 p.m., are equally endearing, especially the short rib version built from a brooding red chile broth and farm-to-table ingredients. Pastries—try the churros—plus fresh-roasted cacao bean-to-cup hot chocolate and agua fresca are ideal accompaniments. (See recipe on p. 351.)

Zealous, 419 W. Superior St., River North, Chicago, IL 60654; (312) 475-9112; www.zealousrestaurant.com; New American; $$$$. Michael Taus's sleek space, storied, contemporary American fare, and lauded wine list remain full of surprises. Seasonally changing menus may include a short stack of mango pancakes with Hudson Valley *foie gras,* a sunny-side-up quail egg, and savory caramel sauce; a Kurobuta, bone-in pork chop with Illinois corn spoon bread, pickled green beans, and red-eye gravy; or *paprikash*-style chicken breast and confit thigh with farmer cheese pierogi and sauerkraut puree. Count on Taus's trusty beauty of a burger, topped with havarti and tomato remoulade on a plush, house-made dill roll. Vegetarian and five- and seven-course tastings are ripe for a splurge. (See recipe on p. 370.)

ZED451, 739 N. Clark St., River North, Chicago, IL 60610; (312) 266-6691; www.zed451.com; Eclectic/Steakhouse; $$$. This stylish, updated *churrascaria* has the same all-you-can-eat bent, but the harvest salads, tableside-carved proteins, and trendy-Zen scene—not to mention the gorgeous rooftop patio—add up to a superior experience. Although availability of soups and composed salads changes, they're always long on flavor. Be seduced by salty, buttermilk-herb bottom sirloin, fire-grilled rib eye, and seasoned rump roast. Proceed to New Zealand red deer and Amaretto-pistachio duck breast. Consider coming for brunch—it provides the perfect balance of sweet (cinnamon rolls) and savory (thick, pleasantly chewy maple bacon and carved meats).

Zocalo Restaurant and Tequila Bar, 358 W. Ontario St., River North, Chicago, IL 60654; (312) 302-9977; www.zocalochicago .com; Mexican; $$. An after-office crowd clocks in at this popular cantina, sought out for its guac trios, perky seviche, and *elotes* (loaded corn-off-the-cob) as well as house-made tamales and shredded beef tostadas zapped with sherry-chipotle vinaigrette. Platters encourage sharing—especially when tequila flights and agave-inspired cocktails come into play.

South

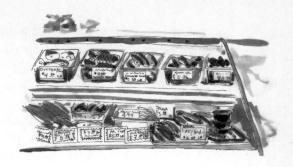

Archer Heights, Ashburn, Beverly, Bridgeport, Bronzeville, Chatham, Chinatown, Englewood, Far South Side, Greater Grand Crossing, Hyde Park, Lawndale, Little Italy, Little Village, Near South Side, Pilsen, Printer's Row, Roseland, South Deering, South Loop, University Village

Chicago's South Side covers more than half of the city's land. The thing is, it's the historic landmarks, museums, and sports teams that most often are touted. That leaves a lot to be discovered by food-minded passersby.

Looking beyond burgeoning Little Italy, Chinatown, and the beloved taquerias of Pilsen, you'll find jerk pits, shrimp shacks, and diners of the detour variety. Come for kebabs, settle in for comfort-driven cuisine, and return (often) for the barbecue of champions.

Abundance Bakery, 105 E. 47th St., Bronzeville, Chicago, IL 60653; (773) 373-1971; Bakery; $. Way-affordable and incredibly satisfying, this Far South Side bakery makes only a handful of coveted, massive, fruit-dappled apple fritters daily. When you can't get your hands on one, the bread puddings, tasty doughnuts—chocolate-glazed long johns among them—and caramel cupcakes are good stand-ins.

Al's #1 Italian Beef, 1079 W. Taylor St., Little Italy, Chicago, IL 60607; (312) 226-4017; www.alsbeef.com; American; $. People go nuts for the shredded, giardiniera-topped Italian beef served here, even if there is an odd, nutmeg-like quality to it. Get it dipped ("juicy" or "wet") and "hot" (with spicy, crushed red pepper–flecked pickled vegetables), or try it "sweet" (with roasted bell peppers). Then, roll up your sleeves and indulge in its sloppy glory while standing or sitting at picnic tables outside. Mind you, the fresh-cut, skin-on fries might just steal the show. There are locations throughout Chicagoland.

Barbara Ann's BBQ, 7617 S. Cottage Grove Ave., Greater Grand Crossing, Chicago, IL 60619; (773) 651-5300; Barbecue; $$. Real, down-home 'cue is dreamy enough to have you breaking appointments in favor of a trek to this cash-only carryout, which exhibits the  smokiness aficionados crave. However, the custom-made links may mean you forget about slabs and plump, juicy rib tips entirely.

Birrieria Reyes de Ocotlán, 1322 W. 18th St., Pilsen, Chicago, IL 60608; (312) 733-2613; Mexican; $. A shining example of its kind, this humble spot does goat proud—its *birria* a steaming, restorative consommé mounded with tender hunks of goat, onions, *chile arbol,* and cilantro spurted with lime. If the mood strikes, work your way through some goat tacos, while eyeing the comically tragic goat head adorning the wall.

Birrieria Zaragoza, 4852 S. Pulaski Rd., Archer Heights, Chicago, IL 60632; (773) 523-3700; Mexican; $$. There are excuses to eat out, and then there are things that *necessitate* a meal out. A visit to this *birrieria* falls squarely in the latter camp, a fact made clear when smoldering goat stew arrives. The *molcajates* of fresh-made salsa, handmade tortillas that are good enough to eat solo, and peerless goat tacos brightened with lime all pop with flavor.

Bridgeport Bakery, 2907 S. Archer Ave., Bridgeport, Chicago, IL 60608; (773) 523-1121; Bakery; $. Fans of the other white meat savor the plush, insanely cheap, and routinely sold-out bacon buns; come early and get them while they're warm. Other morning wake-up calls include hot-cross buns, crullers, and *paczkis*. Meanwhile, cheese or fruit-filled *kolacky* are a wonderful midday pick-me-up.

Brown Sugar Bakery, 328 E. 75th St., Greater Grand Crossing, Chicago, IL 60619; (773) 224-6262; Bakery; $. Dangerously delicious when calories are a matter of concern, Stephanie Hart's sweet tooth haven has cobblers—from peach to pear, apple, and sweet potato—down pat. Be sure to get a slice of her storied caramel cake, keeping in mind the cookies, brownies, and banana pudding—available by the serving, half, and full pan—are contenders, too.

Cafe Bionda, 1924 S. State St., South Loop, Chicago, IL 60616; (312) 326-9800; www.cafebionda.com; Italian; $$. Lovers of red sauce find much to like in the bounteous portions of Old Country standbys (fried calamari, antipasto salad, spaghetti and meatballs). Other rib-stickers include rigatoni with slow-simmered, pot roast-infused "gravy," jumbo shells cloaked in vodka tomato cream, and crisp-skinned, boneless brick chicken with rosemary potatoes. Sandwich-centric sis **Bionda to Go** is at 400 S. Financial Pl., (312) 435-0400.

Cafecito, 26 E. Congress Pkwy., South Loop, Chicago, IL 60605; (312) 922-2233; www.cafecitochicago.com; Deli/Cuban; $. Be forewarned: these pressed sandwiches—some simple, others stylin'—result in post-visit cravings. The crusty Cubano strikes the perfect balance between porky goodness, briny pickles, piquant mustard, and heaven-sent cheesiness, while the Provoleta is a griddled marvel of provolone, roasted red pepper, and garlic-laden *chimichurri*. Sip eye-popping Cuban espresso while making room for round two: a meltingly tender *ropa vieja* sammie with black beans and sweet plantains.

Cafe Trinidad, 557 E. 75th St., Greater Grand Crossing, Chicago, IL 60619; (773) 846-8081; www.cafetrinidad.com; Caribbean; $. Munch on curry goat, hell-fire jerk chicken with pea-studded rice, and potato and *chana* (curried potatoes and chickpeas) while island beats and a friendly environ transport you someplace else. Roti wraps—great stuffed with the aforementioned jerk chicken— require hibiscus-esque sorrel to quell the habañeros' burn.

Calumet Fisheries, 3259 E. 95th St., South Deering, Chicago, IL 60617; (773) 933-9855; www.calumetfisheries.com; Seafood; $$. The buxom, smoky peel-and-eat crustaceans from this circa-1928 shrimp shack will steal your heart. Strictly takeout, cash only, and located near the famed "Blues Brothers bridge," it's where you'll see patrons— parked in cars—plucking chubs, fried oysters, and fried shrimp from paper sacks. Call ahead to special order its stellar smoked fish.

Calypso Cafe, Harper Court, 5211 S. Harper Ave., Hyde Park, Chicago, IL 60615; (773) 955-0229; www.calypsocafechicago .com; Caribbean; $$. The spirited setting is half the draw at this pastel-hued, decorative-toucan-adorned Jamaican jerk shack with a penchant for big flavors. While not necessarily at the top of its class, there are plenty of things to like, including plantain nachos, an oyster po 'boy with cilantro-lime mayo, and grouper baked in parchment with veggies and white wine. Cajun cousin **Dixie Kitchen & Bait Shop** is located in Evanston.

Carnitas Uruapan, 1725 W. 18th St., Pilsen, Chicago, IL 60608; (312) 226-2654; Mexican; $. Light on frills but long on flavor are the *carnitas* served here—available in by-the-pound, moist, straight-up pork, or whole-hog configurations. They arrive with warm corn tortillas, pickled jalapeños, and salsa verde for build-your-own fun. You'd be wise to get some *chicharrones* (fried pork rinds) and nopales to go with. And—if it's the weekend—go all-out with an order of hangover-helping menudo.

Cedars Mediterranean Kitchen, 1206 E. 53rd St., Hyde Park, Chicago, IL 60615; (773) 324-6227; www.eatcedars.com; Mediterranean/Middle Eastern; $$. You'll find all the Med stalwarts—gently spiced lentil soup, standout falafel, kebabs—at this sleek, strip-mall dining room. Yet it's the tender hunks of slow-braised lamb in garlicky yogurt sauce and the well-wrought stews and sandwiches that are most memorable.

Chicago's Home of Chicken and Waffles, 3947 S. King Dr., Bronzeville, Chicago, IL 60653; (773) 536-3300; Regional American; $$. Crunchy, salty chicken and sweet, syrup-doused waffles are the benchmark of this soul-food spot. Nonetheless, there are other finds for the after-church crowd, including smothered gizzards, red beans and rice, and gooey mac and cheese. It has a suburban sibling in Oak Park at 543 Madison St., (708) 524-3300.

Couscous, 1445 W. Taylor St., University Village, Chicago, IL 60607; (312) 226-2408; www.couscousrestaurant.com; African/ Middle Eastern; $. Co-eds and post-op docs from the nearby medical campus rub elbows here over Maghrebin cuisine. Turn to the tagines and meaty soufflé-like creations, which go down well with house-made lemonade. Don't discount the more familiar fare, though, be it hummus or falafel.

Custom House Tavern, Hotel Blake, 500 S. Dearborn St., South Loop, Chicago, IL 60686; (312) 523-0200; www.customhouse.cc; New American; $$$. Since Shawn McClain parted ways with Sue Kim-Drohomyrecky and Peter Drohomyrecky, changes ensued at this earthy-chic Printers Row dining room, though it still highlights seasonal, local ingredients. When available, Goose Island 312–steeped mussels with chorizo and herbs; seared scallops with braised pork belly, grits, and green tomato preserves; and balsamic-accented roasted quail with country ham, fresh figs, and farro are a great way to go.

Daddy-O's Jerk Pit, 7518 S. Cottage Grove Ave., Chatham, Chicago, IL 60619; (773) 651-7355; Caribbean; $. Expert jerk preparations are dished out by an affable pitmaster in a cheery, no-frills, mostly carryout storefront, which emanates with reggae beats. The butterflied birds—set aflame by a Scotch bonnet and allspice-based rub—get tempered by plantain and rice and bean accompaniments. Braised oxtail and curry goat are enviable alternatives.

Dat Donut, 8249 S. Cottage Grove Ave., Greater Grand Crossing, Chicago, IL 60619; (773) 723-1002; Bakery; $. This homespun, handcrafted doughnut shop, located in the same building as Leon's Bar-B-Q, makes its fresh-glazed and buttermilk cake creations—both types feather-light—24-hours a day. When you're really hungry, order the Big Dat—a super-sized version of its signature sweet treat. There's also a location at 1979 W. 111th St., (773) 298-1001.

Davanti Enoteca, 1359 W. Taylor St., Little Italy, Chicago, IL 60607; (312) 226-5550; www .davantichicago.com; Italian/Small Plates/Wine Bar; $$. Scott Harris's rustic, cavernous-feeling Little Italy wine bar—across from the Taylor Street's Mia Francesca—is a happening joint for brick oven-fired pizza topped with pork belly, potato, and a farm egg; charcuterie and cheese spreads; tastily topped polenta boards; and smearable snacks served in  Mason jars with crostini. Wines by the glass and quartino, coupled with an affordable price point, heighten its appeal.

Don Pedro Carnitas, 1113 W. 18th St., Pilsen, Chicago, IL 60608; (312) 829-4757; Mexican; $. If it's Sunday, come early—this spot does a brisk business with the post-mass crowd. A bit confusing unless you know the drill, there are two counters serving various wonderments: *barbacoa, birria, nopales* and *chorizo, plus chicharrones* and *carnitas* sold by the pound and chopped to order. Step up and order to go, or wait for a table in the bare-bones dining room in back. Then, customize with green and red salsas, onions, cilantro, and limes to your heart's content (and tune of a mariachi serenade).

Double Li, 228 W. Cermak Rd., Chinatown, Chicago, IL 60616; (312) 842-7818; Chinese; $$. Serious Szechuan-style eats, courtesy of Ben Li, bypass all that has given Americanized Chinese a bad name. Rather, the bold, deeply nuanced, fiery, and intricate dishes set tongues tingling. Take the dry chile chicken, its crisply fried nubs of meat wok-tossed with scallions and dry chile; the cumin-scented lamb; and the rich, brow-mopping, battered fish swimming in brick-red chile broth as examples. Not oversights are dishes such as sweet-savory, garlicky black-pepper beef, hoisin-glazed, house-made "bacon," dumplings, and excellent twice-cooked pork.

Eleven City Diner, 1112 S. Wabash Ave., South Loop, Chicago, IL 60605; (312) 212-1112; www.elevencitydiner.com; Deli; $$. The food at Brad Rubin's retro-chic South Loop diner is on the pricy side, yet the Jewish staples do the trick when cravings hit. Best are the oversized sandwiches—take the Woody Allen, a double-decker corned beef and pastrami number—though melts on challah and brisket with potatoes and carrots are tempting, too. If none of these seem worthy of a mini-splurge, phosphates, floats, and egg creams prepared by an in-house soda jerk just might.

Epic Burger, 517 S. State St., South Loop, Chicago, IL 60605; (312) 913-1373; www.epicburger.com; Burgers; $. For fast food of another variety, head to this environmentally conscious joint serving burgers packed from pasture-fed, antibiotic and hormone-free beef topped with low-mileage ingredients (cage-free eggs, Wisconsin cheese) alongside hand-cut, skin-on fries crisped in trans fat–free oil. Likewise, chicken sandwiches are for those with a conscience. Thick shakes and a fab lemon squeeze smoothie are among the added perks. There's another location at 1000 W. North Ave., (312) 440-9700.

Ferrara Original Bakery, 2210 W. Taylor St., Little Italy, Chicago, IL 60612; (312) 666-2200; www.ferrarabakery.com; Bakery; $. The cannoli is every bit as good as the hype suggests, though the dizzying selection of pastries and cookies—including tiramisu, éclairs, pignoli cookies, and baba au rhum—are distractions of note. This standby also serves cafe fare, such as sandwiches, salads, and pastas.

5 Loaves Eatery, 405 E. 75th St., Greater Grand Crossing, Chicago, IL 60619; (773) 891-2889; www.5loaveseatery.com; American; $$. Big breakfasts, including fluffy omelets, powdered sugar-dusted Belgium waffles, and thick-cut French toast, give way to po' boys, stuffed baked potatoes, and satisfying salads with a loyal following. The quaint cafe also features all-you-can-eat "soulful" Saturdays and Sundays, when down-home Southern fare can be had on the cheap.

Flo & Santos, 1310 S. Wabash Ave., South Loop, Chicago, IL 60605; (312) 566-9817; www.floandsantos.com; Italian/Polish; $$. The folks behind Zapatista offer up this nostalgic ode to contrasting Polish and Italian cuisines. Here, pierogi and pizza exist in harmony, and families of South Siders even tolerate a touch of Cubbie Blue. The garlicky kielbasa—served in sandwich form and as a pizza topper with kraut—is a standout, and the lacy potato pancakes are good—especially when accompanied by a few brews or Polish vodka.

Grandaddy's Subs, 2343 W. Taylor St., Little Italy, Chicago, IL 60612; (312) 243-4200; Deli/Italian; $. The Sicilian subs hit the spot, as do the straightforward corned beef and BLT sandwiches. Then again, the old-school vibe of this sammie stand is endearing all on its own.

Han 202, 605 W. 31st St., Bridgeport, Chicago, IL 60616; (312) 949-1314; Chinese; $$. When en route to The Cell—or, frankly, just because—consider this exceptionally affordable diversion, a BYOB beacon of fine Asian fusion from Guan Chen (formerly of Ninefish in Evanston). Hunker down and choose your own adventure with a five-course prix fixe ($25), opting for beef-lemongrass salad with tart matchsticks of Granny Smith and blazing miso soup with contrasting bits of sweet king crab. Also worthy of consideration is the dish of clams with white truffle sauce and the expertly prepared shrimp-scallop red curry, which smacks of a five-star affair.

Harold's Chicken Shack No. 2, 6419 S. Cottage Grove Ave., South Side, Chicago, IL 60637; (773) 363-9586. American; $. It's impossible to single out one of the countless, mostly South Side institutions, which vary in quality, have slightly different menus, and waver in terms of environment. Some are too rough around the edges to be called charming. However, one thing is certain: when Harold's is good, it's so fine. Just look for the sign emblazoned with a crazed, chicken-chasing cook, cleaver in hand. Then, order a crackly-skinned, half chicken mix, fried "hard" and peppery, with juicy white and dark meat. It'll arrive cloaked in piquant hot sauce, atop fries and slices of white bread. Naturally, there's fried fish, shrimp, and by-the-books sides as well.

Honky Tonk Barbecue, 1213 W. 18th St., Pilsen, Chicago, IL 60608; (312) 226-7427; www.honkytonkbbqchicago.com; Barbecue; $$. Owner Willie Wagner got his start as a man about town, setting up his smoker at outdoor festivals and neighborhood events. Now, his Memphis-style smoke shack turns out some amazing pulled pork, flavorful, lightly charred brisket, and fried green tomatoes that downright deserve a championship win. The properly chewy baby backs, with a side of bracing slaw, likewise will not let you down. Weekly specials—perhaps candied bacon or Manchego and shiitake-stuffed empanadas—deviate from the norm.

Izola's, 522 E. 79th St., Greater Grand Crossing, Chicago, IL 60619; (773) 846-1484; Regional American; $$. When you're in need of a good soothing, come to Izola White's cheery, welcoming storefront for home-style chicken soup brimming with chewy, dumpling-like noodles; juicy, golden fried chicken; tender short ribs beneath comforting gravy; caramelized sweet potatoes; and chitterlings, served "seasonally." One more thing: don't pass on the subtly smoky, peppery greens.

Jamaica Jerk Villa, 8 E. 22nd St., South Loop, Chicago, IL 60616; (312) 225-0983; www.jamaicajerkvilla.com; Caribbean; $$. Marinated and rubbed, grilled jerk chicken will set your lips to tingling, building heat with each chomp. Biting callaloo helps to cool the burn ever so slightly. Alternatives, such as stewed or curry chicken and oxtails can be had at a second location (737 W. 79th St., 773-651-2240) as well.

Joy Yee's Noodle Shop, 2139 S. China Pl., Chinatown, Chicago, IL 60616; (312) 328-0001; www.joyyee.com; Pan-Asian; $. Starch-seekers swoon over this one-stop noodle shop, which serves everything from wontons and udon to chow mein and Korean-style seafood soup. There are locations in Naperville, Evanston, and in Chicago's University Village neighborhood. Nearby, **Joy Yee Plus** (2159 S. China Pl., 312-842-8928) expands upon the concept with sushi, sukiyaki, and shabu-shabu. The restaurants also have a great selection of fruity drinks and bubble tea.

Koda Bistro, 10352 S. Western Ave., Beverly, Chicago, IL 60643; (773) 445-5632; www.kodabistro.com; French; $$$. Executive

Chef Aaron Browning (Everest) brings a change of pace to the Far South Side with this sleek, contemporary Frenchie with a seasonal mindset. Sip pours from the LED-lit bar before kicking back in the dim dining room for tarte flambées and produce-driven follow-ups, such as duck confit with spaghetti squash, duck fat–fried fingerlings, and cranberry gastrique.

Kristoffer's Cafe & Bakery, 1733 S. Halsted St., Pilsen, Chicago, IL 60608; (312) 829-4150; www.kristofferscafe.com; Bakery; $. You can nibble on egg preparations (breakfast burritos, a sausage, scrambled egg, and cheese bagel) as well as standard ham and roast beef sandwiches. Not to discourage it, but it is in the moist tres leches cake that you'll find devotion. Whether you choose the classic version or one where creative liberties are taken (egg nog, *cajeta,* Kahlua), be assured it—as well as the magically delicious chocoflan—warrants indulgence.

Kroll's South Loop, 1736 S. Michigan Ave., South Loop, Chicago, IL 60616; (312) 235-1400; www.krolls-chicago.com; American; $$. Don't be deterred by other items on the large, fried food–heavy menu—you come to this Green Bay transplant for your fried cheese curd and butter burger fix. If you're not in the mood, go with the chili, loaded with kidney beans, topped with cheese, onions, and sour cream, and served on a bed of spaghetti.

La Casa de Samuel, 2834 W. Cermak Rd., Little Village, Chicago, IL 60623; (773) 376-7474; Mexican; $. The food of Guerrero informs the cooking at this Little Village taqueria, which serves vegetarian's nightmares (baby eel, grilled bull's testicles, rattlesnake) as well as truly special venison *cecina* with blistered handmade tortillas, silky guac, and acidic pico de gallo. Baked, grilled baby goat with beans and *chiles en nogada* are among the other house specialties.

La Cebollita Grill, 1807 S. Ashland Ave., Pilsen, Chicago, IL 60608; (312) 492-8443; Mexican; $. Tamales morning, noon, and night—that's a very good thing. And so it goes at this inviting, brightly hued haunt, which sauces them with *rojas* or *verde* and also serves them stippled with raisins and pineapple. Also look to *tortas,* tacos, and mole poblano–sauced entrees. When in need of cold weather comfort, try the *champurrado,* a cornmeal-based hot chocolate *atole.* There is also a location at 4343 W. 47th St., (773) 247-0910.

Lagniappe Creole Cajun Joynt, 1525 W. 79th St., Englewood, Chicago, IL 60620; (773) 994-6375; www.cajunjoynt.com; Cajun/Creole; $$. A lively homage to the Bayou, Mary Madison's BYOB gumbo haven has blossomed from a mostly carryout operation to a small—but very popular—powerhouse proffering spicy, homespun dishes you'd be hard-pressed not to love. No visit is complete without the "wangs" and waffles, étouffée, or jambalaya and the garlicky, remoulade-dappled shrimp po' boy. Other Southern faves, including candied sweet potatoes and fried green tomatoes, also fare well. There's also a location along the Chicago Riverwalk at 55 W. Riverwalk South, (312) 726-7716.

La Lagartija, 132 S. Ashland Ave., West Loop, Chicago, IL 60607; (312) 733-7772; www.lalagartijataqueria.com; Mexican; $$. "Little lizards" are a running theme at this Tex-Mex hot-spot, the creation of Laura Cid-Perea, a Bayless protégé, and her husband, Luis Perea. Groove on the noteworthy battered, chipotle-dressed shrimp and brick-red, caramelized *pastor* tacos, both tucked into piping hot, house-made tortillas. Its compadre, **Bombon Cafe,** is just down the block; likewise, sweets-focused **Bombon Cake Gallery** is nearby.

La Michoacana, 2049 W. Cermak Rd., Pilsen, Chicago, IL 60608; (773) 254-2970; Mexican; $. Fans of crispy ends must order the *gorditas de boronas* (available on Sat and Sun), the byproduct of fallen-to-the-bottom bits of lard-braised pork. Any other time, the simple, honest *carnitas* topped with cilantro are sure to suit your fancy.

Lao Beijing, 2138 S. Archer Ave., Chinatown, Chicago, IL 60616; (312) 881-0168; Chinese; $$. Tony Hu's Chinatown sib to **Lao Shanghai** and **Lao Sze Chuan** emphasizes the cuisine of its namesake city, with options that include crispy eggplant, shrimp-pork dumplings with black vinegar for dunking, and a three-course meal of Beijing duck, which appears shredded, as soup, and as a mélange of crisped skin and scallions, scooped into pancakes and daubed with hoisin.

Lao Shanghai, 2163 S. China Pl., Chinatown, Chicago, IL 60616; (312) 808-0830; Chinese; $$. Speaking the Shanghainese dialect, this Tony Hu venture offers *xiao long bao*—broth- and pork-filled dumplings—and tender, braised pork belly in preserved bean curd, but you'll also find showier preps, like a platter of sizzling, spicy lamb and shredded, deep-fried fish.

Lao Sze Chuan, 2172 S. Archer Ave., Chinatown, Chicago, IL 60616; (312) 326-5040; Chinese; $$. Tony Hu's beloved Chinatown fixture, popular with the hot pot–seekers, is every bit as pleasing for the gluttonous solo diner, who will be tempted to keep raging-hot three-chile chicken, cumin lamb, chile oil–drizzled Chengdu dumplings, and the wontons to himself. To eat one's way through the lengthy menu takes time, but it's a commitment that reaps rewards.

La Petite Folie, Hyde Park Shopping Center, 1504 E. 55th St., Hyde Park, Chicago, IL 60615; (773) 493-1394; www.lapetitefolie .com; French; $$$. Cordon Bleu–trained Executive Chef-Owner Mary Mastricola opened this pleasant neighborhood bistro with an all-French wine list to great neighborhood success. Tweaked seasonally, the classic and affordable fixed-price menus feature dishes like an Alsatian tart with Gruyère, smoked duck salad, and braised chicken, served in a quiet, date-appropriate dining room.

Lawrence Fisheries, 2120 S. Canal St., Chinatown, Chicago, IL 60616; (312) 225-2113; www.lawrencesfisheries.com; Seafood; $$. At one time a commercial fishing business, this casual, around-the-clock seafood operation—located along the river, steps from Chinatown's dim sum houses—serves thickly battered fried shrimp, fish-and-chips, wings, and by-the-pound seafood dinners, all of which benefit from a plunk in hot sauce.

Lem's Bar-B-Q, 311 E. 75th St., Greater Grand Crossing, Chicago, IL 60619; (773) 994-2428; Barbecue; $$. These chewy, caramelized, tangily sauced ribs; glistening, smoky tips; and flavorful, fat-riddled links are a gold standard, and they rope in diners who spot the glowing neon sign. It may not win any decorative awards, but this place is long on charm.

Little Three Happiness, 209 W. Cermak Rd., Chinatown, Chicago, IL 60616; (312) 842-1964; Chinese; $. Significant enough that its initials inspired the "LTH" in culinary chat site, LTHForum.com, this Cantonese-style juggernaut dishes up a massive, highlights-heavy menu, ranging from spicy string beans with XO sauce and pork to dry pan-fried noodles with barbecue pork and roast duck. Black bean–sauced clams; head-on or off salt-and-pepper shrimp; and fried chicken, accompanied by a pepper-salt blend, cilantro, and lemon, also spell bliss.

Manny's Coffee Shop & Deli, 1141 S. Jefferson St., University Village, Chicago, IL 60607; (312) 939-2855; www.mannysdeli.com;

Deli; $$. A workingman's slice of life, Manny's has been serving its famed, high-piled corned beef, brisket, and pastrami on caraway-specked rye since 1942. Blue-plate specials—salisbury steak on Monday, oxtail on Thursday—and cold-begone matzoh are among the other common denominators among the blue- and white-collar clientele.

Mario's Italian Lemonade, 1068 W. Taylor St. Little Italy, Chicago, IL 60607; No phone; Italian; $. It's possible to mark the seasons by the operation of this 1954 family-run fixture, turning out the best lemony, slushy, zest-specked Italian ice early May through September 15. (Needless to say, the other fruit-based creations— watermelon, strawberry, tutti frutti, cantaloupe— are equally sublime.) This place embodies Chicago in so many ways; to this day, a cross-section of Chicago floods it on hot summer nights. Skip dessert elsewhere, coming here as a nightcap when meals at the neighboring *cucinas* wind down.

Masi's Italian Superior Bakery, 933 S. Western Ave., Little Italy, Chicago, IL 60612; (312) 733-5092; www.italiansuperior bakery.com; Bakery/Italian; $. With a history dating back to the 1930s (it was formerly called Western Avenue Bread), this stalwart's mad skills are seen in crackly *filone,* bubbly, browned, sausage-topped sheet-pizzas, and Sicilian muffuletta layered with prosciutto, capicola, and sopressata.

May St. Cafe, 1146 W. Cermak Rd., Pilsen, Chicago, IL 60608; (312) 421-4442; www.maystcafe.com; Mexican; $$. Tweaked Latin fare—*mojo criollo*-marinated *lechón,* double-cream Brie, and winter-pear quesadillas, chicken in Michoacan-style mole—enlivens this dreary stretch of Cermak. So, too, does Mario Santiago's spicy sopa de tortilla, with grilled chicken, avocado, and sour cream garnishes.

Medici on 57th, 1327 E. 57th St., Hyde Park; Chicago, IL 60637; (773) 667-7394; www.medici57.com; American; $$. Folks come to this University of Chicago hang because they can count on it for solid sandwiches, burgers, and thin or pan pizza, which leave them with money to bank. The funky, historic BYOB—outfitted with carved and graffitied seating—also has an adjunct, artisan bakery, located at 1331 E. 57th St., (773) 667-7394.

Mercat a la Planxa, Blackstone Hotel, 638 S. Michigan Ave., South Loop, Chicago, IL 60605; (312) 765-0524; www.mercat chicago.com; Spanish; $$. Jose Garces's Catalan cuisine is enough to make the gracious Grant Park view, not to mention the soaring, sensory overload space, fade into the background. Nibble on cured meat and queso with interesting accompaniments while considering the bold options to follow: melty, cider-glazed pork belly with green apples and truffle; comforting-but-chic house-made pork-apple sausage with truffled white beans and carrot escabeche; and perfectly seared *a la planxa* preparations. Try the seasonal sangria and a stylish cocktail or two.

Moon Palace, 216 W. Cermak Rd., Chinatown, Chicago, IL 60616; (312) 225-4081; www.moonpalacerestaurant.com; Chinatown; $$. Shanghainese fare, including plump *xiao long bao* (soup dumplings) and sweet, *shu mai*–style sticky rice, is served in a sedate, contemporary setting that's a notch above its Chinatown counterparts. Safe bets include the tender black-pepper beef and spicy fish. But consider calling ahead to order the pork shoulder, a glistening, group-friendly hunk of heaven. Alternately, take the plunge and dive into the eel preparations.

Mundial-Cocina Mestiza, 1640 W. 18th St., Pilsen, Chicago, IL 60608; (312) 491-9908; www.mundialcocinamestiza.com; Eclectic/ Latin; $$. Changes have ensued at this elevated, approachable, globally influenced Pilsen storefront, but the results still evoke "wows." After perusing the menu of *huauzontle,* wild mushroom, Manchego, and *epazote* fritters with chipotle aioli; chipotle-accented hummus with sweet potato–roasted pumpkin salsa and pita chips; and shrimp with anchos and almond mole and saffron-cream sauces, it's clear just why.

Nana, 3267 S. Halsted St., Bridgeport, Chicago, IL 60608; (312) 929-2486; www.nanaorganic.com; American; $. A welcome addition to the neighborhood, this cheery, exposed-brick cafe melds a menu of American and Mexican-inflected dishes, while incorporating

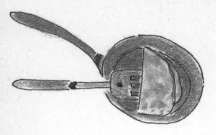

organic and sustainable ingredients to great success. Jump-start the morning with a house-made chorizo, *pupusa,* and cilantro cream riff on eggs Benedict or biscuits with duck-confit gravy. Whether it's the classic burger or smoked pork shoulder with cheesy, peppery grits, it's apparent quality ingredients make all the difference in the world. Even the grilled cheddar-cheese sandwich is a revelation when grilled fig is tucked into the mix.

Nightwood, 2119 S. Halsted St., Pilsen, Chicago, IL 60608; (312) 526-3385; www.nightwoodrestaurant.com; New American; $$$. The offerings are ever changing at this Lula sib, where an open kitchen turns out unfussy, farm-to-table dishes with oodles of crowd appeal. Depending on when you dine, that may mean garganelli with arugula-Taleggio sauce, spit-roasted chicken with black beans, creamed corn, and spicy peppers, or wood-grilled Wisconsin trout alongside butter-roasted potatoes, turnips, and escarole. Nightwood is also a popular destination for brunch, given offerings like bacon-butterscotch doughnuts and house-made maple-cinnamon granola with brown sugar and apples.

Nuevo Leon, 1515 W. 18th St., Pilsen, Chicago, IL 60608; (312) 421-1517; www.nuevoleonrestaurant.com; Mexican; $$. The nachos—oh, the individually constructed nachos. They are all the incentive you need to visit this all-around reliable institution with fantastic flour tortillas, genuine service, and a come-casual vibe.

The *guisado* (pork or beef stew) takes the nip out of the chilliest day, and the chicken swathed in mole is a stalwart that is hard to beat.

Old Fashioned Donuts, 11248 S. Michigan Ave., Roseland, Chicago, IL 60628; (773) 995-7420; Bakery; $. A thing of great worth is Old Fashioned's iced, apple-packed fritter. The same is true of the real blueberry-dotted doughnuts, offered seasonally, as well as caramel- and pineapple-frosted sweet things. Greedily indulge in them—and quick-serve burgers and fries—while sitting in the diner-style digs.

One.Six One, 1251 W. Taylor St., Little Italy, Chicago, IL 60607; (312) 226-1611; www.1pointsix1.com; Eclectic/Small Plates; $$. With a name that nods to math's golden ratio, this global small-plates spot is a refreshing alternative to Little Italy's Old-World eateries. The modern, loftlike space, complete with a fireplace, open, late-night kitchen, and roomy patio, serves worldly shareable and large plates, such as *samosas,* clay-oven lamb, duck rolls, and chicken *tinga* quesadillas.

Original Rainbow Cone, 9233 S. Western Ave., Beverly, Chicago, IL 60643; (773) 238-7075; www.rainbowcone.com; Ice Cream; $. You don't have to wait for its appearance at the Taste of Chicago to enjoy treasured chocolate, strawberry, Palmer House (cherry), pistachio, and orange-sherbet beauties, served seasonally from March to November in a vintage soda-shop setting. Cakes and a handful of other scoops are available as well. For a fast (though not nearly as nostalgic) fix, head to the Loop location at 177 N. State St., (312) 931-3354.

The Original Scoops, 608 W. 31st St., Bridgeport, Chicago, IL 60616; (312) 842-3300; www.scoops1. com; Ice Cream; $. Tap your inner child (or glutton) with classic cones, sundaes, and gut-busting banana splits, crafted from 32 flavors of hand-packed ice cream. When in need of a warm-up, turn to the array of coffee concoctions.

Park 52, 5201 S. Harper Ave., Hyde Park, Chicago, IL 60615; (773) 241-5200; www.park52chicago.com; American; $$$. Jerry Kleiner, in all his excess, succeeded in creating yet another swanky, riotously colorful dining room, this one with a chef's table offering a view of the action. Seared, hand-sliced strip steak with Parmesan–blue cheese grits, braised short ribs, and pork chops smothered in sweet-onion gravy with collard greens are among the mid-priced crowd-pleasers. It's also a popular brunch option, drawing plenty of U of C students.

Parrot Cage, South Shore Cultural Center, 7059 S. South Shore Dr., Far South Side, Chicago, IL 60649; (773) 602-5333; http:// kennedyking.ccc.edu/washburne/parrot_cage/home.html; New American; $$. Lovely lake views frame this genteel Washburne Culinary Institute student dining room in the architecturally stunning South Shore Cultural Center. Wednesday and Thursday evenings usher in affordable, choose-your-own, set-price meals; otherwise, snag braised lamb shank or seared salmon, prepared by chefs in training and served a la carte.

Pearl's Place, 3901 S. Michigan Ave., Bronzeville, Chicago, IL 60653; (773) 285-1700; Regional American; $$. Dishing out more Southern comforts than you can shake a stick at—juicy fried chicken, catfish, mac and cheese—this simple fixture oozes octogenarian appeal, though its down-home peach cobbler shows nothing short of all-ages charm.

Phoenix, 2131 S. Archer Ave., Chinatown, Chicago, IL 60616; (312) 328-0848; www.chinatownphoenix.com; Chinese; $$. Come early to avoid the crowds that flock to this popular dim-sum destination. Expansive windows overlooking Chinatown Square are built for people-watching from the comfort of the upscale, banquet-like space. When roving carts reveal sweet, flaky barbecue pork buns; shrimp dumplings; curried baby octopus; and toothsome, pork-filled *bao,* snag them. When ordering off the menu, splurge on succulent Peking duck, dipping it—and all else—in the superb oily, spicy chile sauce that tops tables.

Pompei Little Italy, 1531 W. Taylor St., Little Italy, Chicago, IL 60607; (312) 421-5179; www.pompeipizza.com; Italian; $$. Blocks of doughy pizza, baked in sheet pans, have lured loyalists to this bakery since 1909. It's true the cafeteria-style place, named in homage to Our Lady of Pompeii church, is a fuss-free and generally likeable option when in the neighborhood. Consider the stromboli-like pizza strudel and the Italian sandwiches, perhaps pepper and egg, when deviating. There are additional locations in Chicago and the suburbs.

Potsticker House, 3139 S. Halsted St., Bridgeport, Chicago, IL 60608; (312) 326-6898; www.potstickerhouse.com; Chinese; $$. In-the-know-diners ask for the translated Chinese language menu. Items that woo include *xiao long bao* (pork-filled soup dumplings); "cigar" potstickers; a sweet, smoky, scallion-flecked pork cake; glazed, garlicky eggplant; and flaming-hot, aromatic cumin lamb.

Pupuseria el Salvador, 3557 E. 106th St., Chicago, Far South Side, Chicago, IL 60617; (773) 374-0490; Salvadoran; $. Pupusas (stuffed masa cakes), griddled in a compact basement kitchen and oozing with cheese, are addictive—and all the more so with *curtido* (vinegary Salvadoran cabbage relish). Stout, glistening chorizo and moist *budin* enjoy followings, too.

Ramova Grill, 3510 S. Halsted St., Bridgeport, Chicago, IL 60609; (773) 847-9058; American; $$. Belly up to the lunch counter at this circa-1929 diner where breakfast is served all day. Most come for the hearty bean or no-bean chili, though, which makes an appearance in the off-menu mother-in-law sandwich, a Chicago original consisting of a chile-doused tamale. Joining it are other bites of Americana, such as a hamburger and BLT.

Ribs 'N' Bibs, 5300 S. Dorchester Ave., Hyde Park, Chicago, IL 60615; (773) 493-0400; Barbecue; $. The hickory-smoked ribs may warrant, well, bib-wearing when visiting this South Side pit. Hokily named western dinners and "chuck wagon" combos with all the fixings appease 'cue-seekers, who also secure oddities like the char-crusted bronco burger and the gunslinger, a drinker's delight of a sausage sandwich with fries.

Ristorante al Teatro, 1227 W. 18th St., Pilsen, Chicago, IL 60608; (312) 784-9100; www.alteatro.us; Italian; $$. A follow-up to Caffè Gelato in Wicker Park, this elegant *cucina*—set in historic Thalia Hall—has art-adorned walls that nod to the 1893 World's Columbian Exhibition. The menu of antipasti, wood-fired pizzas, and homemade pasta dishes as well as main courses of the Vesuvio-variety, provides a change of pace amid a sea of neighborhood taquerias. End on a sweet note with its selection of two-dozen gelati, made in-house daily.

The Rosebud, 1500 W. Taylor St., Little Italy, Chicago, IL 60607; (312) 942-1117; www.rosebudrestaurants.com; Italian; $$. This is where the Rosebud empire began, and it remains a force to be reckoned with still. Yes, more serious Italian dining destinations exist, but it's safe to assume the standards—stuffed artichokes, minestrone, chicken Vesuvio—won't lack crowd appeal or scrimp on portion size. There are numerous outposts, with varying bents, scattered about town.

Saint's Alp Teahouse, 2131 S. Archer Ave., Chinatown, Chicago, IL 60686; (312) 842-1886; www.saints-alp.com.hk; Taiwanese; $. As the name implies, tea of many stripes is the emphasis at this Hong Kong transplant, which most notably serves Taiwanese-style, milkshake-like bubble tea dotted with tapioca pearls. Quick bites (*yakitori,* spicy vermicelli, sweet milk toast)—though not the main draw—serve a purpose.

Shui Wah, 2162 S. Archer Ave., Chinatown, Chicago, IL 60616; (312) 225-8811; Chinese; $$. Setting a standard with cooked-to-order, Hong Kong–style dim sum is addictive salt-and-pepper squid, fried taro and delicate, translucent shrimp dumplings. If hunger permits, pork *siu mai,* slippery shrimp, or barbecue pork crepes and leaf-wrapped sticky rice are great grabs, too. The less enthralling menu hosts sweet-and-sour chicken, a tangy pork and eggplant hot pot, and a salty, flavorful olive and minced pork mixture atop rice.

Sikia, Washburne Culinary Institute, 740 W. 63rd St., Englewood, Chicago, IL 60621; (773) 602-5200; www.ccc.edu/sikia; African; $$. Located on the Kennedy-King College campus, this contemporary, African-inflected, expertly student-run dining room provides real-life experience, while tapping the flavors of Brazil, Jamaica, and even New Orleans. Nosh on the likes of Senegalese peanut soup, fry bread, and black-eyed pea fritters, followed by *berbere*-spiced spare ribs, and grilled rib eye with house-made *harissa.* Note that as of now, it's open for Sunday brunch only.

Soul Vegetarian East, 205 E. 75th St., Greater Grand Crossing, Chicago, IL 60619; (773) 224-0104; Vegetarian/Vegan; $$. Those with vegan and vegetarian leanings find a lot to like in the food from this mainstay, where options such as the mock-meat BBQ Twist are something a meat-eater could endure—even enjoy. What sets this place apart, though, is its flavor-driven dishes, such as chicken-like "protein tidbits." Maybe it's because they're not always as straight-up-healthy as the concept suggests. The restaurant also operates a vegan food truck, which may be followed via Twitter.

Southside Shrimp House, 335 W. 31st St., Bridgeport, Chicago, IL 60616; (312) 567-0000; Seafood; $. Steps from "Sox Park," this chill seafood shack fries up butterflied, lightly breaded shrimp that's redolent of garlic. While it's hard to recommend this as an alternative to a ballpark dog, it certainly makes the case for a pre- or post-game visit.

Spring World, 2109 S. China Pl., Chinatown, Chicago, IL 60616; (312) 326-9966; Chinese; $$. A magic Yunnanese mushroom menu (including a multiple variety-packed hot pot) sets the tone at this stellar, simple cornerstone in Chinatown, which also serves cold sesame and Chengdu-style noodles; Szechuan-style lamb stew; and crisp, scallion-flecked pancakes to a satisfied collective. For a rock-bottom deal, come during lunch.

Stax Cafe, 1401 W. Taylor St., Little Italy, Chicago, IL 60607; (312) 733-9871; American; $$. Stacks of pancakes—ricotta topped with rhubarb compote, butterscotch, upside-down pineapple—are the specialty at this modern daytime diner, though it makes sense to take your time with the braised-brisket hash, French toast, and eggs Sardou, too. When the hours wane, expect a fresh, affordable selection of soups, salads, and sandwiches to come into play.

Take Me Out, 1502 W. 18th St., Pilsen, Chicago, IL 60608; (312) 929-2509; www.takemeouthotties.com; Chinese; $. Affording a break from the Mexican-heavy cuisine populating the 'hood, this destination showcases the soy-chile-lacquered Chinese chicken wings made famous at Great Seas on Lawrence Avenue. Nai Tiao's daughter, Karen Lim, decided to serve the fabled "hotties" in hipper digs, along with shrimp-topped fried rice and crab Rangoon.

Tao Ran Ju, 2002 S. Wentworth Ave., Chinatown, Chicago, IL 60616; (312) 808-1111; Chinese; $$. James An's hip Spring World follow-up serves superb, steaming *xiao long bao* (soup dumplings)—though it's primarily known for serving hot pots, which are prepared upon individual tabletop burners. When going that route, choose your broth—the hot, spicy version fares well—customizing from an a la carte selection of ingredients, both familiar (pork, lamb) and adventurous (duck tongue, goose intestines). Not to be missed are the skewers and the biting, beef-noodle soup finished with pickled veg.

Taqueria El Milagro, 1923 S. Blue Island Ave., Pilsen, Chicago, IL 60608; (312) 433-7620; www.el-milagro.com; Mexican; $. This taqueria adjunct of the beloved, local tortilla producer serves fab tamales of several stripes, crafted from fresh masa, plus tacos, chile rellenos, and chicken swathed in mole at rock-bottom prices. Afterward, head to the store to pick up tortillas and chips for the road. There are additional locations in the Little Village neighborhood and North Riverside.

Taqueria Tayahua, 2411 S. Western Ave., Little Village, Chicago, IL 60608; (773) 247-3183; Mexican; $. You don't have to spend a lot to reap the rewards of this off-the-beaten-track taqueria, outfitted with a telltale spit for roasting *carne al pastor*. Feel confident in ordering the comforting *carne en su jugo,* which arrives with a bevy of lively accompaniments—limes, cilantro, radishes, chiles— or settle on the *huitlacoche* quesadillas.

That's-a-Burger, 2134 E. 71st St., South Side, Chicago, IL 60649; (773) 493-2080; Burgers; $. Although service lags—and lags— people are willing to wait for what this exclusively carryout operation, bulletproof glass and all, has to offer: two-fisted, five-napkin burgers both classic and—at least in the case of the cheesy, split

Polish-topped Whammy burger—tricked out. Also good: the TAB, topped with a fried egg, sport peppers, onions, and chili. A rarity, the turkey burger is fantastic. So are the superior hand-cut fries.

Top Notch Beefburgers, 2116 W. 95th St., Beverly, Chicago, IL 60643; (773) 445-7218; Burgers; $. For a real-deal diner experience, visit this throwback, a landmark burger joint owned by Diran Soulian; it has griddled up house-ground round patties with beef-tallow fries since 1954. Get yours topped with American and grilled onions, adding on some onion rings and a thick, indulgent shake. Then, bask in the simple deliciousness amid a beige, wood-paneled dining room hung with landscape paintings.

Troha's Shrimp & Chicken, 4151 W. 26th St., Little Village, Chicago, IL 60623; (773) 521-7847; www.chicagoshrimphouse.com; Seafood; $. Lightly breaded, nicely spiced crustaceans are the main attraction at this circa-1920 seafood house, which claims to be the original of its (nearly extinct) kind. You'll find plenty of other artery-clogging fry-daddy delights as well, including near-perfect chicken, frog's legs, and smelt.

Tropic Island, 553 E. 79th St., Chatham, Chicago, IL 60619; (773) 224-7766; www.original jerkchicken.com; Caribbean; $. Those who head to this carryout are determined to procure one thing: smoky, spicy, and incredibly juicy jerk chicken. There's also oxtail, curry goat, and stewed chicken as well as classic sides, from red beans and rice to steamed cabbage and callaloo. There is a second location at 570 Torrence Ave., Calumet City, (708) 730-0033.

Tufano's Vernon Park Tap, 1073 W. Vernon Park Pl., University Village, Chicago, IL 60607; (312) 733-3393; www.tufanosrestaurant.com; Italian; $$. Looking as though it's from a mobster movie set, this cash-only 1930s relic—famous for its sprightly lemon chicken—exudes a back-in-the-day vibe. It's the sort of place where families celebrate landmarks over shared spaghetti *aglio e olio* and linguine with red or white clam sauce, presented by a veteran waitstaff. It's not particularly polished and certainly not trendy, but no one comes here looking for that.

Uncle Joe's Tropical Dining, 1461 E. Hyde Park Blvd., Hyde Park, Chicago, IL 60615; (773) 241-5550; www.unclejoesjerk.com; Caribbean; $$. Whole-bird, wood-smoked Jamaican jerk—loaded with habañero heat—begs for sides of plantains and red beans and rice to deliver relief. Jerk also appears on shrimp and fish. Meanwhile, standards, like stewed chicken, oxtail, and curry goat, as well as locally made beef patties, foster the island-like feel. There are a handful of additional locations in Chicago.

Uncle John's, 337 E. 69th St., Greater Grand Crossing, Chicago, IL 60637; (773) 892-1233; Barbecue; $. You'll want the deeply smoky, surprisingly moist rib tips and breakfast sausage-y links combo from this carryout pit, where the magic happens behind glass and the results are just this side of hog heaven. There's only one drawback, really, and it's that you'll have to eat these babies in the car.

Valois, 1518 E. 53rd St., Hyde Park, Chicago, IL 60615; (773) 667-0647; www.valoisrestaurant.com; American; $. U of C coeds, profs, and neighborhood types can't get enough of this casual, landmark cafeteria, and it takes but a visit to agree. As the line snakes around the counter, options such as a Denver omelet or French toast reveal themselves in the morning. Later, roast pork doused with gravy, baked chicken, and hot sandwiches, plus fruit and cream pies, cobblers, and Jell-O replicate what mom makes.

Vito & Nick's, 8433 S. Pulaski Rd., Ashburn, Chicago, IL 60652; (773) 735-2050; www.vitoandnick.com; Pizza; $. What may be the best cracker-thin pizza in the city is found at this institution, which got its start in 1923. Kitted out with carpeted walls, it attracts a blue-collar crowd that knows bright-sauced sausage pies are the boss. Though it serves a roster of sandwiches, pastas, and fried pub grub, plus all-you-can-eat smelt on Friday, it's doubtful anyone notices. There's also a location at 1015 S. State St., Lemont, (630) 257-5426, within Lemont Lanes.

White Palace Grill, 1159 S. Canal St., University Village, Chicago, IL 60607; (312) 939-7167; www.whitepalacegrill.com; American; $. When cravings set in during the wee hours, this classic, all-hours diner has your back. Its diverse menu, available anytime, ranges from corned beef hash crowned with sunny-side up eggs and biscuits and gravy to standard sandwiches, south-of-the-border specialties (enchiladas, burritos), and fried fish or chicken dinners.

Wings Around the World, 510 E. 75th St., Greater Grand Crossing, Chicago, IL 60616; (773) 483-9120; www.flavorsto infinity.com; Eclectic; $. A dizzying number of globally inspired hot wings—maple-glazed Canadians, Indian Curry, Szechuan-style— ensure you'll never tire of this take-out joint. In the event you do, fried fish and shrimp are options as well.

Yolk, 1120 S. Michigan Ave., South Loop, Chicago, IL 60605; (312) 789-9655; www.yolk-online.com; American; $$. The masses wait in anticipation for eye-openers, such as pot roast eggs Benedict and *huevos rancheros* as well as skillets, frittatas, and fresh fruit and granola–topped oatmeal. However, it doesn't end there, what with all the banana-nut French toast, crepes and fresh, chock-full salads. Look for its breakfast brethren at 747 N. Wells St., (312) 787-2277; and 355 E. Ohio St., (312) 822-9655.

Zaleski & Horvath Market Cafe, 1126 E. 47th St., Kenwood, Chicago, IL 60653; (773) 538-7372; www.zhmarketcafe.com; Deli; $. Locals swing by this charming specialty cafe and international gourmet grocer for its attractive selection of cheeses. They also seek sustenance from the chalkboard menu touting panini and cold sandwiches, plus daily soups (try the rustic garlic). Its pastries are perfect for pairing with macchiato con panna, espresso, and *café au lait*. There's also an outpost at 1323 E. 57th St., (773) 538-7372.

Zaytune Mediterranean Grill, 3129 S. Morgan St., Bridgeport, Chicago, IL 60608; (773) 254-6300; www.zaytunegrill.com; Mediterranean/Middle Eastern; $. You've got to hand it to a from-scratch place, especially when the results are this good. The brainchild of Kendall College grad Daniel Sarkiss, the spot's fresh, quality ingredients and made-to-order approach shines in flavorful, grilled kebabs; crisp outside, downy inside falafel; and rosemary- and garlic-marinated chicken shawarma. An added advantage is the food—free of trans fats and preservatives—is healthy.

Suburban Stunners, Stalwarts & Surprises

City-dwellers—at least those not already in the know—call the suburbs a wasteland. That's just fine with outlying addressees, who happily keep their fortunes hush-hush.

Look beyond low-lying, indistinguishable office complexes, and see communities ripe with culinary aplomb, restaurants quaint and cultured, and plenty of jaunting material.

North & Northwest

Bank Lane Bistro, 670 N. Bank Ln., Lake Forest, IL 60045; (847) 234-8802; www.banklanebistro.com; New American; $$$. Located in a building that in part dates back to 1901, the heart of this South Gate Cafe adjunct is its wood-burning oven, visible through an open kitchen. In the intimate setting, fail-safes (poke tartare, fillet with mashed potatoes, chicken roulade) never deviate too much, making it a haven for families and neighborhood couples.

Barrington Country Bistro, Foundry Shopping Center, 718 W. Northwest Hwy., Barrington, IL 60010; (847) 842-01300; www .barringtonbistro.com; French; $$$. A charming locale for a romantic night out, this snug, French bistro has a comfy country interior, with warm-weather seating outdoors. The seasonal menu changes often but usually includes bubbly, gratinéed French onion soup topped with Raclette, garlic-forward escargots, charcuterie plates, and twice-cooked, apple-glazed duck leg with celery remoulade.

Bavaria Hof, 933 S. Roselle Rd., Schaumburg, IL 60193; (847) 891-7997; German; $$. Touting traditional German dishes, this holdout hosts enough steins, schnitzel, sausages, sauerbraten, and strudel to stuff a gorger silly. Specials like roast duck, though, are added for good measure. Friday and Saturday usher in an all-you-can-eat pig roast.

Burt's Place, 8541 Ferris Ave., Morton Grove, IL 60053; (847) 965-7997; Pizza; $$. This is a destination unto itself, thanks to the cheesy, caramelized—okay, charred—mid-weight pizzas from owners Burt and Sharon Katz (Gullivers, Inferno, Pequod's), served at a leisurely pace in a space adorned with antique tchotchkes. A word to the wise: get your fresh, tangy-sauced pie topped with sweet peppers and aromatic coins of Italian sausage. The restaurant is cash only.

Cafe Pyrenees, 1762 N. Milwaukee Ave., Libertyville, IL 60048; (847) 362-2233; www.cafepyrenees.com; French; $$. Some come to sip wine from the thoughtful list, though few leave without engaging in country French meals: a selection of sausages atop white-bean cassoulet, braised beef Bourguignon, a duo of sliced duck breast and crispy leg confit on a bed of mascarpone polenta with lingonberry sauce. Ask about its fixed-price retro menu, which features prices on par with their 1990 originals. Also, grab a bottle of vino from the wine shop for another day.

Campagnola, 815 Chicago Ave., Evanston, IL 60202; (847) 475-6100; www.campagnolarestaurant.com; Italian; $$$. Daters have long adored the dignified simplicity of this Italian in Evanston, its rustic dishes—made from locally procured ingredients—endlessly charming. Begin with a bruschetta of roasted tomato marmalade and whipped feta; bacon-wrapped, wood-fired radicchio with goat cheese and basil aioli; or pillows of ricotta with fragrant wild-boar *ragù,* saving room for brick-roasted chicken or smoky pheasant with bacon, Delicata squash, and cipollini. Its owners are also behind **Union Pizzeria** (1245 Chicago Ave., Evanston, 847-475-2400) and mobile **Hummingbird Kitchen** (847-475-6680).

Capannari Ice Cream, 10 S. Pine St., Mount Prospect, IL 60056; (847) 392-2277; www.capannaris.com; Ice Cream; $. Nestled in a historic general store, this quaint parlor makes its own frozen treats, including scoops of rich hazelnut ganache. Expect over-the-top creamy, standard flavors like chocolate, cake batter, and cookie dough, but don't shy away from lesser-knowns, such as lavender-honey, Nestlé-inspired Drumstick, or chocolate chile pepper. Ice cream samplers, packed in dry ice, may be shipped.

Captain Porky's, 38995 Rte. 41, Wadsworth, IL 60083; (847) 360-7460; www.captainporky.com; Seafood/Barbecue; $$. Not far from the tranquil, rocky shores of Illinois State Beach Park, this relocated, scratch-cooking, smoked meat and fried seafood shack shows attention to detail. As a result, much shines: organic, locally grown produce; its own wild-caught fish; and quality imported ingredients, including olive oil from the family's own fields in Sparta, Greece. Ribs, infused with woody flavor, give way to perch, crawfish tails, and gator as well as a lobster roll po' boy and pulled-pork-shoulder sandwich. **The Shanty** (38995 N. US Hwy 41, Wadsworth, 847-336-0262) is its seafood-centric cohort.

Carlos' Restaurant, 429 Temple Ave., Highland Park, IL 60035; (847) 432-0770; www.carlos-restaurant.com; French; $$$$. The kind of place that keeps on keeping on, this North Shore fancy pants is the lovechild of Carlos and Debbie Nieto. Within its hallowed, wood-swathed confines, classic and unpredictable French cuisine meets one of the area's best wine lists. Fortunately, though, the aura is anything but aloof. Yes, diners are "of a certain age," but artfully plated, roasted cauliflower ravioli with celery espuma is enough to make you forget. Order a la carte or by degustation, and keep an eye out for ongoing events, including a twice-monthly film dinner club. Sister restaurants include **Cafe Central** (455 Central Ave., Highland Park, 847-266-7878) and **Happ Inn Bar and Grill** (305 Happ Rd., Northfield, 847-784-9200).

Chaihanna, 19 E. Dundee Rd., Buffalo Grove, IL 60089; (847) 215-5044; Uzbek; $$. Set in a nondescript strip mall, this Uzbek is a gem of a joint loaded with foods unfamiliar to the large collective. Crisp, five-alarm pickled vegetables; dumpling-like, meat-filled *manti*; moist, flavorful skewers; and baked, samosa-esque *samsas* give way to something not to be missed at meal's end: *chak-chak,* a fried, honeyed dough dessert. The laid-back setting is offset by upscale touches, like lovely place settings.

Charlie Beinlich's, 290 Skokie Blvd., Northbrook, IL 60062; (847) 714-9375; www.charliebeinlichs.com; American; $$. The chin-dribbling cheeseburgers from this wood-paneled tap get props, though the shrimp cocktail has a fan base as well. The edited menu has a handful of other options—grilled ham and cheese, chili, a tuna salad sandwich—but no one pays them much mind.

Chef's Station, 915 Davis St., Evanston, IL 60201; (847) 570-9821; www.chefs-station.com; New American; $$$. The warehouse ring to its name is a misnomer. Rather, this funky, anything-but-institutional Euro bistro is set in the Davis Street Metra station. Raves go to the American eats, six-course tasting menu, and winning selection of over 350 wines. Pluck your flatware from a trademark jeans-pocket-cozy, and cuddle up to a Manchego-caramelized Vidalia tart with 25-year aged balsamic; seared duck breast with mushroom bread pudding and red-wine reduction; and a turtle sundae topped with shaved chocolate, caramel sauce, and whipped cream.

Cho Jung Restaurant, 952 Harlem Ave., Glenview IL 60025; (847) 724-1111; Korean; $$. Come for the judiciously prepared *pan-chan* (behold the pickled apple); fresh, pancake-like *pajeon* specked with green onion and seafood; fried, dumpling-like *mandu;* and restorative *sundubu jjigae* (steaming, spicy stew). You'll also get a taste of the good life in vibrant, heartwarming *dolsot bibimbap,* christened with a yolky fried egg.

Cross-Rhodes, 913 Chicago Ave., Evanston, IL 60202; (847) 475-4475; www.crossrhodes.biz; Greek; $. On the surface, this is just another Greek diner—that is until a plate of über-crisp, feta-showered fries bathed in lemony, white wine-herb sauce is placed before you. Round out your diet with avgolemono soup and accolade-worthy gyros. The restaurant is cash only.

D&J Bistro, 466 S. Rand Rd., Lake Zurich, IL 60047; (847) 438-8001; www.dj-bistro.com; French; $$. A hidden, though always bustling, crowd-pleaser, this chef-owned bistro does the standards and does them well, be it cheesy French onion soup, chicken braised in white wine with earthy root vegetables, or steak frites with shallot butter. This is a labor of love, so expect ground-to-order steak tartare and elaborate tarts and cakes for carryout. Menus catering to vegetarians and children are available.

Dung Gia - Annam, 1436 Miner St., Des Plaines, IL 60016; (847) 803-4402; www.dunggiarestaurant.com; Vietnamese; $$. David Tran relocated his popular Vietnamese from Evanston, and the fans followed, ordering sizzling *banh xeo* (a shrimp and veggie crepe); customizable *pho* and acidic *canh chua tom* (shrimp-tamarind soup); and garlicky beef skewers. The lunch menu is a steal.

Edzo's Burger Shop, 1571 Sherman Ave., Evanston, IL 60201; (847) 864-3396; www.edzos.com; Burgers; $. Culinary-school graduate Eddie Lakin (Spruce, Tru) is among the contingent of chefs gone casual (but still mindful of quality). His house-ground chuck burgers—available in charred, pink-centered half-pound; flat-griddled; and patty melt configurations—don't need much gussying up. Yet, it's futile to resist garlic butter and giardiniera, let alone versions using Dietzler Farm meat. For a lesson in discipline, try bypassing the double-fried, Merkts-topped fries and the shakes, which range from Nutella to Mexican chocolate with a kick.

El Tipico, 3341 Dempster St., Skokie, IL 60076; (847) 676-4070; www.eltipico.net; Mexican; $$. The margaritas are good, the mole-sauced enchiladas even better at this trusty spot dispensing generous portions of Mexican and Americanized south-of-the-border fare. There's also a special menu dedicated to seafood-based appetizers and entrees (think fish tacos, fiery camarones with a myriad of peppers, and whole red snapper).

Francesco's Hole in the Wall, 254 Skokie Blvd., Northbrook, IL 60062; (847) 272-0155; www.francescosholeinthewall.com; Italian; $$. Enjoying a cult following, this North Shore Southern Italian with distressed walls, a marker-board menu, and handful of perpetually packed tables wafts with scents of snapper Vesuvio and Bolognese-sauced tortellini.

Frank's Karma Cafe, 203 S. Main St., Wauconda, IL 60084; (847) 487-2037; www.frankskarma.com; Deli; $. Named for a German shepherd with purportedly good luck, this ambitious deli specializes in seasonal soups, substantial salads, and sandwiches made from fresh ingredients. Adding interest are daily specials, available in limited quantities. Come on Monday when Mediterranean meatloaf may appear or on Thursday, when bacon-and-egg salad sandwiches take center stage. Real fruit smoothies, fresh-baked desserts, and afternoon-to-evening tea service—not to mention a back-door drop-off service geared toward harried moms—are added charms.

Froggy's French Cafe, 306 Green Bay Rd., Highwood, IL 60040; (847) 433-7080; www.froggysrestaurant.com; French; $$$. Upscale but approachable, this longtime, art-adorned French fave features a menu where old-school (escargot) meets new and improved (Gulf shrimp with orange, coconut, and leaf lettuce in cayenne vinaigrette). Finds from the large, notable French and American wine list are kept in a temperature-controlled cave. Its ami, **Gourmet Frog Bakery,** is at 316 Green Bay Rd., Highwood, (847) 433-7038.

Gabriel's, 310 Green Bay Rd., Highwood, IL 60040; (847) 433-0031; www.egabriels.com; French/Italian; $$$. CIA graduate Gabriel Viti's mahogany-trimmed dining room has little to hide: both its kitchen and glassed-in wine cellar are on full display. And while the setting is white tablecloth, this French-Italian hybrid sticks to what's familiar, resulting in silky lobster bisque with Gulf shrimp, sautéed Hudson Valley *foie gras* with leeks and black-truffle sauce, and crespelle, filled with spinach and Taleggio in Parmesan sauce. The wine list is excellent, a fact that's supported by Viti's by-appointment wine shop.

Gene & Jude's Red Hot Stand, 2720 River Rd., River Grove, IL 60171; (708) 452-7634; Hot Dogs; $. Lines snake out the door of this simple, true blue stand, a beacon for snappy, Chicago-style dogs topped with sweet relish, mustard, onions, and sport peppers in a steamed bun with hand-cut fries. There's not much else in the way of pomp, save the option of a perfectly steamed tamale.

Hackney's on Harms, 1241 Harms Rd., Glenview, IL 60025; (847) 724-5577; www.hackneys.net; American; $$. The history is interesting—founder Jack Hackney began selling these trademark burgers from the back porch of his Glenview home during Prohibition. The family tradition lives on here with the fresh-ground Hackneyburger on dark rye, served on a pretty patio shaded by silver poplars when it's warm. Be sure to get the fried onion rings, too. There are six area locations.

Himalayan Restaurant, 8265 W. Golf Rd., Niles, IL 60714; (847) 324-4150; www.himalayanrestaurant.com; Indian/Nepalese; $$. Serving a popular, varied lunch buffet in comfortably casual digs, this place provides an alternative to Devon Avenue (and the parking conundrum that goes with visits). Start with the ginger-flecked *momo* (dumplings) and Masala chicken wings, which arrive sputtering atop herbaceous onions. And while tandoori dishes are downright commonplace, here they taste better—smokier, in fact. But that's not to say *ko masu,* stew-like goat or chicken fragranced with Nepalese spices, falls flat. Others are at 398 Army Trail Rd., Bloomingdale, (630) 523-5100; and 3747 Gran Ave., Gurnee, (224) 637-3000.

Inovasi, 28 E. Center Ave., Lake Bluff, IL 60044; (847) 295-1000; www.inovasi.us; New American; $$$. John des Rosiers (formerly of Bank Lane Bistro) has his way with food in an off-the-beaten-path, blue-hued storefront where it seems anything can happen. Known for off-the-cuff flavor profiles, des Rosiers concocts fleeting dishes, such as delicate, corn powder–dusted Great Lakes walleye, roasted and served with creamy red Inca quinoa, ginger-lime tree honey sauce, and threads of crisped leek. Although many options come loaded with bells and whistles, impressive, too, is the pared down, three-day pork shoulder, marinated, grilled, turned to confit, smoked, and poached in goat's milk. Desserts are inventive, without being overwrought. Tasting and loose-leaf tea menus are available, as is a menu for children that isn't dumbed down.

Jacky's on Prairie, 2545 Prairie Ave., Evanston, IL 60201; (847) 733-0899; www.jackysonprairie.com; French; $$$. Jacky Pluton no longer heads this comfortable French bistro, but the seasonally inspired menu, like the window-lined space, still holds allure. Look no further than dishes like cauliflower-pear soup with hints of Maharaja curry, braised short ribs with tangerine-ginger sauce, and Dover sole *pour deux* as evidence. There are two tasting menus, one vegetarian, available with or without wine pairings.

Ko Chi Jip, 773 Milwaukee Ave., Glenview, IL 60026; (847) 486-8048; Korean; $$. As is custom, meals at this frills-free Korean begin with a selection of *panchan* before tabletop cooking begins (or orders arrive). Chief choices include *dukbokki* (fiery rice cakes), spicy *cham-bong* seafood soup, *dolsot bibimbap,* and *bulgogi.*

La Casa de Isaac, 431 Temple Ave., Highland Park, IL 60035; (847) 433-5550; www.lacasadeisaac.com; Mexican; $$. This North Shore hacienda serves a stable of familiar, traditional Mexican meals during breakfast, lunch, and dinner, including fresh-hewn salsas and guacamole, comforting *caldo de pollo* (chicken soup), *posole*, and chicken sauced with rich, traditional red mole. Take note that the restaurant closes for the Jewish Sabbath after Friday lunch service, reopening after sunset on Saturday.

Le Titi de Paris, 1015 W. Dundee Rd., Arlington Heights, IL 60004; (847) 506-0222; www.letitideparis.com; French; $$$$. Michael and Susan Maddox tirelessly preside over this elegant, though not uppity, homage to French fare. The results—as in a crispy phyllo "brique" of shredded duck confit with braised red cabbage, dried cherries, Boursin, and orange-cognac sauce—are clearly labor-intensive, but with benefits. When in need of a warm-up, get the hunter's plate of semi-boneless quail and braised rabbit leg, and always consider the tasting menus and wine from the lauded list.

The Lucky Monk, 105 Hollywood Blvd. South Barrington, IL 60010; (847) 898-0500; www.theluckymonk.com; American; $$. With a name that nods to Trappist monks, whose dedication inspires its house-crafted ales and lagers, this buzzing suburbanite serves a prime, bigger-than-mouth-sized burger with hand-cut fries; soupy poblano chili verde; and crisp, hand-stretched pizzas adorned with béchamel, mozzarella, and fontina cheeses, or a trio of button, cremini, and oyster mushrooms. Then again, it's the fried pickle chips that may make it worth the haul.

Maria's Bakery, 530 Sheridan Rd., Highwood, IL 60040; (847) 266-0811; Bakery/Italian; $. Savory and sweet Italian nibbles made with *amore*— that's what you get at this quaint bakery (formerly Il Mulino). Whether you settle on a roll of sugared raisin bread, a crusty loaf, layer-laden sfogliatelle dusted with powdered sugar, or arancini, you're in good hands at this superior Sicilian. Rather than simply grab and go, get a cup of joe and a cannoli—which is filled to order—eating at one of two tables in house.

Michael, 64 Green Bay Rd., Winnetka, IL 60093; (847) 441-3100; www.restaurantmichael.com; French; $$$. Michael Lachowicz (Le Français, Les Deux Gros) has culinary kahunas to name his "personal creation" as such. Fortunately, it's swagger you can count on. Confirmation arrives with a duo of Alaskan king crab with Tahitian vanilla–scented fennel-crab salad and tempura king crab leg; grilled, wild escolar atop lobster mushrooms and Pernod-spiked yellow tomato coulis; and warm blueberry-almond financier cake.

Mizrahi Grill, Crossroads Shopping Center, 215 Skokie Valley Rd., Highland Park, IL 60035; (847) 831-1400; www.mizrahigrill.com;

Israeli; $$. Whether you order the crisp-crumbly falafel, marinated, spit-carved turkey-lamb shawarma, or the bright cabbage, diced Israeli, or *matbucha* (tomato and roasted pepper) salads, expect that they're fresher than fresh. Moist kebabs and *sufganiyots* (fried jelly doughnuts) are further pleasures to succumb to.

Myron & Phil's, 3900 W. Devon Ave., Lincolnwood, IL 60712; (847) 677-6663; www.myronandphil.com; Steakhouse; $$$$. This dark, moody steakhouse of yore has a tried-and-true formula that includes relish trays with pickled green tomatoes and chopped liver, flavorful Romanian skirt steak, super-garlicky shrimp de Jonghe, and lightly breaded lake perch. Entrees may be customized, so try your meat with burnt onions or a Parmesan crust, and opt for creamed spinach on the side.

New York Bagel & Bialy, 4714 W. Touhy Ave., Lincolnwood, IL 60712; (847) 677-9388; www.newyork-bagelandbialy.com; Deli; $. Offering the best local example of what a bagel should be, this brusque beacon beckons with chewy salt and poppy and mish-mosh creations. Bring cash, and get yours piled high with pastrami, chicken salad, or a simple slather of house-label cream cheese.

Nozumi Asian Cuisine, The Arboretum, 100 W. Higgins Rd., South Barrington, IL 60010; (847) 783-0001; www.nozumiasian cuisine.com; Japanese; $$. Executive Chef Andy Park knows how to tweak Asian staples so as to make them appear brand new. Here, in a sleek, loungelike, dark-wood space, that means Moscato ginger duck, Wagyu tataki with yuzu-soy jus, and signature rolls, such as the Black Widow with soft-shell crab tempura, snow crab, mascarpone-lime spice, avocado, and pickled red–onion encased in *mamenori*. The same restaurant group is also behind **Blue Ginger** (6320 S. Rte. 53, Woodridge, 630-353-6000) and **Blue Ocean**.

Oceanique, 505 Main St., Evanston, IL 60202; (847) 864-3435; www.ocean ique.com; Seafood/French; $$$$. Mark Grosz makes a solid case for seafood in Middle America with French-influenced fins, presented in a fancy schmancy setting. The menu changes often, but opting for the three- or-seven-course tasting menus is always prudent. It may yield a plate of day-boat scallops with cabbage kimchee and soy-lobster broth or lemongrass-fragranced Holland turbot with pea tips. A wine cellar 900-labels-strong houses rare Champagne, Bordeaux, and Burgundy. Keep an eye out for occasional wine dinners.

Paradise Pup, 1724 S. River Rd., Des Plaines, IL 60018; (847) 699-8590; Burgers; $. It's no wonder lines swell beyond the walls of this matchbox-sized stand, run by two ever-present brothers. Once bitten, the legendary char-burgers cause cravings. Get yours slathered with Merkts cheddar and a nest of sweet, grilled onions. Complete with experience with artery-clogging three-layer fries, mounded with cheese, bacon, and sour cream and a mighty fresh raspberry shake. Bring cash, and expect to eat in your car—or at an outdoor picnic table when it's warm.

Pho Ha, 1971 Bloomingdale Rd., Glendale Heights, IL 60139; (630) 894-4000; www.phohaglendaleheights.com; Vietnamese; $. Small in stature but big on flavor, this bare-bones Vietnamese makes a fresh, crusty *banh mi* as well as lip-smackingly good *pho* in several configurations. Get a fruit smoothie with tapioca pearls as well.

Pho Le, 541 S. Schmale Rd., Carol Stream, IL 60188; (630) 588-8299; Vietnamese; $. There's no ambience to speak of, but the brothy, meat- and noodle-packed bowls of *pho*—as well as the fried pork chop piled with shredded pork skin and an egg cake—are enough to endure slow delivery.

Pita House, 365 S. Roselle Rd., Schaumburg, IL 60193; (847) 352-4750; www.pitahouse.com; Middle Eastern; $. A generic façade gives way to someplace where Middle Eastern flavors sparkle. That's true from the zucchini-based mama ghannouj to the lemon-zapped *fattoush* salad and decent shawarma and falafel sandwiches. There's also a location at 340 E. Roosevelt Rd., Lombard, (630) 576-5060.

Poochie's, 3832 W. Dempster St., Skokie, IL 60076; (847) 673-0100; www.poochieshotdogs.com; Hot Dogs; $. Few things in life are as satisfying as this charred (or steamed) Chicago-style red hot, dressed in onion, a generous squeeze of mustard, sweet, neon relish, tomato, a pickle, and a shower of celery salt on a plush, steamed poppy-seed bun. But to ignore the other attributes of this straightforward stand would be a disservice. The hand-cut fries and cheddar burger are five-star, as is the char salami spurted with mustard and dressed with onions—grilled and raw.

Prairie Grass Cafe, 601 Skokie Blvd., Northbrook, IL 60062; (847) 205-4433; www .prairiegrasscafe.com; New American; $$. Disproving the notion that the suburbs suck: Ritz-Carlton Chicago vets Sarah Stegner and George Bumbaris, whose seasonal, stone and wood–hewn dining room that drew city slickers until a mate opened in the West Loop. It's still worth the drive, with a menu that holds baked feta with spicy banana peppers and tomatoes; ancho-marinated skirt steak with white bean–Swiss chard *ragù* and grilled onions; and crispy half-duck with braised greens, quince jam, and crunchy beet slaw. **Prairie Fire** is at 215 N. Clinton St., (312) 382-8300 (see p. 147). (See recipe on p. 368.)

Quince at the Homestead, Homestead Hotel, 1625 Hinman Ave., Evanston, IL 60201; (847) 570-8400; www.quincerestaurant .net; New American; $$$. Sedate and romantic, this is dining for grownups. Featuring a la carte, tasting, and bar menus minded by Andy Motto (Le Lan), its offerings rove from curry-inflected, sunchoke soup with hints of horseradish to ambrosial juniper and rosemary venison with eggplant, raisins and crispy sausage. Composed desserts are hard to resist, especially when a Brie napoleon with dried fruit compote, pine nuts, thyme, and pink peppercorn is available. Selections from the large, tended wine and creative cocktail lists should be savored before the roaring fireplace.

Renga-Tei, 3956 W. Touhy Ave., Lincolnwood, IL 60712; (847) 675-5177; Japanese; $$. Sashimi seekers succumb to this humble hang for Japan's kitchen comforts, such as *tonkatsu, goma-ae,* and *agedashi tofu,* served in a simple setting that is welcoming and warm.

Schnitzel Platz, 729 North Ave., Glendale Heights, IL 60139; (630) 942-9900; www.schnitzelplatz.com; German; $$. Tip back some *bier* at this beloved Bavarian, long plating caloric platters for the restraint-challenged. Tackle one with fried pork cutlets, *frikadelle* (German chopped steak), sausages, home fries, red cabbage, and sauerkraut. The massive menu also hosts dumplings, spaetzle, sauerbraten, and its namesake, prepared endless ways. Come during Oktoberfest for its legendary pig roast.

Tori Shin, 1584 S. Busse Rd., Mount Prospect, IL 60056; (847) 437-4590; Japanese; $$. An izakaya experience awaits at Toshio

"Tony" Kaneko's abiding, no-nonsense Japanese pub, a destination for homey hot pots, sushi, and alcohol-abetting, country-style dishes written in Japanese on a dry-erase board. Make like the salarymen and dive into *agedashi tofu* and chilled monkfish liver in a puddle of ponzu.

Tramonto's Steak & Seafood, 601 N. Milwaukee Ave., Wheeling, IL 60090; (847) 777-6575; www.westinnorthshore.com; Steakhouse/Seafood; $$$$. Although Rick Tramonto has left for other pastures, this steak-and-seafood expert forges on with a menu of prime steaks with customizable sauces and toppers, butter-poached Maine lobster, and wood-fired fish. Sushi, a larger selection of which is available upstairs in the RT Lounge, is on hand as well, and prime rib is served Thursday through Saturday. The large, affordable cellar stocks some serious wine finds.

Union Pizzeria, 1245 Chicago Ave., Evanston, IL 60202; (847) 475-2400; www.unionevanston.com; Italian; $$. Creative Tuscan pizzas are cooked in a wood-fired oven and served alongside an array of Italian small-plates, microbrews, and vino. Meanwhile, daily specials—such as herb-roasted Amish chicken or ziti with meaty, braised Sunday gravy—add to the mix. Its more upscale cuz, **Campagnola,** is at 815 Chicago Ave., Evanston, (847) 475-6100. There's also a mobile kin, **Hummingbird Kitchen.**

Village Creamery, 4558 Oakton St., Skokie, IL 60076; (847) 982-1720; www.villagecreamery.com; Ice Cream; $$. The creative scoops never cease to amaze at this Far East–inspired ice cream parlor from Lito Valeroso. Go on an adventure with varieties such as *buko*, purple yam, or avocado with sweetened young coconut. Or play it safe with mint chip or orange sherbet. Also of note are the bubble teas, shaved ice, and jolting cappuccino with tapioca pearls. There is a second installment at 8000 Waukegan Rd., Niles, (847) 965-9805.

Wiener and Still Champion, 802 Dempster St., Evanston, IL 60202; (847) 869-0100; www.wienerandstillchampion.com; Hot Dogs; $. This red hot stand doesn't reinvent the wheel, but it does tackle convention head-on. Hand-breaded corn dogs take festival food to the next level, while burgers dolloped with Merkts cheese are impossible to ignore. Still, missing fried pickles, country-fried bacon with Argentine garlic and herb sauce, and country-fried gyros would be a shame. Then there's the Chicago-style hot dog, presented as it is intended to be.

West & Far West

Al Bawadi Grill, 7216 W. 87th St., Bridgeview, IL 60455; (708) 599-1999; www.albawadigrill.com; Middle Eastern; $$. There are reasons to zero in on this neighborhood jewel, located on the outskirts of a strip mall amid a number of like-minded destinations. Among them: the sprightly pickles that arrive when you're seated;

the charred, moist, wood-fired kebabs; the creamy hummus. Get some garlicky *motawma* (pureed potato dip) or *foul* (tahini-spiked fava bean dip) to slather on everything, and consider the *arayes*—pita stuffed with a minced lamb mixture or Syrian cheese—and rustic, chopped Arabic salad. Or, take stock in the homey *kufta* casserole.

Alex & Aldo's, 720 E. 31st St., La Grange Park, IL 60526; (708) 354-1390; Pizza; $$. Dark and dive-y, this petite pizza palace has made a name for itself with cracker-crust pies, homespun Italian dishes (veal Parmesan, various pasta preps ladled with "gravy"), and crostini with liver spread. Couple any with crumbly, breading-encased green olives and a finisher of homemade carrot cake, when it's available.

Alfie's Inn, 425 Roosevelt Rd., Glen Ellyn, IL 60137; (630) 858-2506; www.alfiesinn.com; American; $$. Low-lit and decked in stained glass and suits of armor for a medieval feel, this steady supplies baskets of battered mushrooms and onion rings, juicy chuck loinburgers with grilled (or raw) onions, and really cheap drinks.

Amber Cafe, 13 N. Cass Ave., Westmont, IL 60559; (630) 515-8080; www.ambercafe.net; New American; $$$. A relatively affordable choice for upscale eats in comfortable environs, this gem plies diners with seasonal, contemporary American fare, like warm Brie and pear salad, butternut squash ravioli, and crisp whitefish with pearls of couscous and lemon beurre blanc. Ask to be seated on the picturesque, enclosed patio when it's warm. Its sibling, **Topaz Cafe,** is at 780 Village Center Dr., Burr Ridge, (630) 654-1616.

Benjarong, 2138-B S. Mannheim Rd., Westchester, IL 60154; (708) 409-0339; www.benjarong.us; Thai; $$. Blink and you'll miss this cozy, tiny Thai in a strip mall adjacent to a grocery store. Although it does a brisk lunch and carryout business, the petite, artifact-adorned dining room is a respite come evening, making it the perfect time for coarse-ground beef basil with vibrant peppers; devilish, lime-blasted *yum nue* (beef salad); and expertly prepared *pad kee mao.*

Bodhi Thai, 6211 W. Roosevelt Rd., Berwyn, IL 60402; (708) 484-9250; www.bodhithaibistro.com; Thai; $$. To order off the menu at this stellar spot is to miss the point. What you really want to do is ask for the secret menu, or challenge the kitchen to prepare custom, "free-style" dishes just for you. Get the garlicky *sai oua* sausage—an Issan standby—fiery fried chicken (*kai thawt*), and insidious, citrus-y *nam tok* beef salad sprinkled with toasted rice powder, knowing you'll need dense sticky rice to temper the heat.

Chef Amaury's Epicurean Affair, 33 W. New York St., Aurora, IL 60506; (630) 375-0426; www.chefamaury.com; New American; $$$. Chef-Owner Amaury Rosado quietly crafts sophisticated, modern American plates, steps from the Fox River in downtown Aurora. Invest in the weekly three- or-five-course dinner, which may include Alaskan halibut with lobster-coconut sauce, Himalayan red rice, and grilled pineapple. And be sure to get a cheese plate pre-dessert. There's a nice wine list, plus cooking classes are offered.

Chef Paul's Bavarian Lodge, 1800 Ogden Ave., Lisle, IL 60532; (630) 241-4701; www.bavarian-lodge.com; German; $$. Although it isn't inexpensive, this Deutsche delivers what few do by offering an Old-World experience and nearly 200 draft and bottle beers, many of them of German and Belgian descent. It's hard to go wrong with classics, like the basket of Bavarian pretzels or griddled potato pancakes with sour cream and applesauce. The same is true when it comes to entrees, namely the crisp schnitzels, sauced or unadorned; hearty rouladen; and caraway-scented roast pork loin. You may also design your own combinations, adding in smoked sausage for good measure.

Chicago Burgerwurks, 8819 W. Ogden Ave., Brookfield, IL 60513; (708) 387-2333; Burgers; $. It'd be easy to blow past this ketchup and mustard–hued stand, but then you'd miss the dizzying roster of gourmet burgers and corresponding chicken sandwiches, each given its own hand-hewn sauce. It would also mean you'd never meet the full-flavored flank steak sandwich or the brooding cup of chili, made from meat scraps. Running faves include the Lucifurger topped with pepper jack cheese, sweet onions, and chipotle relish and the Au Poivre, finished in black-peppercorn gravy. There's a design-your-own sandwich option as well as *poutine*-inspired, fresh-cut fries. Soups are superior, too; get the smoked tomato bisque when it's available—both here and at its counterpart, **Chicago Soup & Sandwichwurks** (8801 Ogden Ave., 708-387-9757).

Chinese Kitchen, 6551 S. Cass Ave., Westmont, IL 60559; (630) 968-3828; www.chinesekitchenwestmont.com; Chinese; $. What this quick-serve Cantonese lacks in ambience, it more than makes up for in flavor—a fact that is immediately apparent in fried, onion-flecked Japanese tofu salt and spice, which is liberally sprinkled with jalapeños. Reliably tasty hot-and-sour soup, tender Mongolian beef, and fried chicken wings with spicy salt are met by more ambitious options, like crisp Dover sole and braised sea cucumber.

Chinn's 34th St. Fishery, 3011 W. Ogden Ave., Lisle IL 60532; (630) 637-1777; www.chinnsfishery .com; Seafood; $$. It's less about the experience and more about the freshly sourced seafood at this crowd-thronged stalwart, where meals begin with rolls bathed in garlic and proceed to feature some of the best crab legs in town. Additional lures include potent mai tais and a retail market selling seasoned and straight-up selections to prepare at home.

Czech Plaza, 7016 W. Cermak Rd., Berwyn, IL 60402; (708) 795-6555; www.czechplaza.com; Czech; $$. The silver set flocks to this authentic Czech eatery where little has changed—huge portions of crisp-skinned duck, breaded pork tenderloin, and Bohemian-style meatloaf included. Comforting liver-dumpling soup, fruit dumplings, and daily specials—such as Hungarian goulash on Thursday—are added attractions.

Dell Rhea's Chicken Basket, 645 Joliet Rd., Willowbrook, IL 60527; (630) 325-0780; www.chickenbasket.com; American; $$. Serving up road food in the truest sense, this restaurant and cocktail lounge—marked by a vintage neon sign—has been making mouths happy since 1938. Located at mile marker 274 on Historic US Route 66, its setting is of another era, and its food—especially the cornmeal-fried chicken it's known for—is as satisfying as ever. Soul-soothing mac and cheese, homemade chicken noodle soup, and a salad bar where cheesy vegetable spread is king complete the throwback experience.

El Pollo Giro, 991 N. Aurora Ave., Aurora, IL 60505; (630) 896-0755; Mexican; $$. The flavorful, charcoal-grilled chicken—served with smoky jalapeños, knob onions, and bright salsa fresca—calls for visits to this casual quick-serve with a second outpost at 817 Montgomery Rd., Montgomery, (630) 898-5143.

Emilio's Tapas, 4100 Roosevelt Rd., Hillside, IL 60162; (708) 547-7177; www.emiliostapas.com; Spanish/Tapas; $$. The garlic potato salad could ward off vampires; the bacon-wrapped dates are at an avenue where sweet and savory collide. Get both with a pitcher of sangria, and make your way through shareable plates both hot and cold, including tuna-filled cannelloni topped with creamy white-wine vinaigrette and grilled, pepper-crusted beef tenderloin with onions, peppers, and sherry sauce. Its downtown companion, **Sol y Nieve,** is at 215 E. Ohio St., Chicago, (312) 467-7177.

Fabulous Noodles, 4663 Old Tavern Rd., Lisle, IL 60532; (630) 305-8868; www.fabulousnoodles.com; Chinese; $$. Its name doesn't lie: These soup noodles are a testament to how good Chinese food really can be. Get them in a spicy slurry with tender beef, Indonesian-style, or bolstered by sweet, caramelized barbecue pork. Noodles also come braised and pan-fried, with *yu* noodles a fore-runner among the latter.

Freddy's Pizza, 1600 S. 61st Ave., Cicero, IL 60804; (708) 863-9289; www.freddyspizza.com; Italian/Pizza; $. At this ambitious from-scratch corner store, you must choose between steaming plates of chicken Parm, stacks of mozzarella caprese, and platters of hot Italian sausage hidden in a tangle of sweet, sautéed peppers and potatoes—all placed lovingly atop and behind a glass counter. Peer behind the shelf piled with fresh-baked bread, too; you'll see the makings of outstanding, chewy Italian subs with imported meats and cheeses, house-label giardi-niera, tomatoes, and lettuce. Order one, along with a side salad or two. Consider adding on a slice of sheet pizza and ultra-creamy limon-cello or fruits of the forest gelato. A small selection of import goods and a case filled with frozen, homemade pasta leads to wise impulse buys, so bring enough cash since credit cards are not accepted. There's a small, enclosed room adjacent to the restaurant for dining in.

Gaetano's, 7636 Madison St., Forest Park, IL 60130; (708) 366-4010; www.gaetanos.us; Italian; $$$. Don't come looking for your nonna's Italian—Gaetano Di Benedetto's cucina serves anything but. The always changing, sometime impromptu approach keeps things interesting, resulting in a dish of Gulf shrimp in puff pastry with caramelized garlic and Gorgonzola fondue or crab cakes with roasted red peppers singed in a wood-burning oven. One visit may mean spicy shrimp bisque with house-made Italian sausage, another spaghetti *chitarra alla sorrentina,* "guitar-string" pasta tossed with tomatoes, olive oil, basil, and homemade mozzarella. True flavor-seekers should order the personalized, free-style dinner, served in four-course, family-style fashion at the chef's counter.

Golden Steer, 7635 W. Roosevelt Rd., Forest Park, IL 60130; (708) 771-7798; www.goldensteersteakhouse.com; Steakhouse; $$. Make no mistake: this dark, mirrored meat-house is of another era, one in which brassy servers deliver food on rolling metal carts, drinks are stiff, and no-fuss food is matter-of-fact good. Stubbornly steadfast, this haunt does that and more, prepping the best, bubbly crocks of French onion soup, salads with flavor-saturated croutons, and affordable steaks with heavily condimented, baked potatoes wrapped in aluminum foil. Get a side of the weirdly wonderful mushrooms, and consider the moist, herb-swathed Grecian chicken as a red-meat alternative. The burger—served on dark rye—is tasty as well.

Goldyburgers, 7316 Circle Ave., Forest Park, IL 60130; (708) 366-0750; Burgers; $. It's not easy on the eyes, but this cash-only dive bar makes a mean blue cheese and bacon–topped burger and fried cheese balls, meant to counteract overindulgence of tap brews. There's also a Friday night perch fry, best enjoyed from the seasonal beer garden.

Grand Dukes Eatery & Deli, 6312 S. Harlem Ave., Summit, IL 60501; (708) 594-5622; www.granddukesrestaurant.com; Eastern European; $$. Uncommon decor—suits of armor, medieval-looking artwork—paves the way for hearty dishes, many Lithuanian, at this unassuming eatery. That means sauerkraut soup, *cepelinai* (potato zeppelins), and bacon-wrapped boar in tangy paprika-cream sauce. Be sure to visit the deli in back—it's packed to the gills with made-on-site meats, salads, and dumplings as well as condiments and breads.

Highland Queen Drive-In, 1511 W. 55th St., La Grange Highlands, IL 60525; (708) 246-1846; Ice Cream; $. Those who grew up in these 'burbs encountered this institution; others should seek it out. The old-time not-so-quick-serve is hopping during summer—and after Little League games—so expect a wait for your cherry-dipped soft-serve cone, pineapple shake, and chocolate malt. The cooked fare is passable at best.

Il Poggiolo, 8 E. First St., Hinsdale, IL 60521; (630) 734-9400; www.ilpoggiolohinsdale.com; Italian; $$$. Jerry Kleiner branched out to the 'burbs, and it was an apparent act of business savvy. This ever-crowded, artifact-filled dining room—located in a one-time silent movie house—is as vibrant as any of the restaurateur's ventures, and the modern take on Italian fare generally delivers. Get seated on the balcony for a bird's-eye view, and begin with carpaccio or Taleggio and mushroom-filled arancini. Then move onward to the handmade *chitarra* topped with Bolognese or the pappardelle with red wine–braised duck *ragù*. Among the comforting mains: pork shoulder with creamy polenta and sautéed rapini in apple-cider reduction. Co-owners Peter and Dana Burdi are partners at **Nabuki** down the street.

International Mall, 665 Pasquinelli Dr., Westmont, IL 60559; Various; Asian; $. This dingy food court next to Asian grocer **Whole Grain Fresh Market** (see p. 309) features a handful of booths, brimming with varied Chinese nibbles (spicy pork dumplings) and soups (spicy-sweet beef noodle). Take note that it gets crowded on weekends, and you should be sure to bring cash.

Johnnie's Beef, 7500 W. North Ave., Elmwood Park, IL 60707; (708) 452-6000; American; $. Surly staffers expect you know your order in advance. Here's what to get: boldly seasoned Italian beef or a combo sandwich (Italian beef and Italian sausage). Order it juicy with hot peppers and a side of Italian ice. When it's warm out, sit at one of the picnic tables; otherwise, eat in your car, an exercise that necessitates a bib. Arrive early on weekends, as this standing-room spot sees lines before doors ever open. There is a second location at 1935 S. Arlington Heights Rd., Arlington Heights, (847) 357-8100.

Johnson's Door County Fish, 908 E. Roosevelt Rd., Lombard, IL 60148; (630) 629-6520; Seafood; $. This nostalgic, Wisconsin-style seafood shack is the kind of mom-and-pop spot where you order at the counter and have magically delicious, fried fare brought to your table. Extra-crunchy, batter-encased shrimp and lake perch are standouts, splashed with lemon from squeeze bottles and dunked into mild cocktail sauce. There's also a passable selection of bottled beer. The same family also operates a location in Indiana at 2619 Central Ave., Lake Station, (219) 962-1956.

Kama Indian Bistro, 8 W. Burlington Ave., La Grange, IL 60525; (708) 352-3300; www.kamabistro.com; Indian; $$. Talk about a pleasant surprise. Located in a narrow storefront across from the Metra station, this pillow-strewn, stylishly lit Indian exhibits the kind of dedication few do. Everything is made from scratch, including the spice blends and sauces; the ingredients are quality; and the heat is no-holds-barred. Planks of crispy, "chilly" potatoes and elegant, delicately flavored shrimp Sunnaina in white-wine garlic-tomato concassé are hits. However, nothing can prepare you for the complex chicken or lamb Kama-Kaze vindaloo set ablaze with ghost peppers—except, perhaps, a gallon of water to tame the flames. Consider, too, the dishes that employ a slow-fired house blend of 18 pickled spices, incorporated into a gentle tomato, onion, and garlic sauce. Numerous vegetarian and gluten-free dishes are available.

Katy's Dumpling House, 665 N. Cass Ave., Westmont, IL 60559; (630) 323-9393; www.katysdumpling.com; Chinese; $. If you're looking to be coddled—heck, even treated with civility—this may not be your place. However, if you're a lover of hand-pulled noodles and house-made dumplings, see past the service and spartan setting of this strip-mall Chinese. Witness the artistry in action beyond the counter, and focus on dishes that utilize its strong suit: spicy dan-dan noodles and oily, chile-flecked Szechuan cold noodles dotted with nubs of ground pork and cooling cucumber. All manner of oddities are in the carryout case, but you'll want to grab handmade, frozen pork-and-chive dumplings for later. A second location is at 790 Royal Saint George Dr., Ste. 115, Naperville, (630) 416-1188.

Klas Restaurant, 5734 W. Cermak Rd., Cicero, IL 60804; (708) 652-0795; www.klasrestaurant.com; Czech; $$. Part of a dying breed, this Old-World Czech is both strange and wondrous—not to mention a criminal bargain. The setting—all castlelike with vaulted archways and weird-looking chandeliers—is a focal point. However, the Bohemian-style eats are easy to love, if treacherous on the waistline. Whether you get the paprika chicken, Pilsner-simmered goulash, or Wiener schnitzel à la Holstein crowned with anchovies, capers, and a fried egg, belt-loosening is sure to ensue. Dishes come with soup or salad, bread or potato dumplings, boiled or mashed potatoes and sauerkraut, sweet-sour cabbage, or a daily veg, plus a homemade *kolacky*. Let the food coma settle in over a beer at the oddly outfitted bar, or take a peek at the ornate banquet space upstairs.

Macarena Tapas, 618 S. Rte. 59, Naperville, IL 60540; (630) 420-8995; www.macarenatapasnaperville.com; Tapas; $$. Don't let its suburban-sprawl setting deter you—this Nuevo Spaniard deserves more than a passing glance. Executive Chef John Borras, who trained with Ferran Adrià, prepares what's sought after (rustic bread brushed with tomatoes and olive oil and topped with *jamon; croquetas;* garlic shrimp). He also fashions more modern Catalan-type fare, like grilled chicken with avocado salsa verde, bacon-wrapped scallops atop romesco sauce, and tilapia with artichoke-spinach sauce. Gluttons will appreciate the availability of a varied, all-you-can-eat menu.

Maijean, 30 S. Prospect Ave., Clarendon Hills, IL 60514; (630) 794-8900; www.maijean.com; French; $$$. Nadia Tilkian's decoratively dramatic country-French bistro is equal parts eclectic and sophisticated. Whatever your camp, one thing is clear: She has a way with seafood. Traditionalists can have their deftly prepared lyonnaise salad, duck confit, and coq au vin. Meanwhile crispy lamb shoulder with garlic confit and mustard sauce; butter-poached flounder with crisp Japanese mushrooms; and a glam Berkshire pork belly sandwich topped with onion frizzles, a fried egg, and smoky paprika are reserved for seekers of something more present-day.

Marion Street Cheese Market, 100 S. Marion St., Oak Park, IL 60302; (708) 725-7200; www.marionstreetcheesemarket.com; New American; $$. A paradise for food lovers, this market, cafe, and wine shop emphasizes products from local purveyors, while featuring small plates inspired by those procurements. Nosh on cheese and charcuterie, design your own cheese flight, or snack on duck confit bruschetta with red wine–fig jam and pickled onions. You'll also find a shareable Raclette plate and full-fledged main courses, such as barramundi with celery-root puree, roasted fingerlings, and fennel-orange slaw dusted with crushed Marcona almonds. Wine and beer dinners are offered regularly, and brunch is served on Saturday and Sunday.

Nabuki, 18 E. First St., Hinsdale, IL 60521; (630) 654-8880; www.nabukihinsdale.com; Japanese; $$$. This venture from Peter and Dana Burdi (also of Il Poggiolo a few doors down) rolls out a menu of specialty maki in a setting rife with undulating, modern details. Get in the spirit with the Japanic roll, maki built from spicy tuna, cream cheese, avocado, and Japanese mint, topped with black and red tobiko. Or, see what the kitchen can do with glazed, Asian-style ribs. There's also a menu for kids that includes fan favorites, like panko-crusted chicken fingers.

Naf Naf Grill, Freedom Commons, 1739 Freedom Dr., Ste. 109, Naperville, IL 60563; (630) 904-7200; www.nafnafgrill.com; Middle Eastern; $. It's impossible to be ambivalent about Naf Naf's pillowlike, homemade pita. Use it to cradle freshly carved chicken shawarma, *kifta* kebabs, and falafel, or plunk it in creamy hummus or baba ghannouj loaded with chunks of char-grilled eggplant. You may also grab stacks of pitas by the steaming bagful to go. Look for a handful of authentic Israeli offerings, including a light salad of cucumbers, tomatoes, cilantro, and onions.

New Rebozo, 1116 Madison St., Oak Park, IL 60302; (708) 445-0370; www.newrebozo.com; Mexican; $$. On top of having a consummate host—one with a trademark tagline, no less—this intimate mole and margarita master offers an authentic, *madre*-inspired menu made with love. Kick back in the vibrant space and be wowed by both the familiar and painstaking preparations, from skirt steak topped with *mole poblano* or *mole pipian* to 42-ingredient Pueblan mole-sauced chicken and straight up, Americanized chimichangas.

Niche, 14 S. Third St., Geneva IL 60134; (630) 262-1000; www.nichegeneva.com; New American; $$$$. This stylish suburbanite takes a lighthearted approach to American cuisine, teaming its crab cakes with orange and Thai curry, its cheese plates with Honeycrisp apples, and its mushroom risotto with Parmesan foam. Seared duck breast is chaperoned by roasted brussels sprouts, rutabaga, walnut sable cookie, and sour-cherry jus, while monkfish is at one with tomato confit, kalamatas, capers, and garlic puree. Desserts toe the line between being comforting and serious, as in butterscotch pudding or roasted pineapple tart with a pine-nut crust, coconut rum cream, and licorice-y basil sorbet.

Nickson's, 30 S. La Grange Rd., La Grange, IL 60525; (708) 354-4995; www.nicksonseatery.com; New American; $$. This rustic wood dining room is rooted in a familiar-but-tweaked menu of greatest hits: fried green tomatoes, chile-braised brisket tacos topped with corn relish, and a pepper-crusted elk burger gilded with aged white cheddar and a fried duck egg. American craft beers and girly cocktails encourage you to take your time, through the crowd with cranky kids does not. Gluten-free and children's menus are available.

Porterhouse Steaks & Seafood, 15W776 N. Frontage Rd., Burr Ridge, IL 60527; (630) 850-9999; www.porterhouse-ss.com; Steakhouse/Seafood; $$$. Although there was a brief interruption in service—the restaurant closed and is now under new owner-ship—this supper clubby, roadside spot remains in full effect with tasty bread service, *saganaki,* and dynamite steaks brought by old-school servers for a fraction of what you'd expect.

Prasino, 93 S. La Grange Ave., La Grange, IL 60525; (708) 469-7058; www.prasino.com; New American; $$. Appealing to those with eco-conscious sensibilities, this spacious, sleek catchall serves three squares, global bevs, and organic smoothies to a crowd with tots in tow. Start mornings with carrot-cake pancakes stippled with plump raisins; meet midday for a black-bean burger injected with Southwest flavors; and unwind over cocktails and sustainable seafood when daylight wanes. There's also an installment at 51 S. First St., St. Charles, (630) 908-5200.

Priscilla's Ultimate Soul Food, 4330 W. Roosevelt Rd., Hillside, IL 60162; (708) 544-6230; www.priscillasultimatesoulfood.com; Regional American; $$. Give this cozy cafeteria a wide berth if you're watching your waistline, as generously smothered pork chops, mounds of moist, kicking fried chicken, and gooey pie, cake, and cobbler wreak havoc. On second thought, scrap the diet altogether and just go for broke. When in the neighborhood, also check out its sister spot at 1020 S. Barrington Rd., Streamwood, (630) 736-3399.

Q BBQ, 70 S. La Grange Rd., La Grange, IL 60525; (708) 482-8700; www.q-bbq.com; Barbecue; $. The interior of this popular, pint-sized storefront isn't especially smoky. Come to think of it, neither is its namesake 'cue. Still, the pulled-pork and brisket sandwiches—garnished with slaw, crumbled blue cheese and tangy, Carolina-style sauce—are satisfying specimens when coupled with toasted cheddar mac and cheese and greasy-good hush puppies.

Red Herring, 31 S. Prospect Ave., Clarendon Hills, IL 60514; (630) 908-7295; www.redd-herring.com; New American; $$. This may be food and wine for ritzy suburbanites, but it turns out there's something for everyone at this modern American bistro from socca chef-owner Roger Herring. Given chef David Gollan (Girl & the Goat, Spiaggia) is in the kitchen, though, that's no surprise. Grab bench at the copper-top bar or in the sleek dining room decked with artwork from Jesus Salgueiro, Art Smith's hubby. Either is a fine place for Allen Brothers steak Diane bites with crumbled blue cheese and Cabernet-thyme sugo, prized pizzettes, or more substantial plates, like pappardelle with spring lamb, asparagus, and Midwestern Manchego.

Riverside Family Restaurant, 3422 S. Harlem Ave., Riverside, IL 60546; (708) 442-0434; Czech; $$. Offering plenty of bang for your buck, this geezer-favored locale has things going for it, namely crispy duck and breaded pork tenderloin. Prepare for the after-church masses—though trade-offs whenever you dine include superior liver-dumpling soup, bread dumplings, and other lovingly rendered classics, like *svickova*. Remember to bring cash.

Salerno's on the Fox, 320 N. Second St., Saint Charles, IL 60174; (630) 584-7900; www.salernosonline.com; Italian; $$. There aren't many places serving good pizza with a waterfront view, but that's what you get at this casual, family-friendly Italian along the banks of the Fox River. Other Italian-American staples (fried calamari, baked cavatelli, fettuccine Alfredo dotted with ham) are okay alternatives.

Schmaltz, 1512 N. Naper Blvd., Ste. 152, Naperville, IL 60563; (630) 245-7595; www.schmaltzdeli.com; Deli; $. The cases of this Jewish delicatessen brim with possibility, from the broccoli-cheddar knishes to the lacy latkes and house-made salads. Moving beyond matzoh ball and other fine soups, you'll find the meat of the matter: overstuffed sandwiches on plush marble rye. Not to be missed is the Reuben-like Sloppy Paul, a warm number with layer upon layer of pastrami or custom-cured corned beef, Swiss, kraut, and Russian dressing. Equally gut-busting-good is the cold pastrami and corned beef-mounded Adams sandwich, which is smeared with spicy mustard.

SugarToad, Hotel Arista, 2139 CityGate Ln., Naperville, IL 60567; (630) 778-8623; www.sugartoad.com; New American; $$$. Hailing from the South Carolina's Low Country, Chef Geoff Rhyne designed a menu around what he knows: just-caught fish, farm-fresh vegetables, and meat from local purveyors. On the menu, that means a forgotten-parts farmer's board (corned beef heart, face bacon), pasture-inspired pork cassoulet, and pastrami-spiced Blackmouth salmon with artichokes, hedgehog mushrooms, and guanciale in barigoule broth.

Taco Grill & Salsa Bar, 111 W. Ogden Ave., Westmont, IL 60559; (630) 353-0964; Mexican; $. Even a fire hydrant's worth of water won't suppress the flames ignited by this taqueria's condiment bar; horchata at least helps. Contend with the full-flavored skirt steak, cone-carved *al pastor,* and *carnitas* tacos, helping yourself amply to the peppery, pickled radishes and carrot-jalapeño toppings, which are in endless supply when dining within the counter-service digs. The *tortas* and burritos are pretty fantastic, too. Its more upscale cousin, **Fonda Isabel,** is at 18W333 Roosevelt Rd., Lombard, (630) 691-2222.

Taste of Himalayas, 110 N. Third St., St. Charles, IL 60174; (630) 444-1575; www.tasteof himalayas.com; Indian/Nepalese; $$. In an area not exactly flush with exotic offerings, this place stands out. But that's not to diminish the good stuff at play: clay oven–roasted garlic and ginger-spiked chicken *chhola;* dry chile chicken;  and aromatic, "village-style" goat stew. There is a lineup of Indian stalwarts and a lunch buffet that is hard to beat when maintaining a budget.

Topaz Cafe, Burr Ridge Village Center, 780 Village Center Dr., Burr Ridge, IL 60527; (630) 654-1616; www.topazcafe.com; New American; $$$. It's not just seasonal fare for tame palates coming from this stylish, modern American. Look to smoked beef carpaccio with pickled red onions and Manchego or harvest-y grilled Texas quail alongside sweet potato puree, pecans, watercress, and balsamico. Its predecessor, **Amber Cafe,** is at 13 N. Cass Ave., Westmont, (630) 515-8080.

Totopo, Oak Brook Promenade, 3041 Butterfield Rd., Oak Brook, IL 60523; (630) 573-8686; Mexican; $$. Dudley Nieto, who has clocked time at both Adobo Grill and Zapatista, has appeared at this counter-service Mexican inspired by *antojerías* (market stores). Expect tamales to tacos, several types of guac, and salsa paired with flavored chips. Nieto is also the chef and partner at **La Fonda del Gusto** (1408 Milwaukee Ave., 773-278-6100) in Chicago's Wicker Park neighborhood.

Uncle Bub's, 132 S. Cass Ave., Westmont, IL 60559; (630) 493-9000; www.unclebubs.com; Barbecue; $$. This roadhouse shack, outfitted with farm tool decor, sets a gold standard for so many reasons: its pulled pork with caramelized bits, deeply smoky brisket, positively addictive rib tips, and moist barbecue chicken. Risking sacrilege, though, you may find singular slaw and fried mac and cheese shine almost as brightly. Its regular pig roasts can go mobile. Also, during the holidays Bub's smokes turkeys and hams for at-home use.

Vie, 4471 Lawn Ave., Western Springs, IL 60558; (708) 246-2082; www.vierestaurant.com; New American; $$$$. Superlatives fail to describe Paul Virant's sedate, hyper-seasonal destination, where intricate dishes pay homage to the local farmers supplying ingredients. Having clocked time at Blackbird, Charlie Trotter's, and Everest, Virant (also of Perennial Virant downtown) now wields enough house-pickled produce to rocket American cuisine to new heights. Sit at the bar for cocktails laced with house syrup, or immediately find your place in the black-and-white dining room punctuated by Mies van der Rohe chairs and tufted banquettes. Then, suss out dishes of pan-roasted ocean trout with black lentils, spicy La Quercia coppa, pickled celery, and organic crème fraîche sauce or roasted sturgeon with a crispy bone-marrow dumpling, earthy-sweet parsnips, baby leeks, and bordelaise sauce. Later, you'll realize sheep's milk cheesecake— served with warm mandarin oranges—never had it so good. Cooking classes are offered. (See recipe on p. 362.)

Villa Nova, 6821 Pershing Rd., Stickney, IL 60402, (708) 788-2944; Pizza; $$. Fitting into the category of things so simple-but-sublime, words don't do justice: this thin-crust pie hole with a perfect sauce, bubbly brown cheese, and paper-thin crust ratio. And while the fennel-flecked sausage is worth touting, better yet is the plain-Jane cheese, which revels in simplicity. Nothing else on the menu is worth a hoot at the mostly carryout joint, so you need not look further. Additional locations are in Lockport and New Buffalo, Mich.

Westchester Inn, Westbrook Commons Shopping Center, 3069 Wolf Rd., Westchester, IL 60154; (708) 409-1313; Czech; $$. Tucked in a strip mall at the corner of Wolf and 31st, this Old-World European cafe doles out bountiful portions of Bohemian staples, complete with soup or tomato juice, dumplings or potatoes, sauerkraut or cabbage, and dessert. Topping the list of choices: rich, roasted duck, fruit dumplings, and breaded pork tenderloin—all of which allow for leftovers in abundance.

Xni-Pec de Yucatan, 3755 Grand Blvd., Brookfield, IL 60513; (708) 290-0082; www.xnipec.us; Mexican; $$. Situated in a triangular corner storefront in sleepy downtown Brookfield, this family-run Mayan has quietly but steadily earned a reputation for its tender *cochinita pibil,* Yucatecan tamale steamed in banana leaf, and tender, achiote-perfumed *poc chuc*. When it's available, get the *chile en nogada,* sweet-savory poblano stuffed with meat and fruits in walnut-cream sauce with a shower of pomegranate seeds. Be careful not to fill up on salsa, even if it's unrivaled.

Zak's Place, 112 S. Washington St., Hinsdale, IL 60521; (630) 323-9257; www.zaksplace.com; New American; $$. Named after a departed pet, this clubby bistro and wine bar has sway—in a country club membership sort of a way. Its offerings are nearly as conservative as the crowd, but there can be comfort in what is familiar: tender, chocolate-braised short ribs with white-truffle orzo, roasted chicken with honeyed walnut pan sauce, and sesame-seared ahi with citrus-y red quinoa and soy vinaigrette.

South & Southwest

Aurelio's Pizza, 18162 Harwood Ave., Homewood IL 60430; (708) 798-4548; www.aureliospizza.com; Pizza; $$. Located in the town where it all began, this pizza place has stood at its current address since 1977, dishing up signature, sweetly sauced pizzas to the generations. Come hungry and get the Super Six, a thin-crust version loaded with sausage, ham, pepperoni, mushrooms, and green peppers—or have it shipped overnight throughout the US.

Bottoms Up Bar & Grill, 1696 Thornton Lansing Rd., Lansing, IL 60438; (708) 418-3877; www.bottomsuponline.com; American; $$. Easy to overlook, this welcoming—if rough around the edges— biker bar features entertainment (horseshoes, bags, bocce) and an expansive beer garden. But the thing that makes it destination-worthy is its fish fry. Configure your own platter, choosing from perch, walleye, and shrimp, and be sure to order the house-made potato chips.

Chuck's Southern Comfort Cafe, 6501 W. 79th St., Burbank, IL 60459; (708) 229-8700; www.chuckscafe.com; Barbecue; $$. There's a bit of an identity crisis going on at this barbecue-themed, down-home cafe, serving everything from pulled pork, hot links, and a heaping plate of barbecue nachos to *huevos* or *chorizo rancheros, pain perdu,* and a daily lineup of specials that may include a Taylor Street sub, smoked corned-beef dinner, Cajun meatloaf, or camarones *en mojo de ajo* (shrimp in garlic sauce). When *cochinita pibil* is available, give it due diligence.

Cooper's Hawk Winery, 15690 S. Harlem Ave., Orland Park, IL 60462; (708) 633-0200; www.coopershawkwinery.com; New American/Wine Bar; $$. Gussied-up American—served in a working winery—is what you'll get from this mid-price, family-friendly eatery with never-fails like drunken, bacon-wrapped shrimp, Thai chicken flatbread, and rich crab and lobster bisque. Pair them with its house vinos, bottles of which may be purchased from its retail store. Offshoots are in Burr Ridge, Wheeling, South Barrington, and Indianapolis, IN.

Courtright's, 8989 S. Archer Ave. Willow Springs, IL 60480; (708) 839-8000; www.courtrights.com; New American; $$$$. Fringed by the forest preserve, this idyllic, upscale fine-dining destination is a natural for special occasions, given seasonally inspired creations like shaved fennel, sunchoke, feta, and roasted-beet salad dressed with lemon and dill; grilled Texas Cross quail breasts with chanterelles, bacon, and cider gastrique; and duck breast with quince compote, cranberries, cashews, and rutabaga caramelized with maple syrup. Consider the three-course prix fixe, and take time to explore the extensive wine list.

Cunis Candies, 1030 E. 162nd St., South Holland, IL 60473; (708) 596-2440; Ice Cream; $. The homemade ice cream—including first-rate, seasonal peach and blueberry—comes with a dose of nostalgia at this South Suburban super scooper. Whatever the time of year, real-deal sundaes—topped with a gorgeous goo of chocolate fudge—do more than fill a void.

Fasano's Pizza, 8351 S. Roberts Rd., Justice, IL 60458; (708) 598-6971; www.fasanospizza.com; Pizza; $$. Everything a good pizza should be—crisp-crusted, cheesy, and sauced with tang—this longtime pizza counter has stood head and shoulders above most since opening in 1972. There are a handful of Italian dishes on offer—veal Parm, a meatball sandwich—but, really, it's all about the 'za. You can get pizzas shipped or pick one up frozen for baking at home. Admittedly, though, nothing compares one turned fresh from the oven and sealed in a paper sleeve.

Fox's, 9655 W. 143rd St., Orland Park, IL 60462; (708) 349-2111; www.foxsrestaurantsandpub.com; Pizza; $$. Although it serves other slices of Americana (prime rib, chopped sirloin beneath a blanket of mushrooms and onions), this vaguely castlelike haunt is best-known for its super-thin-crust, top-of-the-heap pizzas, which sport the perfect savory sauce-to-cheese ratio. Live entertainment takes place on weekends. There are additional locations at 11247 W. 187th St., Mokena, (708) 478-8888; and 31 N. River St., Batavia, (630) 326-9355.

Gayety's Chocolates & Ice Cream Co., 3306 Ridge Rd., Lansing, IL 60438; (800) 491-0755; www.gayetys.com; Ice Cream; $. Scoops, ice-cream pies, and old-fashioned sundaes—as well as shippable, hand-dipped chocolates—define this South Suburban icon. The dense, hand-churned ice cream—rich with 14 percent butterfat—includes flavors from tropical banana, strawberry cream, and vanilla bean to seasonal peach or coconut during summer. Its candies are available here and at other area locations, including Horseshoe Casino in Hammond, IN, and the gift shop of the Fairmont Chicago.

Hog Wild, 14933 S. Pulaski Rd., Midlothian, IL 60445; (708) 371-9005; www.originalhogwild.com; Barbecue; $$. It's billed as a sandwich, but the juicy, monster pork chop that made a name for this cabinlike, cash-only place is more akin to fork-and-knife eating. Other slim-wallet specialties include boneless rib, Cajun chicken, or filet sandwiches and rib tips.

Jack Gibbons Gardens, 14700 Oak Park Ave., Oak Forest, IL 60452; (708) 687-2331; www.jackgibbonsgarden.com; Steakhouse; $$$. A dimly lit mainstay since 1922, this vintage steakhouse is a worthy small-town alternative to big-box meateries—especially since its aged steaks, too, arrive sizzling in butter. Get au gratin potatoes on the side, and end with the Irish cream cheesecake for a solid meal.

Krapils the Great Steak, 6600 W. 111th St., Worth, IL 60482; (708) 448-2012; www.krapilssteakhouse.com; Steakhouse; $$$. Don't let them sit you in the bar—or the expanded, enclosed patio. To get the real experience, you want to sip your pink squirrel before one of three roaring fireplaces in the darkish, main dining rooms. There, hunter's trophies—large-mouthed bass, deer, and fox heads and a hornet's nest—adorn the walls in supper club fashion. Chummy, "hi-ya" service complements the menu of simply prepared, dry-aged steaks, which arrive after metal trays of fresh veggies and marinated cucumbers and tomatoes. House soups are of note (get the baked potato with hunks of ham if you can), and splurge on lemony, garlicky shrimp de Jonghe, which does the breadcrumb-laden Chicago original proud.

Mabenka, 7844 S. Cicero Ave., Burbank, IL 60459; (708) 423-7679; www.mabenka.com; Polish/Lithuanian/Eastern European; $$. One thing is for sure—you won't leave this home-baked hybrid hungry. It specializes in rib-sticking Polish and Lithuanian fare, including a solo meal that could feed the masses: a combo of roast beef, roast pork, Polish and Lithuanian sausages, a meat-filled-blintz, chicken breast, a veal cutlet, and a pork chop with a bounty of sides. Don't ignore tasty apple or potato pancakes or the dumplings. Come on polka nights, when the scene gets raucous. Frozen dumplings may be purchased to cook at home.

Mr. Benny's Steak and Lobster House, 20857 S. Cicero Ave., Matteson, IL 60443; (708) 481-5800; www.mrbennyssteakhouse .com; Steakhouse/Seafood; $$$. Fans of old man joints will have an affinity for this gentle-manly steak and seafooder, where you may kick things off with raw oysters Moscow, topped with caviar and horseradish cream. Follow-ups range from prime rib (Wed and Sat only) to various char-grilled cuts of beef and Italian-style walleye dressed with olive oil, rosemary, and garlic. There is a sib at 19200 Everett Ln., Mokena, (708) 478-5800.

The Patio, 9100 S. Harlem Ave., Bridgeview, IL 60455; (708) 598-2099; www.patioribs.com; Barbecue/American; $$. Casual with a counter-service approach, this barbecue joint makes celebrated racks of baby backs. Offering just enough resistance, these slabs don't fall off the bone and are coated in tangy, sticky, lightly spicy sauce. The other pit preparations are fine enough, but better is the double-decker burger cluttered with 'shrooms, grilled onions, green peppers, and gooey, melted American cheese. There are a handful of Chicago locations.

Petey's Bungalow Lounge, 4401 W. 95th St., Oak Lawn, IL 60453; (708) 424-8210; www.peteysbungalow.com; Steakhouse; $$$. A vintage, fluorescent sign marks the location of this treasure, where career servers present relish trays and meat-centric dinners, followed sherbet for dessert. Tackle the juicy, Greek-style pork chops, zippy chicken Vesuvio, or any of the properly cooked steaks. The hand-packed burger is a thing of beauty as well. There is another Petey's at 15900 S. LaGrange Rd., Orland Park, (708) 349-2820.

The Plush Horse, 12301 S. 86th Ave., Palos Park, IL 60464; (708) 448-0550; www.theplushhorse.com; Ice Cream; $. Truth be told, the cones at this 1937 parlor are excessively large, but the cases filled with homemade, candy-colored 'screams—rum raisin, blue moon, black cherry, cake batter—simply can't be denied. You'll also find gelato, shakes, malts, and other sweet treats. When it's warm, get your slicks in on the quaint patio, as the nostalgic interior is usually jam-packed.

Rosangela's Pizza, 2807 W. 95th St., Evergreen Park, IL 60805; (708) 422-2041; Pizza; $$. Get your wafer-thin, tavern-style pizza topped with big hunks of sausage, giving thanks that this generations-old institution remains untouched by time. Also storied are its sandwiches, especially the Italian beef. Do yourself a solid, though, and don't mention the Cubs—this is Sox country after all.

Schoop's Hamburgers, 695 Torrence Ave., Calumet City, IL 60409; (708) 891-4270; www.schoophamburgers.com; Burgers; $$. This Indiana import with many area locations turns out lacy-edged two-slice cheeseburgers, topped with relish, onion, mustard, and "catsup" in old-fashioned environs. Bringing the retro diner experience full circle are happy endings, like chocolate sundaes and Green River milkshakes as well as sodas and floats.

Siam Marina, River Oaks Mall, 80 River Oaks Center Dr., Calumet City, IL 60409; (708) 862-3438; www.siammarina.com; Asian; $$. Upscale-casual Thai and Asian fusion goes beyond the basics to include avocado crispy rolls, banana curry duck, and sizzling chicken in a tangle of pliant, brightly hued vegetables. All the handy Thai standbys, like pad Thai and basil fried rice, are available, too. The first and third Fridays of the month usher in live jazz. There is a Calumet City cousin at 1669 Sibley Blvd., (708) 868-0560.

Tallgrass, 1006 S. State St., Lockport, IL 60441; (815) 838-5566; www.tallgrassrestaurant.com; New American; $$$$. Recalling a time when dining out was an affair, this jackets-requested sophisticate is worth the drive. And while the reservations-required, wood-paneled opulence suggests stodginess, there's plenty to leave you surprised. Diners mix and match three-, four- or five-course meals. Look to the reliably intriguing soup trio; it may include parsnip-apple, potato-porcini, and carrot-fennel. From heirloom pork with prosciutto,

Stilton polenta, pear chutney, and port emulsion to butter-poached prawns strewn with pancetta and oranges with pink peppercorn rice, the classiness continues. For dessert, the soufflé and silky lemon panna cotta don't disappoint. Be sure to explore the carefully cultivated wine list, which is strong on Russian River Valley and Oregon Pinot Noirs.

Tin Fish, 18201 S. Harlem Ave., Tinley Park, IL 60477; (708) 532-0200; www.tinfishrestaurant.com; Seafood; $$$. Colin Turner's boisterous, clubby catch keeps the maritime spirit alive with seafaring touches and a design-your-own menu of creatively plated, super-sauced fish. Start with selections from the raw bar (oyster shooters, fresh-shucked oysters, and clams), a half-pound of uncommonly good buffalo shrimp, or lime-licked Asian tuna tartare. Then, start devising the main event, choosing your protein preparation and accompaniments. Birthday dish–worthy is the cornmeal-crusted Lake Superior whitefish on a mound of mashed potatoes bathed in sherry vinegar–pickled giardiniera. Alternately, try the halibut with bashed spuds, roasted tomatoes, prosciutto, and lemon-balsamic butter. Cooking classes are hosted regularly.

White Fence Farm, 1376 Joliet Rd., Romeoville, IL 60446; (630) 739-1720; www.whitefencefarm-il.com; American; $$. An on-site petting zoo and antiques museum help pass the time when waiting

for a table at this always-clucking fried chicken farm, set in a labyrinth of ancient-feeling rooms. Served family-style with bowls of sweet beets, tangy slaw, and kidney-bean salads; powdered sugar–dusted corn fritters; cottage cheese; and mashed potatoes with highlighter-hued gravy, the moist mound of fried chicken retains its charm. Cheap cocktails are poured with a generous hand, a fact that shows in the bitingly boozy brandy ice dessert. Come early on Sunday, or expect to hold court with the after-church crowd.

Outlying

The Brat Stop, 12304 75th St., Kenosha, WI 53142; (262) 857-2011; www.bratstop.com; American; $. This ramshackle restaurant just off the highway does its namesake proud. Ask for it grilled, and order the cheese soup as well. Affordable tap beer, live entertainment, a small cheese store, and a game room that contains a vintage Showbiz ride-on truck are finishing touches.

Cavalier Inn, 735 Gostlin St., Hammond, IN 46327; (219) 933-9314; www.cavalierinn.net; Polish; $$. Paneled walls and pierogis are the name of the game at this jovial, family-run institution dating back to 1949. Many come for the fried chicken livers with onions, the meat-heavy Polish platter, and the *golabki* (stuffed cabbage), though picky eaters are easily sated with American standbys.

Freddy's Steakhouse, 6442 Kennedy Ave., Hammond, IN 46323; (219) 844-1500; www.freddyssteakhouse.net/html/welcome_page.html; Steakhouse; $$$. Come for the prime rib, the battered lake perch, and the broiled, massive cowboy steak, served in a time-trap setting by servers who know their stuff. Dinners come with a relish tray and all the fixings, including a fab double-baked potato.

Green Gables, 17485 E. 2500 North Rd. Hudson, IL 61748; (309) 747-2496; Burgers; $. The unassuming tackle shop-meets-grocer, bar, and grill is known for its greasy, griddled burgers, battered corn bites, and fried cheese cubes. According to lore, the simply sublime meat owes credit to the sizzling, seasoned grill, where the beef simmers in its own juices.

John's Pizzeria, 247 Ridge Rd., Munster, IN 46321; (219) 836-8536; www.theoriginaljohns.com; Pizza; $$. With a history that dates back to 1943, the original pizzeria in Calumet City no longer stands. However, its predecessor warrants a trip due east. Sure, you'll have to eat in your car, but such indulgences are worth the fuss. What sets this place apart? The robust tomato sauce, the midweight, cornmeal-dusted crust, and—above all—the house-ground, crumbled fennel sausage coating the whole thing. There's also a location at 2356 Schrage Ave., Whiting, IN, (219) 659-1046.

June, Heritage Square, 4450 N. Prospect Rd., Ste. S1, Peoria Heights, IL 61616; (309) 682-5863; www.junerestaurant.com; New American; $$$. Emphasizing fresh, organic cuisine—the fruit of area farms—this Modern American from rising chef-owner Josh Adams has its own geothermal greenhouse brimming with fresh produce year-round. Everything here is handcrafted, from the Maple tables made by a neighboring artisan to the house-made duck pâté with aigre doux cherries and cocoa nib crostini. Butchering is done in-house; the wine list leans organic and biodynamic; and the cocktails are inspired by the seasons.

Miner-Dunn Hamburgers, 8940 Indianapolis Blvd., Highland, IN 46322; (219) 923-3311; Burgers; $. Smashed, griddled burgers with crisp edges are the claim to fame at this simple, show-stopping, and atmospheric diner, where a great meal is made even better with helpings of fries and orange sherbet.

Stop 50 Wood-Fired Pizzeria, 500 S. El Portal Dr., Michiana Shores, IN 46360; (219) 879-8777; www.stop50woodfiredpizzeria .com; Pizza; $$. Plan a road trip to this Neapolitan-style pizzeria for slightly charred, fire-blazed pies laden with fresh, high-quality ingredients. Start with the smoky, fire-roasted seasonal vegetables or wood-roasted, sausage-stuffed Italian peppers. There's no wrong choice to be had among 'zas, though the Parmigiano graced with red onion, nutty cheese, pistachios, and rosemary offers chewiness of the most satisfying kind. Finish with house-made gelato or s'mores.

Teibel's Restaurant, 1775 US Hwy. 41, Schererville, IN 46375; (219) 865-2000; www.teibels.com; American; $$. Seniors favor this Indiana holdout for granny-style fried chicken; a hassle-free roast turkey dinner; and fabled buttered, deep-fried pike with sides of cole slaw, beets, and cottage cheese, presented within these charmingly old-fashioned, hallowed walls since 1929.

Cocktail Culture

There's no Thirtieth Street, San Diego equivalent. It lacks the Wine Country way of life. And it's not unique in knowing there's a cocktail renaissance. But when Chicago does something, it does it right.

From its craft breweries and beer sommelier-styled lists to its chef-like mixologists and masterful sommeliers, one thing is clear: Chicagoans hit the bottles with the best of them.

Hops Havens

America's Historic Roundhouse, 205 N. Broadway St., Aurora, IL 60505; (630) 264-2739; www.rh34.com. First of all, the structure—a historic roundhouse adjacent to the Aurora Transportation Center, complete with comedy club, live music, and restaurant paying homage to the late developer, Walter Payton—is quite a sight with its soaring ceilings. But it's what comes from the gleaming brew-tanks that deserves a fan base. Brewmaster Mike Rybinski's gold medal–winning, small-batch selections range from Payton Pilsner to Bourbon Barrel Imperial Stout.

Clark Street Ale House, 742 N. Clark St., River North, Chicago, IL 60654; (312) 642-9253; www.clarkstreetalehouse.com. Spacious and convivial, this watering hole is marked by a sign encouraging you, logically, to STOP & DRINK. It's not a bad proposition, considering the reward: 100 beers, plenty of them specialty craft and many on draft, as well as a hefty selection of scotches and cognacs.

Edgewater Lounge, 5600 N. Ashland Ave., Andersonville, Chicago, IL 60660; (773) 878-3343; www.edgewaterlounge.com. Light filters through stained-glass windows at this friendly neighborhood watering hole with a thoughtful accrual of independent American and import beers—think Scrimshaw Pilsner from California and special-edition Rogue Ale. The grub is hardly an afterthought, though: Smoked-pepper brisket or grilled ham and cheddar on caraway rye are fine foils.

Emmett's Ale House, 128 W. Main St., West Dundee, IL 60018; (847) 428-4500; www.emmettsalehouse.com. The Burns family conceived this handcrafted microbrewery in the 1870s-era Hunt's Block building, listed on the National Register of Historic Places. Known for its traditional water, malt, hops, and

yeast-based, classically crafted beers, it furnishes everything from English-style A.M. Ale to jet-black, Double Barrel Oatmeal Stout. Upscale bar fare—beer-battered walleye bites, cheddar-ale soup, shrimp Boursin pasta—buffer debauchery. Locations are at 5200 Main St., Downers Grove, (630) 434-8500; and 110 N. Brockway St., Palatine, (847) 359-1533.

Flossmoor Station Restaurant & Brewery, 1035 Sterling Ave., Flossmoor, IL 60422; (708) 957-2739; www.flossmoorstation .com. This boisterous brewpub, residing in the historic Flossmoor train station, made a name for itself with festival-winning takes on tradition. Cases in point range from orange blossom honey–scented Gandy Dancer Honey Ale to lightly spicy Station Master Wheat Ale. The menu goes beyond dressed-down basics to include tempura Zephyr Golden Ale–battered green beans and house beer–spiked teriyaki chicken.

Fountainhead, 1970 W. Montrose Ave., Ravenswood, Chicago, IL 60613; (773) 697-8204; www.fountainheadchicago.com. Those in the know come to this welcoming tap from Bar on Buena's Aaron Zacharias for its carefully culled beer and whiskey lists—the former with a dizzying 200-plus choices. Then there's the grub from a Kendall Collage grad, like Gorgonzola-bacon monkey bread with sweet potato chips; seared duck breast with ginger-onion chutney and crisped curry polenta; and a sandwich of lager-braised pork shoulder with aged cheddar, Dijon, and pickles on sourdough.

Goose Island, 1800 N. Clybourn Ave., Lincoln Park, Chicago, IL 60614; (312) 915-0071; www.gooseisland.com. Standing proud as Chicago's most widely recognized (and consistently lauded) brewpub, Goose Island's handcrafted beers have been making mouths happy since 1988. Coming to the original location isn't without added return; there are seasonal brews you won't find elsewhere. A regular rotation of 20 drafts is available, plus brewmaster Brett Porter collaborates with local chefs to make limited-edition labels, such as FairytAle, a pumpkin ale from Tony Mantuano, and Stone Fruit Sour Ale, the wizardry of one sixtyblue's Michael McDonald. Cask creations are available on site, plus brewery tours and tastings take place on Sunday. Its Cubs-loving cohort is at 3535 N. Clark St., (773) 832-9040, near Wrigley Field.

Half Acre Beer Company, 4257 N. Lincoln Ave., North Center, Chicago, IL 60618; (773) 248-4038; www.halfacrebeer.com. Gabriel Magliaro founded the company in 2006, initially creating beers on a contract basis at Wisconsin's Sand Creek Brewery. Years later, he moved the brewing operation to Chicago, opening an on-site retail store in its wake. Stop in for bottles and growlers of aromatic Gossamer Golden Ale and bold Baumé, and keep your eyes peeled for tastings, which occasionally take place. The shop also stocks a selection of other local brews and spirits, including potables from Koval Distillery.

Hamburger Mary's (see p. 15). Co-owner Brandon Wright—a one-time chemical engineer—turned his home-brewing hobby into a career, which now means poured-in-house bevs at sports-loving complement, Mary's Rec Room. Consider yourself charmed if citrus-forward Mary Hoppins, a pale ale, or hopped-up amber, Gangster, are among the small-batch, bottle-conditioned, or on-tap selections.

Harrison's Restaurant & Brewery, 15845 S. La Grange Rd., Orland Park, IL 60467; (708) 226-0100; www.harrisonsbrewpub .com. The vibe is lively, and the house brews are as honest as the Cajun-tinged food coming from the kitchen of this South Suburban brewery. Whether it's creamy, unfiltered Harrison's Wheat or copper-colored Millennium Pale Ale you crave, shrimp po' boys, jambalaya, and ale-battered fish-and-chips offer sturdy sustenance.

Haymarket Pub & Brewery, 737 W. Randolph St., West Loop, Chicago, IL 60661; (312) 638-0700; www.haymarketbrewing.com. Sure, the house-made sausages, rotisserie chicken, and other workingman's favorites are put to good use. But since this pub and brewery—located near the site of the Haymarket Riot—comes from former Rock Bottom brewer Pete Crowley, it's the Belgian-focused beers that command the utmost attention. Make a point to check out the brew-house and fermentation room, made visible within the century-old building.

Hopleaf, 5148 N. Clark St., Andersonville, Chicago, IL 60640; (773) 334-9851; www.hopleaf.com. This tavern is tops among hops heads, who revel in its 200-strong craft suds selection that emphasizes Belgian-style brews. Food is a big part of the equation, too, with plump thyme, shallot, and bay leaf-scented, Wittekerke white ale–steamed mussels for two leading the way. Other upscale, beer-appropriate bites include a sausage plate with bourbon-pancetta white beans as well as cherry-glazed, St. Bernardus-braised venison ribs with cranberry beans alongside pumpkin, fennel, and celery-root slaw and dried cherry-walnut-sage pesto.

Metropolitan Brewing, 5121 N. Ravenswood Ave., Ravenswood, Chicago, IL 60640; www.metrobrewing.com/brewery. There's no public phone number (reach them via minion@metrobrewing.com), but this small-production brewery from husband-wife team Doug and Tracy Hurst is the talk of the town. Legendary suds include seasonal numbers and flagships like Cologne, Germany-inspired

Krankshaft. You'll find suds at neighborhood bars and specialty stores, and they may be purchased online. Public tours of the facility are offered semi-regularly and by reservation.

Moonshine Brewing Company, 1824 W. Division St., Wicker Park, Chicago, IL 60622; (773) 862-8686; www.moonshinechicago .com. Chill and inviting, this regional American brewhouse features a Southwestern-inflected menu (cast iron–singed shrimp with fire-roasted jalapeños and avocado, a three-pepper burger with habañero aioli, ancho-marinated rib eye) and a unique, changing 10-barrel selection of house-brewed beer, courtesy of Goose Island vet Bob Kittrell. Don't overlook the Bloody Mary bar on weekends— it's loaded with boutique hot sauces for heating things up.

Owen & Engine, 2700 N. Western Ave., Logan Square, Chicago, IL 60647; (773) 235-2930; www.owenengine.com. This boisterous, dimly lit pub is a date-appropriate, Brit-inspired hang that's heavy on surprises. Among its seductions is the lengthy, rotating selection of cask and craft beers overseen by a certified cicerone (beer sommelier); house-cured sausages and charcuterie with homemade pickles; and beyond-basic bar bites like Amish chicken wings with *piment d'espelette* and crème fraîche. The bangers-and-mash and fish-and-chips, too, are ratcheted up from the rest.

Piece Brewery & Pizzeria, 1927 W. North Ave., Wicker Park, Chicago, IL 60622; (773) 772-4422; www.piecechicago.com. Crisp, red, or barbecue-sauced, garlicky "plain," and white New Haven-style pizzas have their share of enthusiasts, though it's Jonathan Cutler's painstakingly crafted, small-batch brews—Top Heavy Hefeweizen, Fornicator, Dark & Curvy Dunkelweizen—that accrue the awards. Enjoy cold ones in-house, or grab them by growler with a pie on the fly.

The Publican (see p. 149). This pad is as much about beer as it is pork and sustainable seafood. The list of amber-hued libations features coveted Trappist and Abbey-style Belgian ales, Flemish finds, lambics, and much more. And although it changes often, it remains cutting edge.

RAM Restaurant & Brewery, 1901 McConnor Pkwy., Schaumburg, IL 60173; (847) 517-8791; www.theram.com. This gregarious, Washington-based brewpub has chains in several states. Don't rule it out since you imbibe locally brewed but nationally honored suds, like Total Disorder Porter, while attacking loaded waffle fries, buffalo wings, or beer-bread pizza. Additional local outposts are at 9520 Higgins Rd., Rosemont, (847) 692-4426; and 700 N. Milwaukee Ave., Wheeling, (847) 520-1222.

Revolution Brewing, 2323 N. Milwaukee Ave., Logan Square, Chicago, IL 60647; (773) 227-2739; www.revbrew.com. Handlebar's Josh Deth is the man with the plan, and his serious gastropub is centered on signature fist-pump taps, replenished with the lifeblood of Brewer Jim Cibak. Toss them back with orders of bacon-fat popcorn with crispy sage or curry-spiced sweet potato cakes with red-pepper cream. Then, grab a to-go growler before hitting the road.

Rock Bottom Brewery, 1 W. Grand Ave., River North, Chicago, IL 60654; (312) 755-9339; www.rockbottom.com. Although its home base is in Colorado, this popular brewery and restaurant holds its own among local microbreweries, thanks to signatures like Chicago Gold, an American-style pale ale, and Walleye, which appears as Hefeweizen, Wit or Dunkelweizen in style depending on Brewer Chris Rafferty's whim. Expect a lineup of crispy salt-and-pepper shrimp with Thai chile sauce, slow-braised short ribs, and chicken-fried chicken with white-cheddar mashed potatoes as complements.

Three Aces, 1321 W. Taylor St., Little Italy, Chicago, IL 60607; (312) 243-1577; www.threeaceschicago.com. A rock-and-roll edge pervades at this loud, Italian-bent, small-plates spot serving *arancini* atop braised oxtail and garlicky beef heart *spiedini* with shaved fennel, fashioned by Matt Troost (ex-Fianco). Amid big flavors and light fixtures obtained from Joliet's prison, it'd be easy to ignore the massive, carefully selected beer list. However, options like Lagunitas Brewing Co.'s Censored and Lakefront Brewery's Organic E.S.B. are worth paying mind.

Three Floyds Brewing, 9750 Indiana Pkwy, Munster, IN 46321; (219) 922-3565; www.3floyds.com. Demanding a short jog out of town, especially on Saturday when free brewery tours are offered, this artisanal Alpha King has its own brewpub, serving a sausage-encased Scotch egg with garlic mayo; braised chicken leg with greens in bacon broth with fried chicken skin; and house-made tagliatelle with fennel sausage and tomatoes. Plan ahead and attend its annual Dark Lord Day, an over-the-top beer fest.

Two Brothers Brewing Company, 30W315 Calumet Ave., Warrenville, IL 60555; (630) 393-2337; www.twobrosbrew.com. Big ideas benchmark this operation from real-life bros Jim and Jason Ebel, whose warehouse opens for tours on Saturday. Of course, there's no need to plan ahead when devouring Cane & Ebel-battered Holland sole or dry-rubbed pulled pork at its companion restaurant, **Two Brothers Tap House.** While you're there, throw back ultra-fresh, cask-conditioned ales and drafts that are only available on site. Beer tastings and dinners often take place.

Vino Venues

Atrium Wine Bar, within **Fox & Obel** (p. 293). Come to this cozy, riverside destination for seasonal small plates as well as glasses, flights, and bottles of wine hailing from Italy to Australia. Team them with the artisan cheeses—available, along with *vins,* in the grocers' respective departments—as well as tender beef stew or a heartwarming fruit crisp.

avec (see p. 114). Blackbird's kin remains a frequented destination for small plates inspired by the seasons. It also has a worldly wine list that's appealing (and relatively affordable) to the food-loving masses. Whether it's a glass of 2009 Triennes Rosé from Provence or 2006 Lar de Paula "Madurado" Rioja you seek, unearth it amid a list loaded with lesser-knowns.

Beviamo Wine Bar, 1358 W. Taylor St., Little Italy, Chicago, IL 60607; (312) 455-8255. This canoodler's paradise is romantic, stylish, and global—not to mention a welcome, wine-centric relief amid Taylor Street's sauce-saturated scene. The fabric-draped, loungelike vibe extends to the deejay-curated beats and lineup of live piano.

bin wine cafe (see p. 72) and **Bin 36** (see p. 117). Both kin serve great food, though plenty consider the approachable wine lists a true come-on. Fruits of the vine are proposed as pairings with dishes. Many by-the-glass, flight, and bottle options—each with engaging, easy-to-relate-to descriptors—complement Wine Director Brian Duncan's endlessly sippable, Chicago-conceived California wines, which may be enjoyed on site, purchased, and shipped.

The Bluebird, 1749 N. Damen Ave., Wicker Park, Chicago, IL 60647; (773) 486-2473; www.bluebirdchicago.com. Emphasizing

wine and beer in equal measure, this exposed-brick haunt from the owners of Webster's Wine Bar is also serious about its plates, from an impressive, artisanal cheese selection to shareable selections and more substantial mains, such as Berkshire pork cheeks braised in Dark Horse Raspberry Ale with grapes. The beer-steamed mussels are most worth revisiting.

Blue Star Wine Bar, 1209 N. Noble St., Noble Square, Chicago, IL 60642; (773) 278-2233; www.bluestarwinebar.com. Sample mostly familiar flights and a small selection of by-the-glass and bottled wines at the granite-topped bar, weighted by Mediterranean small plates, such as pork-pine nut meatballs with romesco sauce, salumi, and wine-poached swordfish with roasted lemon-artichoke vinaigrette.

Davanti Enoteca (see p. 172). Scott Harris's red-hot spot hits the right notes with an Italian menu of polenta boards, Mason jar smears, and antipasti. However, thrifty, boot-based grapes—poured by the glass, bottle, and quartino and also available for purchase—offer perks beyond chow.

D.O.C. Wine Bar, 2602 N. Clark St., Lincoln Park, Chicago, IL 60614; (773) 883-5101; www.docwinebarchicago.com. Named for the Italian wine designation, this down-to-earth vino bar—a sibling of Dunlays on Clark and Dunlays on the Square—pours globe-trotting *vins* alongside bacon-wrapped, chorizo-stuffed dates, meat and cheese platters with apricot-Merlot jam, and a chocolate chip cookie skillet. It—and its mall-centered counterpart at 326 Yorktown Center, Lombard, (630) 627-6666—often host tastings.

ENO, Intercontinental Chicago, 505 N. Michigan Ave., Gold Coast, Chicago, IL 60611; (312) 321-8738; www.enowinerooms.com. Wine, cheese, and chocolate—that pretty much sums up the sins at this hotel-centered wine bar that manages to be esoteric without a trace of snootiness. (Sign up for its Eno-versity classes to experience firsthand.) Ask about featured, hand-crafted wines, which are sometimes highlighted by flight, and do visit the tap vinos—one white, one red—blended by Wine Director Scott Harney. A second location is at the Fairmont Chicago, 200 N. Columbus Dr., (312) 946-7000.

Enoteca Roma (see p. 85). This is an intimate option for Italian eats, though it's the international wine list, featuring more than two-dozen options by the glass and many more by the bottle, that leaves budget-minded oenophiles aflutter.

Fion Wine & Spirits, 426 W. Diversey Pkwy., Lincoln Park, Chicago, IL 60614; (773) 549-5400; www.fionwineandspirits.com. A step up for aging Duffy's and McGee's rabble rousers, this marble bar disburses martinis, classic cocktails and, notably, more than a dozen wines from an air-tight system.

404 Wine Bar, 2856 N. Southport Ave., Lakeview, Chicago, IL 60657; (773) 404-5886; www.404winebarchicago.com. Warmed by a fireplace, this global addendum to Jack's Bar & Grill pours flights, glasses, and bottles, serving cheese and charcuterie plates, house-made tapenade, steak frites, and flatbread alongside.

Frasca Pizzeria & Wine Bar (see p. 46). More than a place for Italian-bent fare, this is also a sensible, jovial joint where you may swirl flights, clink glasses of sparkling wine, and idle over house-made sangrias.

Joie de Vine, 1744 W. Balmoral Ave., Andersonville, Chicago, IL 60640; (773) 989-6846; www.joiedevine.com. There's a hidden charm to this quiet, narrow wine establishment on a residential street, its long, wood bar turning out more than two-dozen by-the-glass vintages. Take in its ambient, jazzy soundtrack, and nibble on small plates and cheese platters.

LUSH Wine and Spirits, 1257 S. Halsted St., University Village, Chicago, IL 60607; (312) 738-1900; www.lushwineandspirits.com. It started as a funky wine shop in 2006, rapidly expanding its off-beat beer, spirit, and wine selection. Come on Sunday afternoon from 2 p.m. to 5 p.m. for complimentary wine geek–guided tastings or stop by—pretty much whenever—when samples are uncorked for sheer fun. Locations are at 2232 W. Roscoe St., (773) 281-8888; and 1412 W. Chicago Ave., (312) 666-6900.

LOCAL BUBBLERS, NOT BUBBLY

Local soda companies and restaurants making house sodas prove theirs are worthy, specialty sips without a bit of booze.

Filbert's Old Time Rootbeer (3430 S. Ashland Ave., McKinley Park, Chicago, IL 60608; 773-847-1520), is a local, glass-bottle soda company known for its namesake as well as flavors that include black cherry, pineapple, and blue raspberry. Pick them up in the store or keep a lookout for them at select spots around town. Restaurateurs are getting in on the action as well. At **grahamwich** (see p. 129)—a sandwich joint from celeb chef Graham Elliot—you'll find seasonal, house-concocted lemongrass-lime leaf and citrus-ginger sodas. Meanwhile, at **DMK Burger Bar** (see p. 45), homemade flavors include blood orange. **Prairie Grass Cafe** (see p. 217) periodically makes a booze-free bev, too, with ingredients sourced from the farmers' market. DIY-types may also get in the game at **American Soda Fountain** (455 N. Oakley Blvd., Near West Side, Chicago, IL 60612; 312-733-5000; www.americansodafountain.com). The trip of a family-run spot specializes in custom bubblers, soda fountains, and milkshake mixers for both commercial and residential installation.

Pops for Champagne, 601 N. State St., River North, Chicago, IL 60610; (312) 266-7677; www.popsforchampagne.com. Expect swanky, bubbly-minded plates that don't take a back seat to the 160-strong Champagne and sparkling-wine list. Then again, the still-wine, beer, and cocktail offerings are every bit as splendiferous.

Quartino, 626 North State St., Chicago, IL 60656; (312) 698-5000; www.quartinochicago.com. This late-night Italian kitchen features over 30 Italian wines by the carafe, which are natural bedfellows for John Coletta's house salumi, Neapolitan pizzas, and fresh pasta. Large-format wines are also available on the easy-to-navigate list, and a surfeit of cocktails—some utilizing house-made "grapefruit-cello"—satisfy spirit-seekers.

Red Rooster Wine Bar & Cafe, 2100 North Halstead, Lincoln Park, Chicago, IL 60614; (773) 929-7660; www.cafebernard.com/ Redrooster. This casual counterpart behind **Cafe Bernard** (see p. 78) has a handful of tables and plenty of dollar-conscious France-focused wines by the glass and bottle. Sample some with—or without—baked Brie *en croûte*.

Rootstock, 954 N. California Ave., Humboldt Park, Chicago, IL 60622; (773) 292-1616; www.rootstockbar.com. The brainchild of Webster's Wine Bar veterans, this unfussy boutique hang has judicious wine, bubbly, and beer lists, along with a menu—served until 1 a.m. nightly—of note. Chef Duncan Biddulph's sustainable, locally driven, shareable plates range from nibbles (croquettes with roasted chicken, bacon, pickled chile, and tomato aioli) to anchoring fare, like Madeira-braised ham with cranberry beans, saffron, and cabbage. There's a nice selection of cheese and charcuterie, too.

The Stained Glass Wine Bar, 1735 Benson Ave., Evanston, IL 60201; (847) 864-8600; www.thestainedglass.com. The cubbies filled with wine—32 of them available by the glass and many more by the bottle—are offset by a *foie gras* BLT on toasted brioche; pork belly with chilled coconut custard, spicy tamarind-curry barbecue, and hearts of palm salad; and miso-glazed salmon with bamboo rice, baby bok choy, and lobster-uni emulsion. Ask about wine classes.

Swirl Wine Bar, 111 W. Hubbard St., River North, Chicago, IL 60654; (312) 828-9000; www.swirlwinebarchicago .com. There's zero pretension at this relaxed, low-lit River North wine bar with live nightly jazz and late-night DJs as well as a docket of flights, glasses, and bottles priced for all budgets. There's a large craft beer list, too. Monthly wine dinners and tastings focus on a regional varietal.

The Tasting Room, 1415 W. Randolph St., West Loop, Chicago, IL 60607; (312) 942-1313; www.thetastingroomchicago.com. For over a decade, this loftlike wine bar has been a go-to for fruit-forward finds, available as taste-size pours and flights based on region, season, or varietal. Artisan cheese plates, tweaked American comfort food, and market cocktails—like a smoked, cedar-infused whiskey cordial with wattleseed and Tupelo honey nectar—round out the experience.

The 3rd Coast Cafe & Wine Bar, 1260 N. Dearborn St., Gold Coast, Chicago, IL 60610; (312) 649-0730; www.3rdcoastcafe.com. Breakfast is served all day at this trim cafe and wine bar with a menu from sandwiches to steaks. However, the main event is the easily deciphered vinos, categorized by price (under $25, $40, and $70).

Vintage 338, 338 W. Armitage Ave., Lincoln Park, Chicago, IL 60614; (773) 525-0521; www.vintage338.com. The wine-producing regions of Spain, Italy, and France largely inform the edited list at this attainable, intimate wine bar with mosaic tile details. Almost all are available by the glass or bottle and may be paired with foods of southern Europe, such as crostini and meat and cheese platters.

Volo (see p. 67). While an enjoyable place to savor wine year-round, it is particularly pleasant coming when the hidden cabana patio is swept by balmy breezes. Grab a seat there and pore over its descriptive wine list, decanted by the two-ounce taste, glass, mini-carafe, or bottle. Specials, perhaps half-price bottles on a designated day, are an additional enticement.

Webster's Wine Bar, 1480 W. Webster Ave., Lincoln Park, Chicago, IL 60614; (773) 868-0608; www.websterwinebar.com. The snoot-factor is nil at this friendly, affordable vino 'veyor from folks behind The Bluebird. Global small plates—Moorish pork skewers, smoky ratatouille with slices of baguette—couple with an assemblage of cheese, cured meat, and more substantial (and traditional) large plates. The wine list—featuring many selections by the glass, bottle, and flight—is top-notch.

Cocktails

Bar DeVille, 701 N. Damen Ave., Ukrainian Village, Chicago, IL 60622; (312) 929-2349; www.bardeville.com. Matt Eisler (Empire Liquors, Angels & Kings) is behind this spot with a French name and decidedly low-key aura. Then there's perfectly balanced cocktails—like the Songbird—created by Brad Bolt (an alum of The Violet Hour). Get your pic taken in the vintage photo booth, shoot some pool, and stay for a couple more rounds before hailing a cab.

Bernard's Bar, Elysian, 2nd Fl., 11 E. Walton St., Gold Coast, Chicago, IL 60611; (312) 646-1300; www.elysianhotels.com. You don't have to shop until you drop to appreciate the tranquil sophistication of this haute haunt just off the Mag Mile. Whether you sit at the marble bar or plop down at a plush, pin-tucked velvet banquette, you get when you pay for: flawless Negronis, Sidecars, and cultured craft beers—not to mention luxury morsels.

The California Clipper, 1002 N. California Ave., Humboldt Park, Chicago, IL 60622; (773) 384-2547; www.californiaclipper.com. Linger over a board game, or take in the tunes at this vintage-chic tap with an Art Deco bar readying cocktail classics, like venerable Rob Roys and Rusty Nails. More contemporary, though, is the Purple Martin, a lip-smacking coconut rum, lemon, and grape-soda libation.

Chizakaya, 3056 N. Lincoln Ave., Lakeview, Chicago, IL 60657; (773) 697-4725; www.chizakaya.com. This communal izakaya from chef-owner Harold Jurado (Sunda, Charlie Trotter's) is a complete package with backing from chef de cuisine Robert Rubba (L20), and a cocktail program overseen by Chantelle Pabros, a former L20 sommelier. Food-wise, its purveyor-driven bent pays off in share-able Wagyu beef yakitori, fried chicken thighs with dashi mayo, and puffed pig ears. Meanwhile the sake, beer, and wine lists are furthered by creative cocktails, like the Pampelmuse, made from Rehorst Milwaukee gin, lime, and house-made grapefruit liqueur.

C-View, Affinia Chicago, 166 E. Superior St., Streeterville, Chicago, IL 60611; (312) 523-0923; www.c-houserestaurant.com. Few things beat the skyline view from this indoor-outdoor rooftop lounge,

GETTING IN THE SPIRIT

The Midwest is home to boutique distilleries—and some in Chicago proper—which offer interesting alternatives for the cocktail crowd.

Koval Distillery (312-878-7988; www.koval-distillery.com) was created by former academics Robert and Sonat Birnecker. Both organic and kosher, its Lion's Pride whiskey is made from 100% grain bills and is available in oat, dark oat, rye, and dark rye varieties. Other potables include vodka distilled from rye; liqueurs from rose hip to jasmine; pear brandy; and Bierbrand, a hoppy number produced in conjunction with Metropolitan Brewing.

Lake Bluff's **North Shore Distillery** (847-574-2499; www.northshoredistillery.com) is behind some seriously smooth, small-batch vodka as well as botanical gins that range from a flagship modern, dry gin to ones mingled with locally grown rhubarb, exotic Medjool dates from Israel, or Sri Lankan Ceylon tea leaf. It also turns out annual single-batch productions, such as 90-proof Mole Poblano and limited edition CR2, a cocktail-in-a-bottle containing gin, orange liqueur, Lillet Blanc, lemon juice, and absinthe. Plus, the distillery produces Aquavit and Sirène Absinthe as well as Mixologist Adam Seger's hum, a spirited, botanical rum.

provided you can tolerate the scenesters in your midst. Light bites—duck rillettes, house-made, blueberry-filled doughnuts—join creative bevs, such as a beer float or lavender-laced pisco.

Death's Door Spirits (608-441-1083; www.deathsdoorspirits .com) is produced between Wisconsin's Washington Island and the Door County Peninsula. Its wild-grown juniper berry, sourced-from-state coriander, and fennel-infused gin utilizes organic wheat and malted barley, resulting in a full London Dry–type libation that's free of bitterness. Meanwhile, its triple-distilled vodka uses organic wheat and barley, and its white whiskey—sporting a south-of-the-border meets *soju* and sake profile—is double-distilled with hints of dark cherry, chocolate-covered raisins, and vanilla.

Prairie Organic (612-362-7500; www.prairievodka.com) is a Benson, Minn.-based vodka distillery that crafts ultra-smooth booze with pear and melon aromatics.

Grand Traverse Distillery (231-947-8635; www.grandtraverse distillery.com) fashions artisan vodkas and whiskeys in Northern Michigan using glacial waters. Among the stars is handcrafted, small-batch True North Vodka, made from local rye. Cherry-flavored and wheat-based vodkas are produced, too, alongside barrel-aged whiskeys. Distillery tours are offered.

Double A, 108 W. Kinzie St., River North, Chicago, IL 60654; (312) 329-9555; www.doubleachicago.com. Located beneath Mercadito, this spot specializes in custom, made-to-order cocktails—like the Daisy Lightning, with Death's Door white whiskey, Curaçao, hibiscus, lemon, and egg white—made before revelers' eyes at posh banquettes. Not surprisingly, cocktail connoisseurs the Tippling Bros. have something to do with the interactive, experience.

The Drawing Room, 937 N. Rush St., Gold Coast, Chicago, IL 60611; (312) 266-2694; www.thedrchicago.com. Chef Nick Lacasse conceives the progressive New American plates at this sultry boîte, where choices may include veal cheeks with root-vegetable pavé and creamed arugula or a griddled oxtail melt glossed with beet-red onion marmalade atop gooey, aged cheddar. But come for Mixologist Charles Joly's seasonal, culinary cocktails, too, like the Self Preservation, Cabana Cachaça, autumn-spiced cranberry shrub and soda.

The Exchange, 1270 N. Milwaukee Ave., Wicker Park, Chicago, IL 60622; (773) 342-5282; www.theexchangebar.com. Sepia vet Peter Vestinos masterminded the potables at this sleek, dimly lit, and conversation-friendly Wicker Park bar serving punch bowls and a tequila cocktail infused with lapsang souchong tea. Located in the intimate, former home of Lava Lounge, it's now adorned with cool orbs of light and has (quietly) pulsing DJ beats.

Gilt Bar, 230 W. Kinzie St., River North, Chicago, IL 60654; (312) 464-9544; www.giltbarchicago.com. Brendan Sodikoff may have worked with Thomas Keller and Alain Ducasse in the past, but his lounge-y boîte favors simple preparations. Scenesters are attracted to the sleek, low-lit space, breaking the ice over smearable, roasted bone marrow and red-onion jam. Elevated American dishes—perhaps Duroc pork belly with stone-ground grits, brown butter, and cider sauce—favor what's local. Most interesting, though, are libations—like the minty, gin-based Southside—designed by Paul McGee (The Whistler). Tipples are also served at cash-only Curio, its moody, subterranean lounge. Also, see **Maude's Liquor Bar,** 840 W. Randolph St., (312) 243-9712.

In Fine Spirits, 5420 N. Clark St., Andersonville, Chicago, IL 60640; (773) 334-9463; www.infinespirits.com. Next to a wine store of the same name, this bi-level lounge serves its share of vino. But equally, if not more, exciting are the 30-plus intoxicants using artisanal spirits. Try the AK-47, a mix of North Shore #6, Koval Ginger liqueur, Licor Beirão, pear preserve, and Prosecco, or the Vieux Carré, Maison Surrene, Templeton Rye, Benedictine, and vermouth. Absinthe fountain service is offered at the bar; North Shore Distillery Sirene Absinthe Verte cocktails are another way to get up and go. Stave off hangovers with a hip light-bite menu, housing zaatar-spiced Marcona almonds; crispy ricotta gnocchi with red wine–pork cheek *ragù* and tartiflette; and a crock of bubbly browned bacon, potato, and Raclette.

Longman & Eagle, 2657 N. Kedzie Ave., Logan Square, Chicago, IL 60647; (773) 276-7110; www.longmanandeagle.com. People go gaga for this gastropub, and it's got little to do with the six casual rooms available for overnight stays. Jared Wentworth's dishes— iconic wild-boar sloppy Joes, roasted bone marrow crostini—meet a liquor list that's 30 whiskeys strong. Not to be outdone, the extensive beer and biodynamic, boutique wine lists, and house cocktails—including an eponymous Manhattan with Italian Punt e Mes—are lounge-lovers' delights.

Maria's Packaged Goods & Community Bar, 960 W. 31st St., Bridgeport, Chicago, IL 60608; (773) 890-0588; www.community-bar.com. The Sazerac set descends on this artsy drinking den from *Lumpen* editor and publisher, Ed Marszewski. Local artwork decks the walls; musicians and DJs hail from the 'hood; and a cache of whiskey cocktails—like a tongue-in-cheek Old Grand-Dad number inspired by "the Stockyards' drainage canal"—give the place its semblance of collective cool.

The Matchbox, 770 N. Milwaukee Ave., River West, Chicago, IL 60642; (312) 666-9292. If there's one thing most every cocktailer agrees on, it's that the Matchbox is close-quarters-classic, a place where all types can—and should—sip handcrafted cocktails with house-infused spirits. Can't cram inside? Consider owner David Gevercer's other spot, train car **Silver Palm** (768 N. Milwaukee Ave., 312-666-9322). Then again, you won't be disappointed by the superior margarita at **Gunner's** (1467 N. Milwaukee Ave., 773-360-

7650), a Wicker Park lair from Eric Palm (The Matchbox) and Dan Palm (Silver Palm).

Maude's Liquor Bar, 840 W. Randolph St., West Loop, Chicago, IL 60607: (312) 243-9712; www.maudesliquorbar.com. Brendan Sodikoff (Gilt Bar) reimagined the Parisian dive bar, leaving Jeff Pikus (Alinea, Perennial) to prepare rustic French fare—such as a torchon of *foie gras* or daily sausage with long-cooked lentils. While a lot of the menu skews classic, dishes like pork belly with braised red cabbage and apple-pork jus take a slight detour. The sultry, loungelike setting is complemented by fancy smashes, handcrafted cocktails like the floral Smokey Violet. Check out the candlelit, sofa-laden upstairs lounge.

Nacional 27, 325 W. Huron St., River North, Chicago, IL 60654; (312) 664-2727; www.n27chicago.com. This hub is beloved for many reasons, not the least of which is the cocktails from mix-ologist extraordinaire Adam Seger. Belly up for a 10 Cane mojito, muddled with mint, lime, pomegranate, ginger, and habañero or an El Corazon margarita with El Jimador blanco, pomegranate, passion fruit, and blood orange with a salt and pepper rim before salsa dancing ensues. And do tackle the modern Latin menu, which trots from seviche to Brazilian barbecue, paella, and sultry seafood and steak.

Old Town Social, 455 W. North Ave., Old Town, Chicago, IL 60610; (312) 266-2277; www.oldtownsocial.com. There's really no 'tude at this gussied up nightspot, where cocktails are crafted by hand and a house butcher shop induces herbivore fright. Snack on Chef Jared Van Camp's Belgian-style frites, *harissa*-spiced duck wings with cucumber-mint *raita,* or a pork belly Rueben. Or make a meal of the house-made salted, smoked, and cured meats made from local, heritage-breed pork. Then, linger over rounds of the Mont Blanc with Patrón añejo, St. Germain elderflower liqueur, Prosecco, and fresh lemon sour.

Potter's Lounge, Palmer House Hilton, 17 E. Monroe St., Loop, Chicago, IL 60603; (312) 917-4933; www.potterschicago.com. When you're looking for a good, centrally located place to kick back over a well-executed cocktail, succumb to this bi-level spot—located in the city's most historic hotel. Order a prickly-pear margarita or gimlet, or chase the green fairy, as absinthe service is an option.

ROOF, theWit, 201 N. State St., Loop, Chicago, IL 60601; (312) 239-9502; www.roofonthewit.com. Provided you don't mind a good, long wait, you'll dig this hot-spot, perched 27 floors up with glass-enclosed private table. Snag a Tokyo Paloma, Milagro tequila with punchy fresh grapefruit and sparkling sake. Thankfully, an offering of upscale small plates means there's no reason to relinquish your seat when hunger strikes.

Sable Kitchen & Bar (see p. 151). Expect not only great food but also a lineup of liquids that live up to the promise of its radiant, quartz light-box illuminated bar. Of the Prohibition-inspired cocktails coming from Mixologist Jacques Bezuidenhout and Lead Bartender Mike Ryan, try the Silent Partner—a mélange of Milagro blanco, sweet, house-made orgeat, Palo Cortado sherry, house orange bitters, and Angostura. The vinos—compiled by sommelier Emily Wines (yes, that's her real name)—should be considered, too. (See recipe on p. 379.)

Simone's Bar, 960 W. 18th St., Pilsen, Chicago, IL 60608; (312) 666-8601; www .simonesbar.com. Loaded with refurbished fixtures—bowling alley parts, vintage pinball machines—this joint from the Northside crew specializes in kitschy cocktails, like the Give Inn, Tullamore Dew with butterscotch schnapps, brown sugar,  strawberries, and ginger ale. There is tweaked bar fare, some of it Latin-tinged, to go with.

The Southern, 1840 W. North Ave., Wicker Park, Chicago, IL 60622; (773) 342-1840; www.thesouthernchicago.com. This Southern watering hole with a rustic timber bar and steel and wood details showcases soulful American updates from Exec Chef Cary Taylor. That translates to a *poutine*-like mess of house-smoked tasso gravy and seared Laack Brothers cheddar-cheese curds on hand-cut

fries. Thankfully, they help soak up booze-infused punch bowls and Georgia juleps with Bulleit bourbon, peach schnapps, bitters, and mint.

The Terrace at Conrad Chicago, 521 N. Rush St., 5th Fl., River North, Chicago, IL 60611; (312) 645-1500. This stylish, seasonal patio hovers five floors above the action with a roster of Latin-inspired plates accenting its antioxidant-rich cocktails. Plan to quaff when movies are shown on the terrace, usually on Sunday at dusk.

The Terrace at Trump, located off **Sixteen** (see p. 153). This sweeping, seasonal outdoor patio serves sparkling and still cocktails. Meanwhile, year-round **Rebar**—located on the mezzanine level of the hotel—is a sushi-focused sophisticate, with classy cocktails like the refreshing Sakezana, a muddled green-apple libation shaken with sake and vodka.

Vertigo Sky Lounge, the penthouse-level counterpart to **aja** (see p. 112). Located in the dana hotel and spa, this sultry spot features a firepit and modern, modular furniture indoors and out. (Don't rule it out during winter, though—there's a solid ice bar proffering cold-weather comfort). But whether you have a Hot Toddy or citrus-y summer cocktail in hand, it's safe to assume the 26th-floor panoramic views get top billing.

The Violet Hour, 1520 N. Damen Ave., Chicago, IL 60622; (773) 252-1500; www.theviolethour.com. Named for a line in T.S. Eliot's "The Waste Land," this urbane cocktail collaborative involves Toby Maloney of Alchemy Consulting and many types of ice. Savor a Barbed Wire Daisy—Weller 107, lemon, house grenadine, Saigon cinnamon syrup, and house orange bitters—in a regal, high-backed chair. Be sure to order edibles from Chef David Ford, a Blackbird Group alum; étouffée fritters with crawfish, tomato, and red-eye gravy are begging for the splurge. There's a no–cell phone policy, so turn your ringer off.

Watershed, a subterranean parlor below **Pops for Champagne** (see p. 271). Since it's dedicated to regional craft beers and quite-cool liquid creations, you can look to the likes of an Italian Hurricane with hum, Campari, Del Maguey mezcal, lime, and ginger beer. The extensive selection of artisanal spirits is built for aficionados, who take time to examine them in detail while waiting for lamb pâté with violet mustard to arrive.

Weegee's Lounge, 3659 W. Armitage Ave., Logan Square, Chicago, IL 60647; (773) 384-0707. Soak up the classic cocktails—like the Delmonico and Knickerbocker—and a nostalgic feel at this understatedly cool neighborhood tavern named for crime-scene photog Arthur Fellig ("Weegee" was his nickname), whose prints adorn the walls.

The Whistler, 2421 N. Milwaukee Ave., Logan Square, Chicago, IL 60647; (773) 227-3530; www.whistlerchicago.com. Part art gallery, live music venue, and record label, this loftlike den from Paul McGee fashions rapturous classic cocktails. Get with the program over a complicated, frothy Torino Fizz with Plymouth sloe gin, Carpano Antica, Gran Classico Bitter, lemon, egg white, and Peychaud's Bitters. By then, you'll hear the Church Key, a mingling of Bols Genever, Orchard Pear liqueur, lemon, and Allspice Dram, calling your name.

Specialty Stores, Gourmet Shops & Purveyors

Food lovers tend to be compulsive shoppers, stocking their pantries and refrigerators with edibles plentiful enough to outlive many rainy days. Chicago, fortunately, answers that call with plenty of food for thought. From intriguing ethnic grocers to niche boutiques, fishmongers, and butchers, the enticements are endless.

Specialty Stores & Grocers

Al Khyam, 4738 N. Kedzie Ave., Albany Park, Chicago, IL 60625; (773) 583-3077; Middle Eastern. This market and bakery brims

Indoor Eats at Chicago French Market

Chicago's permanent, year-round indoor market doesn't exactly rival Pikes Place Market in Seattle or even Cleveland's West Side Market, but the **Chicago French Market** (131 N. Clinton St., West Loop, Chicago, IL 60661; 312-575-0306; www .frenchmarketchicago.com) has plenty to offer nonetheless. Featuring a collection of 30 specialty vendors, it's stocked with grab-and-go options and ingredients for the home cook. Be sure to check out these standouts.

Fumare Meats (312-930-4220) earns accolades for its sold-by-the-pound, house-smoked pastrami, which also comes tucked between slices of Red Hen bread.

Saigon Sisters (312-496-0094), from Mary Nguyen Aregoni and Theresa Nguyen, serves up tangy, crunchy, chewy *banh mi*. It has a companion restaurant at 567 W. Lake St., (312) 496-0090.

Vanille Patisserie (312-575-9963) is the work of World Pastry Champion Dimitri Fayard, whose handmade chocolates, tarts, and mousse cakes are more than just eye candy.

with temptations, from hot, just-baked pita and baklava to falafel, Middle Eastern cheeses, bulk legumes, pickles, and massive vats of olive oil. Its close proximity to several other specialty stores is another plus.

Andy's Deli, 5442, N Milwaukee Ave., Jefferson Park, Chicago, IL 60630; (773) 631-7304; www.andysdeli.com; Polish. Although the original location on Division Street is no more, thank your lucky stars for what *is* in store at this address: fantastic Polish sausage, country-style bacon, grill-ready meats, and imported pantry items, such as red borscht starters, sauerkraut, and sour-cherry syrup. But that's not to say the delish pierogies and cheeses are something to overlook, nor is the fact that its meats and sausages can be shipped throughout the US.

Andy's Fruit Ranch, 4733 N. Kedzie Ave., Albany Park, Chicago, IL 60625; (773) 583-2322; www.andysfruitranch.com; Grocery. This standout has a vast selection of multiethnic produce (including less familiar varieties) as well as canned and dry goods and an impressive meat and seafood counter. Filled with the requisites for an Asian meal, it also stocks Polish faves, tons of cured meat, and plenty of Middle Eastern necessities, from imported olive oil to *labna*.

A&G International Fresh Market, 5630 W. Belmont Ave., Portage Park, Chicago, IL 60634; (773) 777-4480; www.agfresh market.com; Grocery. This sprawling grocery store is destination-worthy for its multiculti baked goods alone. And although the owners are Italian, the space—at home in the former Goldblatt's department store—houses one of the most diverse selections of exotic produce, many fetas, olive oils from around the globe, and deli meats galore.

Angelo Caputo's Fresh Markets, 2400 N. Harlem Ave., Elmwood Park, IL 60607; (708) 453-0155; www.caputo markets.com; Grocery. Come during off hours to avoid a perpetual mob scene, and explore hundreds of varieties of fruit and vegetables, row upon row of sweet panettone, a dizzying number of olive oils, and countless pasta cuts. The fine meat, seafood, cheese, cured meat, and bakery counters have plenty of wow-factor, too. There are locations in Addison, Bloomingdale, Hanover Park, South Elgin, and Naperville as well.

Bari Foods, 1120 W. Grand Ave., West Loop, Chicago, IL 60622; (312) 666-0730; www.bariitaliansubs.com; Italian. There's a not-to-be-missed deli inside this Old-World Italian grocer, where from-scratch sandwiches—the Italian sub especially—are masterpieces. While you're there, wander down the handful of aisles, which are jammed with imported oil, pasta, and jarred sauces as well as other requisites to culinary wizardry. Incidentally, specialty and custom cuts of meat may be ordered from its butcher.

Bobak's Sausage Company, 5275 S. Archer Ave., Garfield Ridge, Chicago, IL 60632; (773) 735-5334; www.bobak.com; Polish. Seekers of smoked sausage and ham, potato pancakes and pierogies find inspiration at this institution, which dates back to 1967. Anchored by an expansive deli with private-label products, it also features an on-site Polish bakery and hot-food island wafting with scents of anticipated faves.

Caputo Cheese Market, 1931 N. 15th Ave., Melrose Park, IL 60160; (708) 450-0469; www.caputocheese.com; Cheese. The retail arm of family-owned manufacturing and processing company Wiscon Corporation sports upwards of 1,000 cheeses from the world over as well as fresh, house-made sausage, deli meats, and prepared salads and sandwiches alongside aisles of imported olives, orecchiette, and spices, plus a bakery counter doling out Italian cookies. There is also a location at 231 E. Wisconsin Ave., Lake Forest, (847) 482-0100.

Carniceria Jimenez, 3850 W. North Ave., Logan Square, Chicago, IL 60647; (773) 235-3637; www.carniceriasjimenez.com; Mexican. Boasting several locations in the city and suburbs, this well-stocked grocer has all the makings of a good Mexican meal: a meat counter with choice cuts, fresh masa, and way-affordable produce, on top of an in-house taqueria that prepares above average, cheap tortas and tacos.

STREET SENSE

It could be argued that the **Maxwell Street Market** is less about wares and more about Mexican street food. The food-centric Sunday flea market, which takes place on Des Plaines Avenue between Roosevelt Road and Harrison Street, is a lively scene wafting with good scents. Wander its stalls in search of pineapple-laced *atole*; rarely seen Mexican fare (pig esophagus tacos stippled with onion and cilantro); produce from *nopales* to hibiscus; and humble, heartwarming tamales. Then, move on to pork in green mole, *huitlacoche* (corn smut) tacos on fresh-made tortillas and grilled corn *elotes* spurted with lime. Be sure to watch the video and download the guide from LTHForum's David Hammond (www.dchammond.com/index.php?id=7) before pounding the pavement.

Chinatown Market, 2121 S. Archer Ave., Chinatown, Chicago, IL 60616; (312) 881-0068; Chinese. Buy whatever you need to prepare an authentic Chinese meal at this bustling grocery store with a free parking lot in back. Score enoki, bitter melon, and tofu for less than you'd imagine, along with fresh finds from the seafood and butcher counters. Just be sure to come during off-hours since the narrow aisles are hard to navigate when the throngs descend.

City Fresh Market, 3201 W. Devon Ave., Rogers Park, Chicago, IL 60659; (773) 681-8600; ww.cityfreshmarket.com; Grocery. Located at the corner of Devon and Kedzie Avenues, this reasonable ethnic grocer is filled with Eastern European and Balkan essentials like *ajvar* as well as cheese and meat pies, glorious cakes, feast breads, and *cevapcici*. There is also an offshoot at the **Chicago French Market** (131 N. Clinton St., 312-575-0230).

City Olive, 5408 N. Clark St., Edgewater, Chicago, IL 60640; (773) 878-5408; www.cityolive.com; Specialty. Olive aficionados will swoon over the tapenades, nearly four-dozen olive oils, and jarred olives at this schmancy boutique gourmet. You'll also find an array of seasonings and spices as well as an abundance of imported goods, such as honey, canned tuna, vinegar, sauces, and rice. Come hungry—a tasting bar allows you to sample before you buy.

Fox & Obel, 401 E. Illinois St., Chicago, IL 60611; (312) 410-7301; www.fox-obel.com; Grocery. There's much to adore about this luxury grocer and cafe with an adjunct wine bar—starting with its perfect, crisp-chewy, fresh-baked baguettes. The fromagerie, charcuterie, butcher, and prepared-foods counters lead to impulse shopping of the worthwhile variety. The wine-and-spirits department is top-tier, too, further necessitating visits. Produce—though not its strong suit—may include less-common heirloom and out-there finds, like rambutans. Validated garage parking at Illinois and Peshtigo is free for two hours with a $20 purchase.

Go Local

Private-label foodstuffs from Chicago restaurants and locally crafted, artisanal products are not only musts for your own pantry—they are also about the best tourist mementos imaginable.

Midwestern-made bitters from Milwaukee-based **Bittercube** (www.bittercube.com) are used in drinks at **Chizakaya** (see p. 275) and may also be purchased online. Whether you settle on lively grapefruit and hibiscus–tinged Jamaican or chamomile, cinnamon, and dried fruit–based Bolivar bitters, cocktail hour will never be the same. There's a Chicago connection, too: bartender Ira Koplowitz, who clocked time at The Violet Hour, is involved.

Salted Caramel (www.saltedcaramel.net) fashions sweet-savory confections, including fruit chews, stout marshmallows, and bacon-bourbon caramel corn. Buy products online, or look for goodies at **Flavour Cooking School** (see p. 390).

Piccolo Sogno's Chef Tony Priolo (see p. 146) sells private-label balsamic vinegar and Tuscan olive oil, available for purchase at his restaurant.

Fresh Farms International Market, 2626 W. Devon Ave., Rogers Park, Chicago, IL 60659; (773) 764-3557; www.myfreshfarms .com; Grocery. The produce selection is jaw-dropping—that's for sure—but easily navigated aisles crammed with chutneys; cheeses from Bulgaria, Finland, Hungary, and Russia; and bakery items that

Indiana-based **LocalFolks'** honey, cilantro, and jalapeño-infused whole grain mustard, habañero hot sauce, and ketchup are free of high-fructose corn syrup. Find products at **Green Grocer Chicago** (see p. 297); call (317) 727-2730 or visit www.localfolksfoods.com.

Katie Das' **Das Foods** (312-224-8590; www.dasfoods.com) sells crazy-good Caramelini Caramels, christened with fleur de sel. Other options include posh pet treats, macaroons, finishing salts, and spice blends. Buy products online at the **Chicago's Downtown Farmstand** (see p. 332).

Milwaukee-based **Bolzano Artisan Meats** (414-426-6380; www.bolzanomeats.com) dry-cures charcuterie, including guanciale, paletilla Hungara, speck, and black-pepper tenderloin. Purchase it at the Milwaukee County Winter Farmers' Market or online.

Chef Joshua Linton's **Joshua Tree Spice Studio** (www.joshuatreespicestudio.com) is a source for spice blends (hickory-smoked clove-bergamot-orange) and rubs (Aleppo).

include naan, *chapatti,* and French and ciabatta breads are sure to leave you enamored. There's also a full-service deli and quality meat and seafood department, the latter with live, fresh, smoked, frozen, and dried options. There is another location at 5740 W. Touhy Ave., Niles, (847) 779-7343.

Gene's Sausage Shop & Delicatessen, 4750 N. Lincoln Ave., Lincoln Square, Chicago, IL 60625; (773) 728-7243; www.genes sausageshop.com; European. Fans of food may find themselves overwhelmed by the selection at this two-story specialty store in the old Meyer Delicatessen. Featuring a full-service butcher shop with second-to-none, smoked-on-site sausage, it's also rife with packaged edibles and liquors. When it's warm, the rooftop beer and wine garden is a prime perch for scarfing down those house-made sausages—cooked over an open wood grill—and small plates. Decked in steel, wood, and stone with looming chandeliers, the sleek space—owned by the Luszcz family—has a less glossy (but every bit as tasty) sib at 5330 W. Belmont Ave., (773) 777-6322.

The Goddess and Grocer, 1646 N. Damen Ave., Bucktown, Chicago, IL 60647; (773) 342-3200; www.goddessandgrocer.com; Specialty. Stocked with essentials for romantic picnics, many pre-pared, this grocer begins days with muffin sandwiches, moving on to matzoh-ball soup, sweet-potato fries with sage mayo, and drunken chicken salads as well as deluxe hot and cold sandwiches and desserts (cupcakes, chocolate ganache cheesecake). Owner Debra Sharpe delivers, too, in addition to selling fancy gift baskets bursting with tasty treats. There are locations at 25 E. Delaware Pl., (312) 896-2600; and 2222 N. Elston Ave., (773) 292-7100.

Bread Heads

Few things beat biting into a crusty, fresh-baked loaf of bread. **Flourish Bakery & Cafe** (773-271-2253; www.flourishbakerycafe .com) is capitalizing on that fact with its home bread delivery service. Simply select loaves—cinnamon-raisin, sourdough, or Friday-only jalapeño-cheddar or challah—choose a delivery date, and prepay. There's a two-loaf minimum; delivery is free. Also delivering on demand is **Necessity Baking Co.** in Highland Park (847-433-9010; www.necbaking.com), whose breadshare delivery program yields loaves like sun-dried tomato-Parmesan and boule studded with dried prunes and chocolate chips.

Golden Pacific Market, 5353 N. Broadway St., Edgewater, Chicago, IL 60640; (773) 334-6688; Southeast Asian. This bright, approachable and tidy market is a treasure trove bursting with insanely cheap Asian produce, imported dry goods, sauces, and super-fresh seafood. Frankly, it's packed to the hilt with everything the home cook could possibly crave (lotus root, soy sauces, curries, and big bags of rice) or fear (water beetles). There's also a freezer section with a generous smattering of finned finds.

Green Grocer Chicago, 1402 W. Grand Ave., West Town, Chicago, IL 60642; (312) 624-9508; www.greengrocerchicago.com; Grocery. Local and organic—that's the thrust at this neighborhood grocer specializing in sustainable ingredients that have been produced and grown in the Midwest. Turn to never-fail One Sister pierogies, goodies from Bennison's Bakery in Evanston, artisan Potter's Crackers, and beer from Metropolitan Brewing. Free classes, talks, and tastings regularly take place.

Hoosier Mama Pie Co., 1618½ W. Chicago Ave., West Town, Chicago, IL 60622; (312) 243-4846; www.hoosiermamapie.com; Bakery. Paula Haney has rocked the dessert scene with her buttery, lovingly made double-crust apple, lemon chess, and sugar cream pies. The peanut butter and orange cream versions? Uh-huh, they really are all that. Even those preferring the savory side can get their fix with chicken potpie and creamy bacon, onion, and cheddar quiche.

Hyde Park Produce, 1226 E. 53rd St., Hyde Park, Chicago, IL 60615; (773) 324-7100; www.hydeparkproduce.com; Grocery. Affordable, quality produce gives way to a deli scented with mushroom bisque soup, snacks, and prepared grub, such as jerk chicken, guac, and mac and cheese. Tasty deli sandwiches, vegan, gluten-free, and organic items—not to mention a parking lot—seal its wide-reaching appeal.

Joong Boo Market, 3333 N. Kimball Ave., Avondale, Chicago, IL 60618; (773) 478-0100; www.joongboomarket.com; Korean. Often referred to as "Chicago Food Corp.," this import emporium—okay, warehouse—is one of Chicago's best spots to score specialty Asian items, be it sashimi-grade seafood, downright cheap kitchen necessities (stockpots, sake sets, rice cookers), and more ramen varieties than you imagined existed. Make time for a meal at the restaurant in back, which serves rousing renditions of bibimbap, Korean fried chicken, and fiery *kimchee jjigae*.

J.P. Graziano Grocer, 901 W. Randolph St., West Loop, Chicago, IL 60607; (312) 666-4587; www.jpgraziano.com; Italian. This warm, generations-old mom-and-pop Italian grocer stocks high-end, small-production cheeses, whole bean coffee, lardo, olives aplenty, and Sardinian bottarga. But the in-house sub shop—serving cheap, amazing sandwiches, stuffed with quality meats and cheeses—is a feather in its cap.

SIMPLER TIMES

Get fresh noodles, fruits, jams, jellies, meats and cheeses at **Amish Healthy Foods** (1023 N. Western Ave., Ukrainian Village, Chicago, IL 60622; 773-278-1717; www.amishhealthyfoods .com). The market is filled with foods produced from the Amish, many of them—like Miller Amish Country Poultry chickens—hailing from Northern Indiana. You can also load up on Amish edibles, including standout doughnuts and bacon cheese, at **Rise 'n Roll Amish Market** (42 S. Clark St., Loop, Chicago, IL 60603; 312-269-0037; www.risenrollbakery.com).

Kamdar Plaza, 2646 W. Devon Ave., Rogers Park, Chicago, IL 60659; (773) 338-8100; www.kamdarplaza.com; Indian/Pakistani. A Devon Avenue fixture since the 1970s, this joint is jammed with aromatic spices, dhals, and beans, as well as chutneys, sauces, dried fruits, and nuts. Pickles, many types of flour, and a broad array of teas are found here, too. While in store, do grab a bite (or a few) from the vegetarian snack bar. Items may also be purchased and shipped from its online store.

La Casa Del Pueblo, 1810 S. Blue Island Ave., Pilsen, Chicago, IL 60608; (312) 421-4640; www.lacasadelpueblo .com; Mexican. This friendly, family-owned supermercado leans Mexican, though it also has a large Middle Eastern section and imports from Thailand, Italy, India, and beyond. Housewares—including *molcajetes* and tortilla presses—make it a bit of a desti-  nation, as do the fresh, quality produce and availability of organic ingredients.

Lindo Michoacan, 3142 W. Lawrence Ave., Albany Park, Chicago, IL 60625; (773) 279-8834; www.lindomichoacansupermarket.com; Mexican. Check out this Mexican market with an attached restaurant for fresh, affordable produce, prepared Mexican meals, and a nice array of bottled soda as well as sweeter-than-sweet Mexican pastries. But first, start with a bowl of restorative *posole* from next door—it'll limit the likelihood of a hunger-induced shopping spree.

Middle East Bakery & Grocery, 1512 W. Foster Ave., Uptown, Chicago, IL 60640; (773) 561-2224; www.middleeastbakeryand grocery.com; Middle Eastern. House-made zaatar pita; parsley, olive, and cheese pie; and falafel fragrance this fanatically fresh Middle Eastern and Mediterranean market. Hummus of many stripes, pickled vegetables, imported Turkish cheeses, and citrus-y salads have the makings of impromptu gatherings, all of which should be capped off with a spread of fresh-made, pistachio and walnut-dotted baklava, *maamoul,* and semolina honey cake.

Minelli Brothers Italian Specialties & Liqrs, 7780 N. Milwaukee Ave., Niles, IL 60714; (847) 965-1315; Italian. This top-notch Italian deli also features a small butcher counter and a nice selection of imported Italian canned goods, bakery items, and spices.

Mitsuwa Marketplace, 100 E. Algonquin Rd., Arlington Heights, IL 60005; (847) 956-6699; www.mitsuwa.com; Japanese. Regarded as the Midwest's largest Japanese grocery store—a claim few would argue—this sprawling, circa-1991 megastore has not just staggering produce, meat, and seafood sections, but a resident travel agency, bakery, bookstore, and liquor store as well. A food court with many stalls serves sought-after staples: udon and soba noodle soups, tempura, *obanyaki* (red bean paste–filled cakes), sushi, and curry concoctions.

The Curated Co-op

You don't have to be a member to shop at the petite, community-owned **Dill Pickle Co-op** (3039 W. Fullerton Ave., Logan Square, Chicago, IL 60647; 773-252-2667; www.dillpicklefoodcoop .org). But chances are—if you live nearby—you'll want to take part. Brimming with amazing edibles, its selection of locally sourced meat, produce, and dairy is teamed with an array of prepared, refrigerated and frozen meals, dry goods, and personal care products, including basil-scented cleaners from Mrs. Meyer's Clean Day. The emphasis is on vendors who follow sustainable and organic practices, which may mean Kishu mandarins and romanesco calling from farmers' market–type wooden baskets or Justin's peanut butter cups and pork tenderloin from Twin Oak Meats in Fairbury, IL. Even in the dead of winter, bursts of flavor can be found on its wire shelves (look for Tomato Mountain Sun Gold preserves from Madison, WI, or dried herbs and spices from Frontier Natural Products Co-op).

Old Town Oil, 1520 N. Wells St., Old Town, Chicago, IL 60610; (312) 787-9595; www.oldtownoil.com; Specialty. Nestled into a small storefront in a vintage building, this niche purveyor specializes in extra-virgin olive oil from around the world, some infused naturally with fruit, herbs, or citrus. There's also an ample selection of aged and white balsamic vinegars as well as reserve sherry and red-wine vinegars. Best of all is the fact that tasting is encouraged, and the availability of recipes ensures shoppers make the most of their buys.

Pasta Fresh, 3418 N. Harlem Ave., Dunning, Chicago, IL 60634; (773) 745-5888; www.pastafreshco.com; Italian. As its name implies, this pasta shop specializes in fresh-made pasta—not the least of which is its touted ravioli—and toppings of garlicky house-made marinara and vodka sauce.

Patel Brothers, 2610 W. Devon Ave., Rogers Park, Chicago, IL 60659; (773) 262-7777; www.patelbros.com; Indian/Pakistani. This popular, family-owned grocery chain originated in Chicago in 1974, and it remains a go-to for ready-to-eat Swad brand foods, bulk spices, and rarely seen fruits (look for Alphonse mangoes and fenugreek greens). There is also an ample selection of herbs, Ayurvedic products, henna, naan, and roti as well as pickles and chutneys of all sorts. You'll also find kitchen basics—*tava* griddles, steel *masala dabba* spice boxes, pressure cookers—and baking requisites, such as chapati flour, snacks, and sweets. Other locations are at 2410 Army Trail Rd., Hanover Park, (630) 213-2222; and 873 E. Schaumburg Rd., Schaumburg, (847) 524-1111.

Penzeys Spices, 1138 W. Lake St., Oak Park, IL 60301; (708) 848-7772; www.penzeys.com; Specialty. This mail-order business originating in Brookfield, WI, now has stores spread throughout the country. The spice specialist extraordinaire, owned by a member of The Spice House clan, stocks items—be it Ceylon cinnamon, annatto seed, or Maharaja curry—in several sizes. Its rubs, salt-free seasoning blends, and chili peppers from Dundicut to Sanaam and Tien Tsin likewise make meal-making a thing of bliss. Extracts, salad dressing mixes, and corned-beef spices are available, too. There is also a location at 235 S. Washington St., Naperville, (630) 355-7677.

Produce World, 8325 W. Lawrence Ave., Norridge, IL 60706; (708) 452-7400; www.produceworldinc.com; Grocery. Veg-lovers will find it hard to tear themselves away from this world-wise market and deli. A vast, multiethnic selection of fruits and veggies is offset by scores of imported sweets, cheeses, and Balkan, Polish, and Italian goodies. There's a butcher and stellar deli as well. A second location is at 8800 Waukegan Rd., Morton Grove, (847) 581-1029.

Provenance Food & Wine, 2528 N. California Ave., Logan Square, Chicago, IL 60647; (773) 384-0699; www.provenance foodandwine.com; Specialty. Housing needs (and even more wants) for special-occasion soirees and personal indulgences, Tracy Kellner's upscale wine and cheese shop is worth experiencing. Walk away with a bottle of Tempranillo, olive oil from Oleum Vitae, or La Mancha Oro saffron in reward. It also sells gift baskets filled with locally made items, plus there is a vino club showcasing its biodynamically focused sips. There is another location at 2312 N. Leland Ave., (773) 784-2314.

Riviera Italian Foods, 3220 N. Harlem Ave., Portage Park, Chicago, IL 60634; (773) 637-4252; Italian. Imported Italian ingredients fill the shelves of this specialty, family-run grocer, which

APPLES OF YOUR EYE

Space-crunched city dwellers needn't deprive themselves of fruit— or pay through the nose to procure it. They should just sign up for the Rent-a-Tree lease program from Michigan's **Earth First Farms,** (269-815-3370; www.earthfirstfarms.com). For $50, participants choose a certified organic apple tree (Ida Red, Red Chief, Stark Crimson). They then receive its seasonal yield, taking hands-on, u-pick approach. Alternately, for an extra $10, fruit will be delivered to a designated Chicago farmers' market. There is more good news for fruit lovers of late: not-for-profit **Chicago Rarities Orchard Project** (www.chicagorarities.org), is working to establish rare-fruit orchards in reclaimed Chicago spaces.

cures many of its deli meats in house, makes its own mozzarella, and has aisles of pasta and artisan canned goods you can easily lose yourself in. While you're exploring, order the Will Special sandwich from the counter, a heavenly hodgepodge of salami, hot capicola, hot sopressata, prosciutto, and mozzarella with giardiniera.

Sanabel Bakery & Grocery, 4213 N. Kedzie Ave., Albany Park, Chicago, IL 60686; (773) 539-5409; Middle Eastern. Piping-hot spinach and cheese pies, Middle Eastern sweets (try the glistening coconut macaroons), and zaatar flatbread are among the things you'll be plied with, right along with super-cheap, house-made pita, halal meats, and essential dry goods.

The Spice House, 1512 N. Wells St., Old Town, Chicago, IL 60610; (312) 274-0378; www.thespice house.com; Specialty. This Milwaukee-based merchant imports its aromatics from their countries of origin, showcasing a collection of salad seasonings, straight-up spices, spice blends, and herbs, along with stock-starting demi-glaces, lecithin, and rubs. A seasonal garden in back often hosts lectures, book signings, and events. There is also a location at 1941 Central St., Evanston, (847) 328-3711.

Super H-Mart, 801 Civic Center Dr., Niles, IL 60714; (847) 581-1212; www.hmart.com; Asian. Part of a chain, this expansive grocer is chock-full of intriguing Asian ingredients, a lot of Korean ones in particular. In addition to displaying a large selection of seafood, this one-stop-shop brims with fresh produce, baked goods, and frozen fare. An inexpensive food court provides a place to recharge. There's also a location at 1295 E. Ogden Ave., Naperville, (630) 778-9800.

Tai Nam Food Market, 4925 N. Broadway St., Ste. J, Uptown, Chicago, IL 60640; (773) 275-5666; www.tainammarket.com; Southeast Asian. Find fixings for *pho* and much more at this well-stocked Asian supermarket deemed worthy of a detour. Wonder at the live lobster and crabs as well as the plentiful array of fresh-baked bread, marinated and butchered meat, and dim-sum preparations—dumplings included. You'll also spy a fair number of Cambodian and Indonesian items, plus seemingly endless dry goods sold at rock-bottom prices.

Three Sisters Delicatessen, 2854 W. Devon Ave., Rogers Park, Chicago, IL 60659; (773) 973-1919; Russian. Outstanding smoked and cured meats (note the salami), plus herring, caviar by the ounce, a bounty of rarely seen imported ingredients, and whimsical cakes attract loyalists to this established Russian deli, which also features relishes and jams easily put to good use.

Trotter's To Go, 1337 W. Fullerton Ave., Lincoln Park, Chicago, IL 60614; (773) 868-6510; www.charlietrotters.com; Specialty. Charlie Trotter's high-end preparations, such as precious sandwiches, reheatable entrees, and other company-appropriate foodstuffs and wines get a seal of approval from gourmands. Biting into the lavender and honey-glazed Amish chicken, braised beef brisket, or watercress-frisee salad with tart cherry vinaigrette it's understood why—though none of these luxuries come cheap.

Uni-Mart, 5845 N. Clark St., Edgewater, Chicago, IL 60660; (773) 271-8676; www.unimaronestop.com; Filipino. Ready-made *lumpia* and *pancit* give way to an atypical meat counter, candies, and canned goods at this definitive market. No visit is complete without stopping at its snack-centric, in-house Filipino carryout operation. There are locations in Niles, Hoffman Estates, and Woodridge as well.

Viet Hoa Plaza, 1051 W. Argyle St., Uptown, Chicago, IL 60640; (773) 334-1028; Southeast Asian. Durian, fragrant herbs, packaged noodles, curry pastes, and pickled veggies commingle at this

Sweet, Sippable Things

Wild Blossom Meadery & Winery (773-233-7579; www.wildblossomwines.com) produces sustainable, traditional, and more avant-garde honey wines, called mead. They're crafted from nectar collected from bees buzzing around reclaimed city lots and along Lake Michigan's sandy shores. Options range from cinnamon-spiked Apple Cin to semi-dry, Riesling-like Blanc de Fleur.

Southeast Asian grocery store and meat market, which also features kitchen tools and an extensive selection of live fish. Marvel over the sauces, and delve into the cross-cultural Asian ingredients, including many Filipino items.

Whole Foods, 1550 N. Kingsbury St., Lincoln Park, Chicago, IL 60642; (312) 587-0648; www.wholefoods market.com; Grocery. Standing proud as one of the biggest Whole Foods period, this expansive outpost houses a bakery, coffee roaster, wine lounge, and several food venues, and it pre-pares gelato on site, scooping it up alongside locally sourced items not found at other outposts. There's also a music stage and a rooftop, where seasonal food and wellness events take place.

Whole Grain Fresh Market, 665 Pasquinelli Dr., Westmont, IL 60559; (630) 323-8180; Asian. Emphasizing Chinese and Southeast Asian ingredients, this large, well-stocked grocery store has all the pantry standbys, but also less-common produce—like the occasional lily bulb. Shaved beef may leave you longing for sukiyaki. Meanwhile, a large selection of fresh and dry noodles and frozen *bao* leaves carts loaded and wallets lighter.

Winston's Market, 4701 W. 63rd St., Midway, Chicago, IL 60629; (773)767-4353; www.winstonsmarket.net; Irish. Founded in 1967 by Michael Winston Sr., a former stockyards meat cutter, this gem offers up house-made bangers and black-and-white pudding (sausages) as well as its own corned beef and smoked butt. Love Irish soda bread? You'll find that here, too. You'll also encounter enough European imports, including oats, Weetabix, and candy. Another market is at 7959 159th St. (Tinley Park, 708-633-7600), adjacent to adjunct Gaelic restaurant, **The Ashford House**.

Butchers

Bende, Inc., 925 Corporate Woods Pkwy., Vernon Hills, IL 60061; (847) 913-0306; www.bende.com. When you have a hankering for salami, head to this longtime sausage-maker to acquire its equally excellent mild Teli and Hungarian paprika-infused Csabai varieties. You'll also find packaged goods, such as *ajvar,* liver pate, sour-cherry syrup, and noodles both fine and broad. There is another location at 444 Roosevelt Rd., Glen Ellyn, (630) 469-6525.

The Butcher & Larder, 1026 N. Milwaukee Ave., Ukrainian Village, Chicago, IL 60642; (773) 687-8280; www.thebutcherand larder.com. This humanely raised, locally sourced, whole-animal butcher comes courtesy of snout-to-tail chef and modern meat-cutter Rob Levitt (ex-Mado), who offers a regular rotation of

butchering classes alongside the bounty of carved carcasses, house-smoked bacon, sausages, charcuterie, and corned beef. The meat is custom cut, and there's an edited lunch menu available, with the exception of Sunday. Also, family dinners are hosted each month. Craving his wife, Allie's, sweets? A selection of them—including her famed Migas bark—are at hand. (See recipe on p. 346.)

Casey's Market, 915 Burlington Ave., Western Springs, IL 60558; (708) 246-0380; www.caseysmarketonline.com. It's spendy, quaint, and crowded, but the meat this neighborhood butcher does deliver. Ogle bourbon-marinated strip steak; plump, stuffed chicken breast; and salty queso dip sold by the pound, but don't depart without asking for a roll of its comforting cream sausage, which is pulled from the freezer on request. Counterpart **Mike's Market** is at 32 South Villa Ave., Villa Park, (630) 832-1760.

Columbus Meat Market, 906 W. Randolph St., West Loop, Chicago, IL 60607; (312) 829-2480. This small retail store is an arm of the hopping wholesale biz, which affords not just a friendly shopping experience but access to hard-to-find cuts, quality prime meats for the grill, and drool-inducing sausages.

Dreymiller & Kray, 140 S. State St., Hampshire, IL 60140; (847) 683-2271. It's all about the hickory and applewood-smoked bacon at this old-fashioned artisan butcher, where edibles are turned from a signature brick smokehouse dating back to 1941. Mind you, the cured ham and smoked turkey breast are also of note. Look for its products at **Fox & Obel** (see p. 293) and Sunset Foods—as well as at some orchards in northern Illinois.

Gepperth's Market, 1964 N. Halsted St., Lincoln Park, Chicago, IL 60614; (773) 549-3883; www.gepperthsmarket.com. Top-tier cuts, both exotic and trusty, are the thrust of Otto Demke's meatery, taunting passersby with crown roasts of lamb and pork, house-made sausages (try the jalapeño brats), and thick-cut steaks. Alligator, venison, elk, bison, and wild boar are regularly available, and specialty cuts may be procured with an advance phone call. An added boon: items may be FedExed.

Grant Park Packing Co., 842 West Lake St., West Loop, Chicago, IL 60607; (312) 421-4096; www.grantparkpacking.com. Come on Saturday mornings (the only time it's open to the public), and grab fine Italian sausages and economical cuts of pork, which are its true area of expertise. But skirt steak and less common options, such as goose neck and beef feet and head, aren't something to scoff at.

Harrison's Poultry Farm, 1201 Waukegan Rd., Glenview, IL 60025; (847) 724-0132. Supplying to many area restaurants, this retail store and butcher sells crazy-fresh fowl—chicken, turkey, duck—that's no

more than a day old, resulting in revelatory eating experiences. Come here to pick up eggs and butter as well.

Halsted Packing House, 445 N. Halsted St., River West, Chicago, IL 60654, (312) 421-5147. The Davos' generations-old butcher shop specializes in high-end, small animals, slaughtering them on site—a fact that impacts both the shop's aroma and the pleasing end results. Put on a brave face, as the lamb, goat, and pork are hyped for good reason.

Joseph's Finest Meats, 7101 W. Addison St., Dunning, Chicago, IL 60634; (773) 736-3766. A small but inviting butcher, this neighborhood joint is a must for prime dry-aged beef as well as wonderful Italian sausage and homemade giardiniera. Call ahead for custom cuts, and they'll be waiting upon arrival.

Olympia Meat Packers, 810 W. Randolph St., West Loop, Chicago, IL 60607; (312) 666-2222. Don't be shy: stock up on the basics from this reliable meat market, be it lamb, sausages, or meaty ribs. Of course, the marbled prime steaks alone—when available—won't leave you disappointed, especially since the prices are quite low.

Paulina Market, 3501 N. Lincoln Ave., Lakeview, Chicago, IL 60657; (773) 248-6272; www.paulinameatmarket.com. Meat eaters are in hog heaven at this standby, known for its extensive selection of sausages—turducken brats, chubby knackwurst, Serbian *cevapcici*—

as well as stuffed veal breast, a plethora of Swedish specialties, handmade garlic salami studded with peppercorns, and fleshy, vibrant steaks. It's also a go-to for wild game—ostrich filet, guinea fowl, and pheasant—as well as offal. Purchases up to 30 pounds may be shipped, flash-frozen, via FedEx.

Peoria Packing Butcher Shop, 1300 W. Lake St., West Loop, Chicago, IL 60607; (312) 738-1800; www.peoriapacking.com. This wholesaler does a brisk business among retail connoisseurs, who don plastic gloves while meandering down aisle after aisle of fresh-cut beef, sausage and seafood, displayed without flourish—openly—in bins. To the joy of loyal patrons, the availability of less-frequented bits and pieces means little gets ignored within the refrigerated, locker-like space. Custom butchering and whole-animal purchases are options as well.

Prime N' Tender, 777 N. York Rd., Hinsdale, IL 60521; (630) 887-0088; www.primentender meats.com. You'll pay up the wazoo for every-thing at this tucked-away, neighborhood butcher shop that's popular with the well-to-do. The quality prime beef is what really sets the place apart, though the custom-made sandwiches with Boar's Head meats and edited selection of specialty products—peach applesauce from The Elegant Farmer, Peter Luger steak sauce—hardly hurt the cause.

Ream's Elburn Market, 128 N. Main St., Elburn, IL 60119; (630) 365-6461; www.elburnmarket.com. Located about 45 miles west of Chicago, this family-owned shop is a standout for house-smoked bacon and encased meats, including garlic wieners, brats, Portuguese linguiça, and beer salami, not to mention bone-in ham and dried beef and jerky of many kinds.

Schmeisser's Home Made Sausage, 7649 N. Milwaukee Ave., Niles, IL 60714; (847) 967-8995. Established in 1951, this is a deservedly popular, personable destination for prime meat and coils of house-made sausage. Plan on paying by cash or check, and be on the lookout—it's also a source for both pork and goose lard.

Zier's Prime Meats & Poultry, 813 Ridge Rd., Wilmette, IL 60091; (847) 251-4000; www.ziersprime.com. Cut-to-order prime, dry-aged beef is the cornerstone of this old-fashioned North Shore butcher shop, which sells heritage birds during the holidays. The house-cured charcuterie is worth a look, too, as is the house-smoked ham and bacon.

Fishmongers

Burhop's Seafood, Plaza del Lago, 1515 Sheridan Rd., Wilmette, IL 60091; (847) 256-6400; www.burhops.com. Fin enthusiasts find the freshest of catches at this upscale shop, which stocks everything from striped bass and Atlantic char to turbot, clams, and scallops. Frozen preparations are eye-catching, too, as they may include wonton-crusted shrimp; cooked, flash-frozen lobster meat; and house-made soups. You can also find Homer's Ice Cream, pies, sauces, and seasonings that make meal preparation a cinch. There are additional, unaffiliated locations at 1431 Waukegan Rd., Glenview, (847) 901-4014; and 14 Grant Sq., Hinsdale, (630) 887-4700.

Calumet Fisheries (see p. 169). This is a must for peel-and-eat shrimp and sublime smoked fish.

Dicola's Seafood, 10754 S. Western Ave., Beverly, Chicago, IL 60643; (773) 238-7071; www.dicolasseafoodbeverly.com. A mainstay for fresh sea fare, this South Side institution bakes, fries, or grills fillets and also allows customers to select them fresh and frozen to take home. All the basics—catfish, smelt, colossal shrimp, and Alaskan whitefish—also are at the ready. Hot preparations, ranging from New England clam chowder to Maryland blue-crab cakes, are available along with other fixings for feasts at home.

Dirk's Fish & Gourmet Shop, 2070 N. Clybourn Ave., Lincoln Park, Chicago, IL 60614; (773) 404-3475; www.dirksfish.com. This sustainably minded place sells the city's best seafood, from farm-raised Laughing Bird shrimp and grouper to Petrale sole, mild Patagonian toothfish, shucked East Coast oysters, and live lobster. With one-day notice, options like corvina, opah, onaga, and hamachi may be available (season willing). Frozen frog's legs, conch, and crayfish also can be yours. Then again, garlicky, prepared escargots and smoked selections—think Finnan haddie, sable, trout, and salmon—aren't afterthoughts. There's sushi, too. Parties and cooking classes are hosted on site.

The Fish Guy Market, 4423 N. Elston Ave., Albany Park, Chicago, IL 60630; (773) 283-7400; www.fishguy.com. Bill Dugan's retail operation is a no brainer for sushi-grade fish, seasonal seafood, and luxuries like Kobe beef as well as some of the area's tastiest smoked fish (try the pecan wood–smoked trout). He'll also host pre-booked dinners for parties of eight (see www.wellfleetchicago.com); the relaxed, multicourse meals take place in the shop on Friday night.

Hagen's Fish Market, 5635 W. Montrose Ave., Portage Park, Chicago, IL 60634; (773) 283-1944; www.hagensfishmarket.com. Fresh, fried, and smoked seafood is the focus of this institution, which also will smoke what you've plunked with rod and reel. Don't expect a lot of fuss—it's not a sit-down kind of a place; however, the end result is priceless. Stop by for live shellfish as well as scrod, herring, smoked sable bellies, chubs, and lox. Fortunately, there's no reason to leave hungry since the fryer turns out an Alaskan pollack sandwich, cod sticks, and spicy popcorn shrimp, which you'll want to splash with malt vinegar or dunk into zesty tartar sauce.

Isaacson & Stein Fish Co., 800 W. Fulton Market, West Loop, Chicago, IL 60607; (312) 421-2444; www.isaacsonandsteinfishcompany.com. An old-time feel, very fresh fare at reasonable prices, and a chance to don gloves and pick your next meal are the benchmarks of this seafood market. Though potentially overwhelming to newbies, row after row of mahimahi, tilapia, and Copper River salmon—also sold to the city's top chefs—are easily be navigated with help from the friendly staff.

Lawrence Fisheries (see p. 182). Check out this 24-hour institution for heavily battered shrimp and other by-the-pound fried fare.

Mercato del Pesce, 2623 N. Harlem Ave., Montclare, Chicago, IL 60607; (773) 622-7503. This family-owned, Italian seafood specialist jams its cases with slippery catches, such as spigola, massive octopi, and sardines as well as beauteous bivalves. Fortunately, prices are poised for the budget-crunched, and the service welcoming as can be.

Rubino's Seafood, 735 W. Lake St., West Loop, Chicago, IL 60661; (312) 258-0020; www.rubinosseafood.com. Not for wishy-washy types, this primo purveyor boasts an extensive seafood selection, including outstanding shellfish. The knowledgeable staff is more than willing to walk customers though the attributes of halibut, whiting, lake perch, and sea bass—among many other varieties—which are flown in fresh daily and sold at wholesale prices.

Sea Ranch, 3217 Lake Ave., Wilmette, IL 60091; (847) 256-4404; www.searanchstore.com. Lush, sushi-grade fish may be purchased here and prepared at home. However, this Japanese market also has a massive *maki,* sushi, and sashimi menu as well as a spread of sundries. There is another outpost at 518 E. Dempster St., Evanston, (847) 492-8340.

Supreme Lobster, 220 E. North Ave., Villa Park, IL 60181; (630) 834-3474; www.supremelobster.com. Its fleet of refrigerated vehicles is seen rambling around town, delivering more than 3,000 types of high-quality catches throughout Illinois, Wisconsin, Michigan, and Indiana. The retail store, brimming with lanky Alaskan king crab legs, a bevy of fillets, and namesake crustaceans, also ships selections throughout the United States.

Tensuke Market, 3 S. Arlington Heights Rd., Elk Grove Village, IL 60007; (847) 806-1200; www.tensuke-chicago.com. Folks flock to this Japanese fish market for pristine pink snapper, black tiger shrimp, and flounder as well as grocery necessities, stopping by its small food court for prepared fare, such as beef sukiyaki, noodle soups, and *maki.*

Farm Fresh

Chicago weather poses a challenge for those who want to eat locally. Complicating matters further, much of Illinois's production centers around cash-crop agriculture.

The good news is many small family farms share a deep-seated— if seemingly obvious—belief: delicious, wholesome edibles are tantamount to a healthy future. These farmers are busy cultivating a rich food culture; meanwhile, restaurant menus read like a who's who, upending the notion of chefs-as-rock-stars and putting more focus where it belongs: on producers.

For those interested in learning more, **The Local Beet** (www.the localbeet.com) is a resource, too, brimming with practical advice for the sustainably minded. Look to it for features on Midwestern cheese, blog posts on beer, or advice for starting your own organic vegetable garden. It also offers insight on how to prepare goodies, like baked spaghetti squash procured from the farmers' market.

Whether dining at Chicago restaurants or frequenting farmers' markets, there's nothing like experiencing food right from the source. Many area farms offer CSA (community supported agriculture) programs; most will happily arrange tours with advance notice; and some even offer apprenticeship programs.

Local Farms

Arnolds Farm, 997 N. Salem Rd., Elizabeth, IL 61028; (815) 858-2407; www.arnoldsfarm.com, is a hilly, family-run farm located in the picturesque Apple River Valley en route to Galena. It offers pasture-raised, grass-fed, and grain-finished beef; Duroc, Berkshire, or Chester White-bred pork; and all-natural lamb and poultry. All of the meat is free of chemicals, hormones, and antibiotics and is sold by the whole animal, side, mixed package, and by the individual cut.

The bird is the word at John Caveny's **Caveny Farm,** 1999 N. 935 East Rd., Monticello, IL 61856; (217) 762-7767; www.caveny farm.com, which is dedicated to raising heritage-breed Bourbon Red turkeys—sold straight-up or smoked—as well as Rouen ducks and American Buff geese. The juicy, rich poultry is typically sold in advance of slaughter and delivered to pick-up points in Chicago. Alternately, poultry may be grabbed directly from the farm.

Jody and Beth Osmund are behind old timey **Cedar Valley Sustainable Farm,** 1985 North 3609th Rd., Ottawa, IL 61350; (815) 431-9544; www.cedarvalleysustainable.com. Consider signing up for its affordable CSA meat share program, which includes a mixture of fresh, farm-raised eggs and hormone- and antibiotic-free beef, pork, and chicken. And plan on visiting when field days,

An Epicenter of Edibles

Situated about 2 hours southwest of Chicago, rural Livingston County is home to something hidden in plain view: more than two-dozen small family farms doing curious things.

From entrepreneurial 11- and 13-year-old children growing their own chemical-free kohlrabi to farmers reviving lost heirloom seeds, raising heritage animals, and procuring wild pawpaws, nettles, and ramps coveted by chefs, many are members of the not-for-profit **Stewards of the Land** (www.thestewardsoftheland .com). Suffice it to say, they are a force to be reckoned with.

Members, residing within a 50-mile radius of Fairbury, IL, sell their crops to food enthusiasts, farmers' markets, and celebrity chefs. They also stock the produce section of **Dave's Supermarket** (120 S. 3rd St., Fairbury, IL 61739; 815-692-2822; www.davessupermarket.com), a quaint grocer with a fried chicken and pizza counter in back.

festivals, cookouts, and tours are scheduled. Sometimes, there are hayrides and bonfires on the farm, too.

Some of the area's most coveted beef comes from **Dietzler Farms**, W4222 County Rd. A, Elkhorn, WI 53121; (262) 642-7665; www.dietzlerbeef.com. The face behind this family-owned specialty beef ranch—located about 90 miles northwest of the city—is Michelle Dietzler, a spa-journalist-turned-farmhand. Call in advance to arrange a visit, and keep your eyes peeled for beef-centric farm dinners, which feature fare prepped by top Chicago restaurateurs (think Cleetus Friedman from City Provisions Deli). They're held during summer in a light-strung, former dairy barn.

Farm-to-fork is the mantra at **Epiphany Farms Enterprise,** 23676 800 North Rd., Downs, IL 61736; (309) 378-2403; www .epiphanyfarms.com. A labor of love, it's owned by Culinary Institute of America grad Ken Myszka and his wife, Nanam Yoon Myszka. Ken worked under Thomas Keller and Guy Savoy in Las Vegas before having, well, an epiphany. Joined by Mike Mustard (ex-Alain Ducasse's Mix) and Stu Hummel, who worked under Joel Robuchon, the crew hosts educational dinner parties and cooking lessons for eight or more. The sustainable farm also welcomes visitors, the more hardcore of whom may spend the day doing a hands-on, work-and-learn experience.

Vicki Westerhoff's heirloom vegetable–driven, direct-market farm—**Genesis Growers,** 8373 E. 3000 South Rd., St. Anne, IL 60964; (815) 953-1512; www.genesis-growers.com—hosts an April through December CSA program, using hoop houses to extend the growing season. Drop-offs of everything from sunchokes and daikon to Asian greens, dry beans, and eggs take place throughout Chicago and the suburbs; produce from the north-central Illinois farm is also sold at farmers' markets.

Terry and Judy Bachtold raise a small herd of grass-fed cattle without the use of hormones, antibiotics, or steroids at **Grazin' Acres,** 29493 E. 400 North Rd., Strawn, IL 61775; (815) 688-3486; www.thestewardsoftheland.com. The result is deeply flavorful, lean beef with an appealing minerality. Call ahead to visit the property, where you'll learn about the labor-intensive rotational grazing process, importance of a stress-free environment for animals, and the family's steadfast commitment to sustainable agriculture. The meat is sold in advance of butchering by the whole animal, side, quarter side, and individual cut.

Fans of heritage-breed meat will have a field day at **Green Earth Farm,** 8308 Barnard Mill Rd., Richmond, IL 60071; (815) 403-7735; www.greenearthfarm.org. Narragansett, Royal Palm, and Bourbon Red turkeys as well as pasture-raised, heritage-breed chickens and eggs listed on the American Livestock Conservancy breed list are its specialty. Heritage ducks (Rouens, Swedish, and Pekin) and geese are available, too. Its CSA is offered on a first come, first served basis.

Something to Cluck About

There's no need to travel rural roads in order to get farm-fresh eggs—thanks to **City Chickens,** Jennifer Neff's hobby farm in suburban Deerfield. She has 16 hens—plus some Polish Silkies, which produce novel, tiny eggs. What Neff doesn't use in baking, she sells by the dozen. E-mail her to arrange pickup of the multihued orbs at jn8809@aol.com.

Growing Power, 2215 W. North Ave., Chicago, IL 60647; (773) 486-6005; www.growingpower.org, is headquartered in Milwaukee but has a significant presence in Chicago proper. Local projects range from a community garden at the intersection of West Chicago and North Hudson Avenues in the Cabrini-Green neighborhood to an urban agriculture *potager* at Grant Park and a farm in Jackson Park utilizing a biological worm system approach. The latter is also the site of a community garden, where workshops educate the farm-curious about composting, vermicomposting, and vegetable growing. Check out its "market basket" program to get a taste.

Harvest Moon Organics, P.O. Box 302, Viroqua, WI 54665; (773) 472-7950; www.harvestmoonorganics.com, is a 20-acre, certified organic farm in west-central Wisconsin's driftless region, at the South fork of the Bad Axe River. Beginning in November, it offers a CSA of cellar crops, such as potatoes and winter squash, bolstered by homemade egg noodles, beans, and eggs. Farmers also appear at the Friday market in the parking lot of Uncommon Ground on Devon Avenue. Produce emphasizes Ark varieties, endangered fare identified by Slow Food International. Beyond that, its farm-to-school programs teach kids about the benefits of working the land.

Heartland Meats, 204 E. US Highway 52, Mendota, IL 61342; (815) 538-5326; www.heartlandmeats.com, raises long-lashed, black-nosed Piedmontese cattle. The resulting meat from Pat and John Sondgeroth's humanely run farm appears at **Green City Market** and the **Evanston Farmers' Market**. Its products are also sold at **Hyde Park Produce,** 1226 E. 53rd St., (773) 324-7100.

Petite heavyweight **Henry's Farm,** 432 Grimm Rd., Congerville, IL 61729; (309) 965-2771; www.henrysfarm .com, grows more than 600 types of vegetables—many of them heirloom—on a 10-acre, sustainable plot in the Mackinaw River Valley of central Illinois. Its CSA program consists of fresh-picked finery—cabbages, sweet corn, mizuna—that's free of GMOs, pesticides, herbicides, and synthetic fertilizers. Its grub also makes the rounds at markets, such as the **Evanston Farmers' Market.**

A powerhouse on 40 acres of certified organic land, **Kinnikinnick Farm,** 21123 Grade School Rd., Caledonia, IL 61011; (815) 292-3288; www.kinnikinnickfarm.com, is situated 80 miles northwest of Chicago. Its ingredients run rampant on Chicago restaurant menus and appear at farmers' markets citywide. Growing everything from Minestra Nera greens to purslane, Helios Gold radishes, and Cherokee Purple tomatoes, it also hosts occasional events at the farm. Incidentally, many of its seeds have been sourced from small companies in Italy.

Living Water Farms, 29695 E. 100 North Rd., Strawn, IL 61775; (815) 848-2316; www.livingwaterfarms.net, is a small family farm with a 6,000-square-foot, geo-thermal greenhouse that makes grown-year-round, chemical-free produce possible. Advance orders can be made for its unusual salad greens (Red Lollo Rosa, Bronze Arrowhead), watercress, daikon, pea shoots, and cucumbers—not to mention borage, edible violets, and anise hyssop. Sometimes farm tours are offered; farm fans also may call ahead to arrange a visit.

Mint Creek Farm, 1693 E. 3800 North Rd., Stelle, IL 60919; (815) 256-2202; www.mintcreekfarm.com, is a go-to for grass-fed lamb. Harry and Gwen Carr's 220-acre farm utilizes traditional, rotational grazing techniques on lush prairie pastures, resulting in incomparable lamb shank, luxe legs, and sultry stews. The east-central Illinois farm has a CSA, appears at several markets—including Andersonville, Wicker Park, and Logan Square—and ships

MAKING CONNECTIONS

Sustain, one of the country's leading environmental communication groups, is behind not-for-profit **FamilyFarmed.org,** 7115 W. North Ave. #504, Oak Park, IL 60302; (708) 763-9920. Making a difference in Chicagoland, it connects local food producers with buyers and consumers regionally. FamilyFarmed.org also helped fight USDA regulations allowing genetically engineered, irradiated, and sludge-grown food to be labeled organic. Plus, it developed a Buy Local campaign and the Local Organic Initiative, culminating in a study to determine the feasibility of buyers and producers bringing local, organic food to the table. In 2004, the first Local Organic Trade show took place, featuring 50 farmers and hundreds of industry buyers. By the next year, it evolved into the FamilyFarmed EXPO, which took place at Navy Pier and has had subsequent Midwestern shows. Its eponymous website points food lovers to local foods and CSAs, while educating the public on why family farms need support.

meat nationally. Organically fed veal, beef, pork, and goat are options as well.

Grass-fed beef, veal, and lamb as well as pastured pork, duck, turkey, and chicken is the focus at **Moore Family Farm,** 2013 N. 1950 East Rd., Watseka, IL, 60970; (815) 432-6238; www.moorefamily farm.com. Pesticide-free pork and veggies as well as Pekin ducks are finds, too, and may be picked up at the farm by appointment.

Practically a household name around these parts, **Nichols Farm & Orchard,** 2602 Hawthorn Rd., Marengo, IL 60152; (815) 568-6782; www.nicholsfarm.com, is a champion on the farmers' market scene. The 250-acre fruit and vegetable farm propagates a staggering array of unique varieties, such as tangy Black Pineapple tomatoes, Rat Tail radishes, and Fordhook lima beans.

Over a century old, eponymous **Plapp Family Organics,** 23544 McQueen Rd., Malta, IL 60150; (815) 825-2589, raises ducks, chickens, pigs, and sheep, producing most of its own soy, wheat, barley, oats, and corn to feed livestock. Look for its grains, pop-corn, meat, and poultry at **Green City Market.**

Prairie Fruits Farm and Creamery, 4410 N. Lincoln Ave., Champaign, IL 61822; (217) 643-2314; www.prairiefruits .com. Illinois's first farmstead cheesemaking facility fashions fluffy, fresh chèvre and gooey, bloomy-rind goat cheeses as well as Camembert-style creations from the milk of Nubian and La Mancha goats, which thrive on a foraged diet. It also grows seasonal fruits and berries, including white-fleshed peaches and black currants, in a certified organic orchard. Plan to attend one of its idyllic farm dinners from May through November—overseen by on-farm chef Alisa DeMarco, a Culinary Institute of America grad. Goats are available for purchase as well.

Seedling Orchard, 6717 111th Ave., South Haven, MI 49090; (269) 227-3958; www.seedlingfruit.com, grows more than 75 types of fruit, including many heirloom varieties. Its apples, peaches, pears, plums, and nectarines are legendary and grown on acreage that's well over 100 years old. Its cider—which may be purchased at the Green City, Lincoln Square, and Wicker Park farmers' markets—is fantastic. Seedling also offers a monthly fresh, dried and preserved fruit club, which is shipped nationally.

Marty and Chris Travis's influence on local food culture is far-reaching. Learn about it at **Spence Farm,** 2959 N. 2060 East Rd., Fairbury, IL 61739; (815) 692-3336; www.thespencefarm.com. In addition to running the oldest family farm in Livingston County, IL, they raise heritage-breed animals (Jacob's sheep, Dexter cows, Black Cayuga ducks), grow crops in two hoop houses on the farm, and reintroduce rare produce—such as roasted, milled Iroquois White Corn—for consumption. Meanwhile, their son, Will, makes maple syrup in a sugarhouse built with a grant from the Frontera Farmer Foundation. The inspiring farmstead also holds educational programs at a facility on site.

WINTER WARRIORS

Faith in Place and the **Churches' Center for Land and People (CCLP)** are behind a series of indoor winter farmers' markets, featuring provisions from small, local producers. The gatherings feature fresh produce as well as cheese, honey, syrup, meat, poultry, and canned goods. The markets typically take place November through April and are held at various locations. Visit www .faithinplace.org or call (312) 733-4640.

Sustainable, organic agriculture is key at diversified, 65-acre **Tempel Farm Organics,** 17970 W. Millburn Rd., Old Mill Creek, IL 60083; (847) 244-5330; www.tempelfarmsorganics.com. Its pros grow vegetables, fruit, and cut flowers as well as produce pasture-raised poultry, honey, eggs, and all the feed grain for livestock. A roadside store is in the works; a CSA program is offered at present; and its grub appears at area farmers' markets, such as the one held in Logan Square.

Consider buying broad-breasted white turkeys from **TJ's Pasture Free-Range Poultry,** 2773 N. 1500 East Rd., Piper City, IL 60959; (815) 686-9200. Given plenty of room to roam, these birds are raised on a natural diet of chemical-free grass, and one free of animal byproducts and antibiotics.

It's a family affair at all-natural, chemical-free **Triple S Farm,** RR #1 Box 122A, Stewardson, IL 62463; (217) 343-4740; www .triplesfarms.com, a certified organic east-central Illinois farm. In addition to growing veggies, it sells pork, poultry, and beef as well as beef sticks and free-range eggs via a home delivery and pick-up program.

Located on 140 acres of certified organic land in central Illinois is **Wettstein Organic Farm,** 2100 US Highway 150, Carlock, IL 61725; (309) 376-7291; www.wettsteinorganicfarm.wordpress.com. The farm—which grows its own combination of soybeans, corn, and other grains as feed—provides poultry, pork, beef, and eggs directly to customers, all the while maintaining a low carbon footprint.

Farmstands & Farms with Stands

Quality plants and produce can be had at **Big John's Farm Stand & Green House,** 1754 E. Joe Orr Rd., Chicago Heights, IL 60411; (708) 758-2711; www.bigjohnsfarmmarket.com. Everything from shelly beans and Purple Hull peas to garlic, onions, and okra can be purchased from its family-owned farm market as well as at the seasonal Tinley Park and Deerfield farmers' markets. You may also pick your own beets, cabbage, tomatoes, and Crowder peas—among other edibles—from July through October.

Whether you're seeking winter cabbage, cauliflower, or beets, you'll find them May through October at **Bultema's Farmstand**

& U-Pick, 2785 E. Lincoln Hwy., Lynwood, IL 60411; (708) 758-1565; www.bultemasfarmstandandgreenhouse.com. In turn, vegetables may also be picked by the pound, half bushel, or full bushel beginning around the third week of May.

You'll find sustainably grown fruits, vegetables, and herbs in season, many organic, at **Chicago's Downtown Farmstand,** 66 E. Randolph St., Chicago, IL 60601; (312) 742-8419. Featuring produce from a 250-mile radius around the city, it also offers cooking demonstrations. Look, too, for edible treasures like Capriole Farmstead goat cheese; sweet-savory, small-batch preserves from Madison, WI–based Quince & Apple; and dips, oils, and seasonings from Wind Ridge Herb Farm in Caledonia, IL.

City Farm, 1204 N. Clybourn Ave., Chicago, IL 60610; (773) 821-1351; www.resourcecenterchicago.org, is a sustainable farm perched between disparate neighborhoods: Cabrini-Green and the Gold Coast. It turns out over two-dozen varieties of vegetables and herbs, growing them in composted soil made from Chicago restaurant trimmings. A model for urban farming, it welcomes individuals and groups to its once-vacant lot as volunteers. Take a tour of the facility, which creates jobs and propagates the future of sustainable agriculture. Its riches appear on many Chicago menus, including Sepia, Chilam Balam, and North Pond. It also has a small on-site market stand that is open to the public.

The Chicago Board of Education launched the **Farmstand at Chicago High School for Agricultural Sciences,** 3857 W. 111th St., Chicago, IL 60655; (773) 535-2788; www.chicagoagr .org. Part of a nationwide endeavor to foster jobs in the fields of agribusiness and agriscience, it features summer internships in conjunction with the University of Illinois and Michigan State University. The student-run stand also sells what it grows, be it fresh, hand-picked sweet corn, pickles, or peppers as well as baked zucchini bread and honey from 40 hives.

Pick an extensive selection of fruits and vegetables when weather allows—typically June through October—at **Garden Patch Farms & Orchard,** 14154 W. 159th St., Homer Glen, IL 60491; (708) 301-7720; www.gardenpatchfarms.com. Fronted by a stand with pre-picked potatoes, blackberries, gooseberries, and tomatoes—not to mention decorative roosters and jellies and jams—the garden and orchard stretches far behind. You may also buy feed for its chickens.

Keep your eyes peeled for the pumpkin silo—it'll guide you to **Goebbert's Pumpkin Farm & Garden Center,** 40 W. Higgins Rd., South Barrington, IL 60010; (847) 428-6727; www.pumpkin farms.com. In addition to having a large selection of annuals and perennials, it is a must-stop for sweet corn, peppers, melons, and stone fruit. You can also pick up soil, compost, and mulch. The farm has an adjunct pumpkin patch at Route 47 and Reinking Road in Hampshire, where a roadside stand is open mid-July through October.

Support the student agriculture program at Chicago Botanic Garden's **North Chicago Green Youth Farm,** Greenbelt Forest

Preserve, two miles north of Green Bay Road past Pulaski Memorial Drive/14th Street, Waukegan, IL 60085; (847) 835-8352. It hosts a seasonal u-pick farmstand on Wednesday and Saturday from mid-July through early October. Produce is also sold at the Chicago Botanic Garden's farmers' market the first and third Sundays of early June through mid-October. Offshoots are located in the North Lawndale neighborhood—here, there's a seasonal Wednesday farmstand at 3355 W. Ogden Ave.—and at the **Washington Park/Dyett Green Youth Farm,** 555 E. 51st St.

A rarity in these parts, four-season growing takes place at eight-acre **Heritage Prairie,** 2N308 Brundige Rd., La Fox, IL 60119; (630) 443-8253; www.hpmfarm.com. Come to its store for everything from beets and celeriac to summer squash, tomatillos, and turnips as well as year-round micro-greens, such as *pac choi,* pea tendrils, and *shungiku*. Its CSA is an option, too, and there is an apiary on site.

The Kauffman family has been raising turkeys since 1933 on green-minded land. Buy fresh birds in person Monday through Saturday at its **Ho-Ka Turkey Farm,** 8519 Leland Rd., Waterman, IL 60556; (815) 264-3470; www.hokaturkeys.com.

Make a point to stop at family-run, single-source Jersey cow dairy farm **Kilgus Dairy,** 21471 E. 670 North Rd., Fairbury, IL 61739; (815) 692-6080; www.kilgusfarmstead .com. Arranging tours of its farmstead is possible, and seeing the cows milked is quite something. While you're there, step inside the self-service country store for a lush, soft-serve ice cream cone, viewing the bottling process through a large picture window between licks. You can also pluck wholesome, insanely rich, all-natural milk, chocolate milk, half and half, heavy cream, and drinkable yogurt from its coolers. Local cheese and meat are stocked in the refrigerator and small freezer as well. Pay is by the honor system; cash or personal checks are accepted.

For Athena muskmelon, bicolored corn, and crisp orchard apples, pay an in-season visit to **McCarthy Farms,** 10301 W. 159th St. Orland Park, IL 60462; (708) 349-2158; www .mccarthyfarmstands.com. Come fall, you'll also find Howden Biggie pumpkins.

In fall, blue and white pumpkins—as well as mini and giant varieties—abound at patch **Puckerville Pumpkins,** 13332 Bell Rd., Lemont, IL 60439; (708) 508-0906.

You'll find a bevy of locally grown produce—including green beans, corn, onions, and zucchini—at family-run garden center and farm market, **Random Acres Garden Center,** Corner of Roselle & Central Roads, Schaumburg, IL 60194; (847) 524-5296; www.random acres.com. There's also a selection of pickled and canned fruits and vegetables from Door County, WI–based Wienke's.

For traditional broad-breasted white and heritage-breed Bourbon Red turkeys, sniff out **R Family Farm,** 6501 N. Boone School Rd., Poplar Grove, IL 61065; (815) 519-4341; www.r-family-farm.com. Cornish Cross broilers, goat, and Berkshire pork are options as well and may be picked up from the on-farm store, by CSA, or at area farmers' markets, such as the suburban Woodstock and Belvidere markets.

For specialty mushrooms, turn to **River Valley Mushroom Ranch,** 39900 W. 60th St., Burlington, WI 53105; (262) 539-3555; www.rivervalleykitchens.com. Its farm store and market sells button, cremini, shiitake, portobello, and oyster varieties grown on site. Other finds include locally foraged morels, multi-colored, farm-fresh eggs, varied produce, and fresh-baked bread as well as house-label salsas and extra-garlicky bread spread. You can score grow-at-home mushroom kits and mushroom compost, too.

Naturally raising and processing beef, pork, and lamb at its own facility in Forrest, IL, is **Slagel Family Farm,** 23601 E. 600 North Rd., Fairbury, IL 61739; (815) 848-9385; www.slagelfamily farm.com. The bucolic locale is lauded for its high-quality, USDA-inspected products, which are additive-, hormone-, and steroid-free. Sample it via a CSA and at its retail butcher shop, located 5 miles from the farm at 103 E. Krack St., Forrest, IL 61741. Or watch for it on menus, including at **The Publican** and **Vie.**

From mid-June through October, load up on sweet and hot peppers, summer and winter squash, melons, and leeks at **Smits Farms,** 3437 E. Sauk Trail, Chicago Heights, IL 60411; (708) 758-3838; www.smitsfarms.com.

Growing Greats

Nothing beats padding out to your backyard, barefoot, to pluck tomatoes, peppers, and lettuce for a fresh-as-can-be salad. Thankfully, there are amazing spots to purchase fruit and vegetable plants, both individually and by the flat.

Worthy of a day trip: **Woldhuis Farms Sunrise Greenhouse** (10300 E. 9000 North Rd., Grant Park, IL 60940; 815-465-6310); www.woldhuisfarms.com). Featuring a labyrinth of interconnected, fragranced greenhouses flush with bright, unique annuals, it also grows from seed a stunning selection of unusual heirloom and hybrid vegetables and herbs. Sure, you'll find Sugar Baby watermelons, bush pickles, and collards, but you'll also unearth scorching Bhut Jolokia peppers, Green Sausage and Great White tomatoes, and herbs from rue to costmary, comfrey, and epazote. Come early, and grab a map (it gets crowded); then, fortify on hot dogs topped with sour-pickle relish and lemon shakeups from the snack stand.

Provided you need a quicker fix for your perennials, vegetable and herb plants, cacti, and succulents, however, head to **Ted's Greenhouse** (16930 S. 84th Ave., Tinley Park, IL 60487; 708-532-3575; www.tedsgreenhouse.com). You'll find potted chervil and curry leaf, borage and burnet as well as moujean tea, cardoons, and artichokes for planting in plots.

Late-season gourds and pumpkins are available, too. You'll also find its produce and herbs—such as lemongrass, lavender, and lovage—at market locations like Daley Plaza, Lincoln Park, and **Green City Market.**

In addition to raising critically endangered Red Wattle hogs, Donna OShaughnessy and Keith Parrish's **South Pork Ranch,** 32796 E. 750 North Rd., Chatsworth, IL 60921; (815) 635-3414; www .south-pork-ranch.com, also sells unpasteurized, non-homogenized raw milk direct to customers, who appreciate its purity and the presence of body-beneficial bacteria. (Find it at the farm proper.) Meanwhile, procure its antibiotic-, hormone-, and steroid-free, pasture-raised beef and pork from livestock that has been fed certi-fied organic hay.

Gaining a reputation for its Duroc boar and Yorkshire Gilt hogs, crossbred and fed without by-products, is **Twin Oak Meats,** 11197 N. 2300 East Rd., Fairbury, IL 61739; (815) 692-4215; www .twinoakmeats.com. This farm features a retail store chock-full of loin cuts, hickory-smoked bacon, and honey-glazed, spiral-sliced ham as well as roasts, brats, and country-style ribs. While you're at it, pick up some pig's ears and fresh-frozen femur bones for pets. Some items, like crown roast of pork and baby-back ribs, must be special ordered a few weeks in advance.

Filled with vibrant begonias, dahlias, and impatiens, aromatic verbena and annual grasses, you'll also find an array of tomatoes, peppers, and other veggies for sale during the growing season at **Van Kalker Farms & Greenhouses,** 1808 E. Joe Orr Rd., Chicago Heights, IL 60411; (708) 758-1732; www.vankalkerfarms.com. Its produce also appears at the Park Forest and Oak Lawn farmers' markets—as well as at its sister location at 13169 E. 10500 North Rd., Grant Park, (815) 466-0234.

Farmers' Markets

Countless farmers' markets operate throughout Chicago and its suburbs starting in May, though run dates and days of operation may vary by season. A good resource for tracking them down, using the event-search tool, is www.chicagofarmersmarkets.us. You may also call (312) 744-0565 or visit www.cityofchicago.org for location information. Most run though October, though some kick it until the end of November. Increasingly, there are even options during the dead of winter.

It may be small, but the Saturday **Bronzeville Community Market,** 4400 S. Cottage Grove Ave., Bronzeville, Chicago, IL 60653, packs a punch. You'll find produce from nearby Washington Park/Dyett Green Youth Farm, Amish baked items, like cinnamon rolls and fried pies from Candlelight Bakery, and perfect little multicolored potatoes from Kap Farms. On top of offering a great, albeit edited, selection of fresh, healthy food, it's significant in that the market is located in one of Chicago's "food deserts," an area where the availability of fresh food is limited.

Daley Plaza Farmers' Market, 50 W. Washington St., Loop, Chicago, IL 60602, runs on Thursday from mid-May through mid-October in the heart of the Loop. It's a favorite among lunch-breakers, who seek respite from the workaday world by ogling vendors' flowers, meat, and produce, as well as baked goods, honey, and jarred treats.

Operating on Tuesday mid-May through late October is the **Federal Plaza Farmers' Market,** Adams and Dearborn Streets, Loop, Chicago, IL 60606. You'll find fruits, veggies, plants, and flowers galore—all surrounded by the towering skyline.

The festive **Evanston Farmers' Market,** University Place and Oak Avenue, Evanston, IL 60201; (847) 448-8138; www.cityof evanston.org, operates on Saturday from early May through early November. Pick out meat, milk, eggs, and cheese—as well as kaleidoscopic produce, while listening to live musical acts.

The granddaddy of local, organic, sustainable farmers' markets is **Green City Market,** which takes place mid-May through October at Clark Street and Stockton Drive, Lincoln Park, Chicago, IL 60614; (773) 880-1266; www.chicagogreencitymarket.org. In addition to having the largest selection of fresh-picked, unique produce, it hosts ongoing chef demonstrations, a farmer scholarship program, and a heritage and heirloom project. Its annual Locavore Challenge is celebrated, as its beloved chef's barbecue, when nearly 100 restaurants band together to highlight farm-fresh products each July. During winter, Green City moves inside the Peggy Notebaert Nature Museum, 2430 N. Cannon Dr.

For fresh fare on the South Side, head to **Hyde Park Farmers' Market**, cul-de-sac at 52nd Place and Harper Court, Hyde Park, Chicago, IL 60602; (312) 744-3315, on Thursday from June through October. Vendors sell the stalwarts here as well as herbs, cut flowers, and preservative-free baked goods.

There's a decidedly hip vibe at the Sunday **Logan Square Farmers' Market,** Logan Boulevard and Milwaukee Avenue, Logan Square, Chicago, IL 60647; (773) 489-3222; www.logan squarefarmersmarket.org. It's smaller than many of the city markets but has the basics well covered. It's also a great spot to score morning bites, like savory and sweet crepes from Cook Au Vin.

Enter the parking lot next to Pilgrim Church on the last Saturday of the month, May though October, and feel as though times are simpler. Swelling with fresh familiar and atypical produce, the **Oak Park Farmers' Market,** 460 Lake St, Oak Park; (708) 358-5780; www.oak-park.us/farmersmarket, enjoys a following for its piping-hot doughnuts, passed though the church window and coated in powder or cinnamon sugars. Browse stalls offering artisan cheeses, canned goods, and honey, and linger over live music between bites of purchased produce.

Usually running early June through October from 4 p.m. to 8 p.m., there is a Friday farmers' market in the parking lot at **Uncommon Ground,** 1401 W. Devon Ave., Rogers Park, Chicago, IL 60660; (773) 465-9801; www.uncommonground.com. It's also a great time to tour the certified organic rooftop garden. Meanwhile, kid-friendly entertainment means fun for the whole family. Vendors' offerings range from produce to tipples from North Shore Distillery and Casa Noble organic tequila. As an added incentive to shop, there's a benefit component to proceeds from certain purchases.

Sunday from early June through late October, consider swinging by the **Wicker Park and Bucktown Farmers' Market,** 1500 N. Damen Ave., Wicker Park, Chicago, IL 60622; (773) 384-2672; www .wickerparkbucktown.com. You'll find a smallish selection of must-have produce, including apples and heirloom tomatoes, as well as baked goods and pretty, affordable fresh-cut flowers.

Recipes

Get ready to host your own regale. In the pages that follow, Chicago chefs—not ones to be stingy with know-how—offer up recipes for beginners and vets, plate-sharers and sweet-tooths, using ingredients that embody the city's vibrant, seasonal sensibility and inventive spirit.

If you groove on gougères or are sated by salad, if you seek solace in soup or one-pot wonders, this one's for you.

Grilled Shrimp & Avocado Bruschetta

Giuseppe Tentori of BOKA and GT Fish & Oyster favors clean, bright flavors—a fact that shows in this sparkling, easy-to-make starter.

Serves 6

- 12 raw shrimp, deveined and shelled
- 1 tablespoon chile sauce, such as Sriracha
- 3 tablespoons vegetable oil
- 4 avocados, pitted
- 2 limes, divided use
- 2 tablespoons cilantro, chopped, plus additional for garnish
- 1 tablespoon jalapeño, minced
- 1 grapefruit
- 1 store-bought baguette
- 2 tablespoons olive oil
- Kosher salt and fresh-cracked black pepper, to taste
- ¼ cup shelled pistachios, toasted and roughly chopped

Toss the shrimp, chili paste, and vegetable oil in a small bowl. Cover with plastic wrap and allow to marinate in the refrigerator for 30 minutes.

Scoop flesh of avocados into a large bowl. Add the juice of one lime, along with cilantro and jalapeños, mixing until incorporated.

Preheat grill to medium-high.

As it heats, cut the peel and white pith from the grapefruit using a paring knife. Cut between membranes to remove the segments.

Slice the baguette ¼-inch thick on the bias. Brush with olive oil and season with salt and pepper. Place the baguette slices on the hot grill, flipping once half way through, until lightly toasted (about 30 seconds per side). At the same time, place shrimp on the grill, cooking for approximately one minute on the first side. Flip and cook for 30 seconds on the second side. Remove both the bread and shrimp from the grill. Squeeze the remaining lime over the shrimp and season with salt, if needed.

To assemble, spread a generous tablespoon of the avocado mixture on the grilled bread. Place two pieces of shrimp, one grapefruit segment, and a sprinkling of pistachios on each piece. Garnish with cilantro leaves and serve immediately.

Recipe courtesy of Giuseppe Tentori, executive chef of BOKA (p. 75) and GT Fish & Oyster (p. xxii).

Chicken Liver Pâté with Grilled Bread & Pickled Onions

Rob Levitt of The Butcher & Larder preps pound after pound of this insanely popular schmear each week.

Serves 10

- **1 pound chicken livers, soaked overnight in ice water**
- **2 sticks of butter, cut into small chunks, plus 1½ tablespoons for sautéing**
- **1 sprig fresh rosemary, leaves removed from stem**
- **2 cloves garlic**
- **½ cup tomato puree**
- **½ cup chicken stock**
- **Kosher salt, to taste**

Quick pickled onions

- **1 red onion, halved and cut into ½-inch semicircles**
- **1 cup red wine vinegar**
- **½ cup sugar**
- **Pinch of salt**
- **Loaf of country bread, sliced on the bias and grilled**

Drain the chicken livers, pat dry, and set aside. In a nonreactive skillet on medium-high heat, melt 1½ tablespoons of butter. Add the livers and cook on both sides until no more than medium-rare; if parts seem a bit raw, that's okay. The residual heat from resting and pureeing will finish cooking them.

Remove the livers from the pan and set aside somewhere warm. Add rosemary leaves and garlic to the same pan and cook on medium heat until the garlic is softened and fragrant. Add the tomato puree and cook until it is dry and pasty, and the edges have begun to caramelize. Pour in stock and scrape pan to deglaze. Cook until reduced by half.

Place the cooked livers and the reduced liquid in the bowl of a food processor. Add a generous pinch of salt and puree. While the machine is running, add hunks of the remaining the butter piece by piece. Continue to puree until smooth. Place the mixture in a sieve over a bowl and press through with a rubber spatula. This will guarantee a nice, smooth pâté. Taste, and add salt as needed. Put the pâté into a decorative serving container and press a sheet of plastic wrap directly onto the surface to prevent oxidation. Refrigerate for a couple of hours to allow the pâté to set.

Meanwhile, mix together the onions, vinegar, sugar, and salt in a nonreactive, sealable container just large enough to hold them. Seal the container and let stand at room temperature for an hour or refrigerate for up to 2 weeks.

When ready to serve, bring pâté to room temperature. Serve with grilled country bread and pickled onions.

Recipe courtesy of Rob Levitt, owner of The Butcher & Larder (p. 310).

Choose Your Own Corn Dogs
with Apple Slaw & Ale Syrup

At Hearty—owned by Dan Smith and Steve McDonagh of "Party Line With the Hearty Boys"—it's rabbit sausage hidden inside honey-mustard corn batter. Feel free to substitute your favorite encased meat.

Serves 6

3 raw rabbit, game, or other sausages
¼ cup cornmeal
½ cup flour
¼ teaspoon salt
¼ teaspoon baking powder

1 tablespoon sugar
¼ cup milk
1 egg
1 tablespoon Dijon mustard
1 tablespoon honey

Apple slaw

2 cups green cabbage, coarsely shredded
1 cup red cabbage, coarsely shredded
1 cup carrot, peeled and shredded
4 green onions, chopped
1 Granny Smith apple, cored and chopped

2 garlic cloves
¼ cup packed cilantro
¼ cup packed basil
1 cup mayonnaise
2 tablespoons rice wine vinegar
Juice of 1 lemon
2 teaspoons hot sauce
Salt and fresh-cracked pepper, to taste

Founder's Red Rye Ale syrup

2 bottles Founder's Red Rye Ale or other ale
1 cup sugar

2 teaspoons salt
1 teaspoon cayenne

1 quart vegetable oil

Special equipment: 10-inch skewers

It's best to begin by making the slaw, as it needs to refrigerate for at least two hours. Combine the cabbages, carrot, green onions, and apple in a large bowl. Place the garlic cloves, cilantro, and basil in the bowl of a food processor and pulse until finely chopped. Add the mayonnaise, vinegar, lemon juice, and hot sauce and season with salt and pepper, to taste. Pulse until combined. Mix dressing with the cabbage mixture, cover, and refrigerate.

To make the batter, combine the cornmeal, flour, salt, baking powder, and sugar in a mixing bowl. In a separate bowl, whisk together the milk, egg, Dijon mustard, and honey. Pour the wet ingredients into the dry and stir until smooth and thoroughly mixed.

Heat vegetable oil in a deep pot over medium heat.

Meanwhile, place the ale, sugar, salt, and cayenne into a saucepan over high heat. Stir until the sugar dissolves and it comes to a full boil. Lower heat to medium and allow to reduce, simmering until thick but still pourable (about 10 minutes).

Cut each sausage in half and skewer with a 10-inch skewer. Dip the sausage into the batter and drop into the hot oil. Fry until golden (about 3 minutes). Drain on paper towels and plate individually, topping slaw with a battered dog and drizzling the dish with warm ale syrup.

Recipe courtesy of Dan Smith and Steve McDonagh, owners-operators of Hearty (p. 48).

Gougères

At Bin 36, these addictive, cloud-like cheese puffs are served with truffle honey. Have them with a glass (or two) of bubbly.

Makes about 75

2 cups milk

2 sticks butter

1 ½ teaspoons paprika

¾ teaspoon cayenne

1 ½ teaspoons salt

¾ teaspoon black pepper

2 cups flour

4 whole eggs

6 ounces (about 1 ½ cups) Parmesan, shredded

1 ½ ounces (about ¼ cup) Gruyère, shredded

Special equipment:

Pastry bag with wide, plain tip (If you don't have a pastry bag, you can use heavy-duty freezer bag with a snipped corner in its place. You may also spoon the dough onto the parchment paper.)

Parchment paper

Preheat oven to 375° F. Bring milk, butter, paprika, cayenne, salt, and black pepper to boil in large pot over medium heat. Add all of the flour at once, stirring with a wooden spoon until it is thoroughly incorporated. Continue stirring until it is doughlike and pulls away from the side of the pan to form a ball.

Remove from heat and let cool slightly.

Transfer to a stand mixer. On low speed, drop in one egg at a time, waiting for each to be fully incorporated before adding another. Stir in cheeses and pipe 1-inch-round mounds of dough onto parchment-lined baking trays. Bake 20 to 25 minutes, or until golden.

Adapted recipe courtesy of John Caputo, executive chef/partner of Bin 36 (p. 117) and bin wine cafe (p. 72).

Seared Scallops with Chorizo, Potatoes & Green Onions

This tapas-style dish from Rick Bayless appears on season seven of "Mexico—One Plate at a Time."

Serves 6 to 8

4 medium red-skin boiling potatoes, cut into ½-inch pieces

1 tablespoon salt

2 tablespoons vegetable or olive oil

1 pound scallops, cleaned and patted dry

Salt and fresh-ground black pepper, to taste

12 ounces (about 1½ cups) fresh Mexican chorizo sausage, casing removed

4 large green onions, roots and outer leaves trimmed, cut into ½-inch pieces

Warm corn or flour tortillas

Fill a large, 4-quart saucepan half-full of water. Add a tablespoon of salt and bring to a boil. Add the potatoes and simmer over medium heat until tender (about 12 minutes). Drain.

Add the oil to a large, heavy, nonstick skillet on medium-high heat. Season scallops with salt and pepper. When the pan is sizzling, add the scallops in a single layer. Sear—turning halfway through—until golden (about 2 minutes total). Remove and reserve.

Add the chorizo and green onions to the same pan. Cook over medium heat, breaking up any clumps of chorizo, just until the sausage has rendered its fat (6 or 7 minutes). Add the drained potatoes and continue cooking, occasionally scraping up any sticky bits, until the potatoes begin to look crusty-brown (about 15 minutes). Meanwhile, cut the scallops into ½-inch pieces so they resemble the diced potatoes. When the potatoes are browned, return the scallops to the pan. Mix everything together and heat through. Scoop the mixture into a bowl and serve immediately with warm tortillas.

Recipe courtesy of Rick Bayless, 2010, owner-operator of Frontera Grill (p. 126), Topolobampo (p. 158), and XOCO (p. 162).

Shaved Squash Salad

Locally sourced, seasonal ingredients inform Chris Pandel's menu at The Bristol, where this salad is the perfect way to usher in autumn.

Serves 4

- **6 cups butternut squash, peeled and seeded**
- **Kosher salt, to taste**
- **1 to 2 tablespoons of lemon juice, or as needed**
- **1 tablespoon pumpkin seeds, toasted**
- **1 tablespoon sunflower seeds, toasted**

- **3 tablespoons pomegranate seeds**
- **6 fresh basil leaves, torn**
- **6 fresh mint Leaves, torn**
- **2 heads endive, sliced into thin ribbons**
- **2 ounces Dante or dry jack cheese, shaved into shards**
- **1 amaretto cookie**

Slice the squash lengthwise into 1-inch-wide pieces. Using a vegetable peeler, peel squash lengthwise into super-thin strips, until the squash is too thin to peel, leaving you with a big pile of light, fluffy, raw squash.

Place squash in a large mixing bowl. Lightly season with kosher salt and lemon juice, to taste. Gently toss and marinate the squash in the refrigerator for at least 20 minutes.

When ready to serve, remove the squash from the refrigerator. Add pumpkin, sunflower, and pomegranate seeds, along with the basil, mint, endive, and cheese.

Taste the dish for seasoning and add another squirt of lemon juice to brighten it up if need be. Toss to combine.

Marinate for five minutes. Divide evenly between four individual serving bowls. Using a microplane, generously grate the amaretto cookie atop each salad. Serve immediately.

Recipe courtesy of Chris Pandel, executive chef of The Bristol (p. 76).

Apple Salad with Pickled Onions, Gouda Croutons & Tangy Mustard Seeds

Nicole Pederson of C-House likes to use a variety of variably cut heirloom apples for this punchy salad, which often appears on the menu during harvest season.

Serves 6

4 apples of various varieties, cut into slices, matchsticks, and wedges just before plating

½ pound baby mustard greens, such as Ruby Streak, or arugula

Cider vinaigrette

¼ cup shallots, minced

¼ cup cider vinegar

2 tablespoons Dijon mustard

2 teaspoons honey

1 cup olive oil

Sea salt and pepper, to taste

Pickled Vidalia onions

1 Vidalia onion, very thinly sliced

3 tablespoons honey

1 tablespoon salt

½ cup water

½ cup cider vinegar

Pickled mustard seeds

¼ cup mustard seeds

¼ cup cider vinegar

¼ cup honey

Water, to cover

Gouda croutons

½ loaf whole-wheat sourdough, crust removed and torn into large chunks
Kosher salt and pepper, to taste

2½ tablespoons extra-virgin olive oil
3 tablespoons grated Gouda, such as Holland's Family, plus additional to top salad

Macerate the shallots in the cider vinegar for 30 minutes. Whisk in the Dijon, honey and—slowly—the olive oil. Season with sea salt and pepper, to taste.

To pickle the Vidalias, place onions in a small bowl. Prepare the pickling liquid by combining the honey, salt, water, and cider vinegar in a small saucepan. Bring it to a simmer. Remove from the heat and immediately pour over onions. Allow mixture to sit at room temperature until cooled. Refrigerate until you're ready to assemble the salad.

Meanwhile, pickle the mustard seeds by combining all ingredients in a small saucepan. Simmer for 20 to 30 minutes or until tender, adding only enough water to cover and balance the flavor.

Preheat oven to 350° F. Toss bread, salt, pepper, and olive oil together in a medium bowl. Place bread in a single layer on a large baking sheet and toast in the oven for 5 minutes. Toss with 3 tablespoons of grated Gouda and cook for 5 to 8 minutes more, until crisp outside, soft on the inside, and just a little greasy.

To serve salad family-style, combine apples, greens, and drained, pickled onions in a large bowl. Season with salt and pepper and dress with the cider vinaigrette. Add croutons and toss again. Using a vegetable peeler, shave Gouda over the top of the salad and drizzle with mustard seeds.

Recipe courtesy of Nicole Pederson, executive chef of C-House (p. 81).

Seared Tuna with Shaved Fennel and Chermoula Vinaigrette

Kristine Subido of WAVE has an affinity for global flavors. Here, she uses versatile North African chermoula to enliven ahi.

Serves 4

2 pounds sushi-grade ahi tuna steak

1 tablespoon green cardamom, ground and quickly toasted until fragrant

Salt and pepper, to taste

2 tablespoons olive oil, divided use, plus additional for brushing grill

2 oranges, 1 peeled, white pith removed and segmented

1 whole fennel bulb, shaved or sliced very thinly

½ red onion, sliced very thinly

1 tablespoon chopped cilantro

Chermoula vinaigrette

½ cup of lemon juice

½ cup of fresh parsley, chopped

½ cup cilantro, chopped

6 cloves garlic, finely minced

1 tablespoon paprika

2 teaspoons ground cumin

½ teaspoon cayenne pepper

1½ cups fruity olive oil

Preheat grill on high heat.

Rub tuna steaks liberally with ground cardamom, salt, pepper, and a tablespoon of extra-virgin olive oil. Rub grill grates with olive oil to prevent sticking. Sear tuna steaks on all sides for about 30 seconds per side. Remove and allow to rest.

To prepare the salad, whisk juice of 1 orange with remaining tablespoon of olive oil in a medium bowl. Season with salt and pepper to taste, and toss with the shaved fennel, red onion, orange segments, and cilantro.

For the chermoula, whisk first 7 ingredients together in a medium bowl. Slowly whisk in the olive oil.

Slice the tuna steaks into ½-inch inch pieces. Plate family-style or individually by spooning chermoula vinaigrette atop the fish. Finish by topping with the dressed salad. Serve immediately with additional vinaigrette for passing.

Recipe courtesy of Kristine Subido, executive chef of WAVE (p. 109) in the W Hotel-Lakeshore.

Chilled Somen Salad with Shrimp & Watermelon

Bill Kim, the maestro behind urbanbelly and Belly Shack, makes flavors sing in this sweet, spicy, and tangy triumph.

Serves 6

- **1 pound somen noodles or angel-hair pasta**
- **1 pound raw shrimp, cleaned and peeled**
- **3 tablespoons vegetable oil**
- **Salt, as needed**
- **½ jalapeño, minced**
- **6 cloves of garlic**
- **½ cup fish sauce**

- **¼ cup white vinegar**
- **6 tablespoons sugar**
- **2 tablespoons mint, torn**
- **2 tablespoons cilantro, chopped**
- **4 cups of seedless watermelon, cut into chunks**
- **2 tablespoons basil, torn**
- **½ cup bean sprouts**

Cook noodles in salted boiling water according to package directions. Drain and chill.

Rinse shrimp. Pat dry using paper towels. Heat half of the oil in large sauté pan on medium-high. Lightly season shrimp with salt. Cook half at a time, stirring occasionally until done (about 2 minutes total per batch). Repeat process with remaining oil and shrimp. Set aside to cool to room temperature.

Whisk together jalapeño, garlic, fish sauce, vinegar, and

sugar until combined. Place the noodles in a large bowl and lightly dress using approximately half of the vinaigrette.

In a separate bowl, combine mint, cilantro, watermelon, and cooked shrimp. Toss with remaining dressing.

Place noodles on serving platter. Top with watermelon and shrimp mixture and garnish with basil and bean sprouts.

Recipe courtesy of Bill Kim, chef-owner of urbanbelly (p. 66) and Belly Shack (p. 38).

Honeycrisp-Burrata Salad with Peppadew Peppers

The mix of flavors, textures, and colors give this summery dish centerpiece appeal.

½ pound burrata cheese (about 2 balls), in 1-inch-thick slices*

2 medium heirloom tomatoes, such as Black Krim, sliced

1 Honeycrisp apple, cored and thinly sliced

Zest of 1 lemon

1½ tablespoons peppadew peppers, minced

1 teaspoon honey

1½ tablespoons olive oil

2 teaspoons balsamic vinegar

Flaky sea salt and fresh-cracked pepper, to taste

Serves 4

Alternate burrata, tomato and apple slices on a platter. Shower with lemon zest, scatter with peppers, and drizzle with honey, olive oil, and vinegar. Season with salt and pepper and serve.

*Note: Burrata is available at well-stocked cheese shops and at Freddy's Pizza (p. 226).

Recipe courtesy of Jennifer Olvera.

Chestnut & Lavender Soup

Seasons inform the menu at Vie, where Paul Virant delivers a dose of comfort with this rich, silky soup.

Serves 6

½ cup rendered duck fat or
   pork fat*
4 tablespoons butter
3½ onions, finely chopped
2 stalks celery, finely chopped
⅓ cup lavender, minced

¼ to ½ cup honey
3½ pounds steamed, whole
   chestnuts**
1 gallon chicken stock
1½ cups heavy cream

Heat rendered fat and butter in a large stockpot set to medium. Add onions and celery and sweat, stirring occasionally until soft and translucent (about 15 minutes).

Raise temperature to medium-high and add lavender and honey. Allow to caramelize, stirring often (about 7 minutes). Reduce heat and add chestnuts. Sauté over medium heat for another 5 to 10 minutes, until flavors meld and chestnuts begin to take on pan flavors.

Add stock and simmer for 1 hour. Allow to cool slightly. Place liquid in a blender and puree with the cream, working in batches if need be. Strain through a sieve and serve warm.

* Note: Rendered duck fat may be purchased at Paulina Market *(see page 313)*; and pork fat is often found at Mexican markets.

** Note: Ready-to-use chestnuts may be purchased seasonally at Trader Joe's or at Williams-Sonoma in store or online.

Recipe courtesy of Paul Virant, executive chef-owner of Vie (p. 241) and chef-partner of Perennial Virant (p. 100).

Garbanzo Bean Soup with Falafel, Pickled Asian Pear & Sumac

At Blackbird, Paul Kahan christens this hearty stew with a caramelized egg yolk.

Serves 6

4 cups dried garbanzo beans

½ cup plus 1½ tablespoons rice-bran or canola oil, divided use

1 large fennel bulb, diced medium

1 clove garlic, peeled and smashed

2 whole star anise

Salt, to taste

1 tablespoon butter, for later use

Falafel

4 cups garbanzo beans, picked through, rinsed and soaked overnight

2 cloves garlic, minced

1 teaspoon salt, or to taste

½ teaspoon cayenne pepper, or to taste

½ cup canola oil for frying, plus additional as needed

Pickled pear

2 Asian pears, peeled, cored, and finely diced

3 tablespoons honey, plus additional as needed

4 tablespoons cider or pear cider vinegar

Pinch of salt, to taste

Ground sumac, to garnish

Fresh chervil leaves, to garnish

Pick through garbanzo beans, removing any stones, stems, and discolored or damaged beans. Rinse under running water until the water runs clean. Soak in water overnight in the refrigerator, taking care to cover the beans by at least 3 inches. (Note that you will need to follow the same method for the falafel as well.)

Using a colander, strain soaked garbanzo beans and rinse again several times.

Heat 1½ tablespoons oil in a large stockpot over medium heat. Add fennel, garlic, and star anise and sweat until soft (about 10 minutes). Add garbanzo beans and fill pot with enough water to generously cover beans. Bring to a boil and reduce heat to a simmer. Cook until beans are very soft (about 1 to 1½ hours).

Remove star anise from pot. Drain, reserving some of the cooking liquid. Place cooked beans and fennel in a blender and puree, adding reserved cooking water until the mixture is very smooth. While blending, stream in about ½ cup rice-bran oil or canola oil into soup base. When a soup-like consistency is achieved, season with salt, to taste. Pass mixture through a fine sieve and chill.

For falafel, sort, rinse, and soak beans as above. Add uncooked beans to a food processor, along with garlic, salt, and cayenne. Pulse, adding a bit more oil, until beans are finely ground and mixture is pasty.

Prepare the pickling liquid for the pears by whisking together honey and vinegar. Season with salt, to taste. Add the pears and toss to coat. Reserve.

To assemble soup, heat butter in a stockpot over medium heat. Add reserved soup puree and bring to a boil while whisking. Add water as needed to adjust to soup-like consistency. Taste and season with additional salt if necessary.

Heat ½ cup oil in a large frying pan over medium-high heat. Form the falafel mixture into balls and fry in oil in batches of six, turning occasionally until outside is crisp and golden brown on all sides (about 4 minutes).

While the falafel is cooking, spoon pickled pears into the bottom of warmed dishes, and place a small pile of sumac next to the pears. Place cooked falafel atop the pears and garnish with chervil leaves. Serve soup in a separate carafe and pour tableside.

Recipe courtesy of Paul Kahan, executive chef-partner of Blackbird (p. 117), avec (p. 114), The Publican (p. 149), and Big Star (p. 72).

Guajillo-Tortilla Soup

Frank Brunacci of Sixteen can't take this beloved soup off the menu. It's so good, in fact, that he eats it for lunch most days.

Serves 4

½ cup olive oil

1 onion, roughly chopped

2 dried Guajillo chiles, seeds and stem removed, and chopped

3 fresh corn tortillas, roughly chopped

Salt, to taste

1 bunch fresh cilantro, leaves removed and chopped

2 tomatoes, roughly chopped

4½ cups chicken stock

1 avocado, peeled, pitted, and chopped

½ cup chicharrones (fried pork rinds)*

2 tablespoons sour cream

1 lime, cut into wedges

Heat olive oil in a stockpot over medium-high heat. Add the onion and sauté until slightly browned (about 5 minutes). Place chiles in the pot and continue to cook for another two minutes. Add tortillas into the mix and stir constantly until they're crispy. Taste and season with salt, and add most of the chopped cilantro. Continue cooking for about 30 seconds and add tomatoes, cooking for another 4 minutes. Pour in the chicken stock and allow soup to reduce by a quarter. Working in batches, puree soup in blender until very smooth. To serve, evenly divide chopped avocado and chicharrones in the bottom of each of four bowls. Ladle in soup and finish with a sprinkle of the remaining cilantro, a small dollop of sour cream, and a squirt of fresh lime juice.

*Note: Freshly fried chicharrones may be purchased at many Mexican markets and at Don Pedro Carnitas (see p. 172).

Recipe courtesy of Frank Brunacci, executive chef of Sixteen (p. 153).

Grass-Fed Beef Brisket

Sarah Stegner and George Bumbaris of Prairie Grass Cafe and Prairie Fire serve this soul-warming dish with seasonal vegetables, such as a medley of diced carrots, turnips, butternut squash, and celery.

Serves 8 to 10

1 7- to 8-pound piece grass-fed beef brisket

Salt and fresh-ground black pepper, to taste

1 tablespoon olive oil, plus additional, as needed

4 cups onions, diced

1 cup carrots, peeled and diced

1 cup celery, diced

2 tablespoons garlic, minced

4 cups whole, canned tomatoes

4 bay leaves

4 sprigs fresh thyme

8 cups chicken stock

½ cup brown sugar

Juice from 1 lime

2 tablespoons sweet butter

Special equipment: Parchment paper

Preheat oven to 200° F. Season the meat with salt and pepper. Heat olive oil in a large roasting pan over high heat and brown the brisket on both sides until a nice crust forms. Remove meat from pan and reserve.

Add additional olive oil if necessary. Reduce heat to medium and add the onions, carrots, and celery and sauté until vegetables begin to soften (about 5 minutes). Add the garlic and cook another minute. Pour in the tomatoes and cook until they begin to break down. Toss in the bay leaves and thyme, followed by the chicken stock and brown sugar. Return the brisket to the pan. The liquid should cover the brisket.

Cover the meat and liquid with parchment paper and top with a rack to hold it in place. Place meat in oven and braise slowly for 12 hours.

Remove the brisket from the liquid and allow to cool. Strain the liquid and discard the solids. Just before serving, return liquid to a boil. Add the lime juice and the butter and season to taste.

Slice the cooled brisket about ¼-inch thick across the grain. Return to sauce and simmer until heated through.

Recipe courtesy of Sarah Stegner and George Bumbaris, chefs and co-owners of Prairie Grass Cafe (p. 217) and Prairie Fire (p. 147).

HAVE IT YOUR WAY

"Cravers" are paired with "makers," courtesy of http://CookItFor .Us, a service-oriented website that allows people to enjoy home-cooked fare—without wielding a knife. Visitors share recipes they crave, whether found online, in print, or passed down through generations. Then, the dishes are prepared by chefs, restaurants, or bakeries for a prearranged fee. Made meals may be picked up or delivered. At the customer's request, they may also be enjoyed at the maker's place of business or made in the customer's home.

Lamb Pie with Vidalia Onion Sauce & Arugula-French Breakfast Radish Salad

Zealous's Michael Taus takes the nip out of chilly nights with this welcoming, company-appropriate wonder.

Serves 4

1 pound trimmed lamb leg meat, cut in 1-inch cubes

Salt and pepper, to taste

1 teaspoon garlic-infused oil or olive oil

2 tablespoons canola oil

1 tablespoon flat-leaf Italian parsley, chopped

Dough

1½ cups all purpose flour

1 teaspoon kosher salt

1 cup cold butter, chopped

⅓ cup ice water

1 egg, whisked, for brushing on pastry

Onion sauce

2 tablespoons canola oil

6 tablespoons unsalted butter, divided use

2 large Vidalia onions (about 6 ounces, total) peeled and roughly chopped

2 cloves garlic, peeled

1 tablespoon honey

1 tablespoon sherry, such as Lustau East India Solera

2 cups chicken stock

Kosher salt and fresh-ground white pepper, to taste

Arugula-radish salad

1 teaspoon grape-seed oil

1 cup arugula, cleaned and
dried

½ cup French breakfast or
regular radishes, halved and
julienned

Rice-wine vinaigrette

1 tablespoon rice vinegar

1 tablespoon grape-seed oil

1 teaspoon chives, chopped

Salt and fresh-cracked pepper,
to taste

Special equipment

4 3½-inch ring molds

parchment paper

In a large bowl, season lamb with salt, pepper, and garlic oil and toss to combine. Heat canola oil in a large sauté pan set to high heat. When it is smoking, sear lamb, turning occasionally until browned on all sides. Remove from heat, add parsley, and stir. Place meat in a colander to strain off excess oil and juices. Lamb should be rare inside. Cool to room temperature.

Meanwhile, make the dough. Place the flour, salt, and butter in a food processor outfitted with a metal blade. Process for one minute. Slowly add the water until it is just combined. The dough should be dotted with visible pieces of butter. Form into a ball, wrap in plastic wrap, and place in the refrigerator for an hour to chill.

While the dough is chilling, prepare the onion sauce. Heat oil and 3 tablespoons of the butter on medium heat in a heavy-bottomed pan. Add onions and garlic and sauté, stirring occasionally, until golden brown (about 10 minutes). Add honey and stir, cooking for a few minutes longer to caramelize. Deglaze pan with sherry, dislodging any browned bits. Add chicken stock and bring to a boil. Reduce heat and simmer for 30 minutes. Transfer to a blender, along with the remaining 3 tablespoons of butter. Season with salt and pepper and blend until smooth. Strain mixture and cover to keep warm.

Spray ring molds with nonstick cooking spray and place on a parchment-lined sheet pan. On a floured surface, knead the dough until it is pliable. Roll out dough to a thickness of ⅛ inch. Cut into 8 circles slightly larger than the ring molds.

Fill each mold with one round of tart dough, allowing for overhang. Fill each with lamb mixture. Lay another circle of tart dough on top of the filled pies and crimp the edges to seal. Place in the refrigerator for 20 minutes.

Preheat oven to 375° F. Lightly brush the top of each meat pie with egg wash. Bake for 30 minutes or until browned. Cool slightly and remove from rings.

To make arugula-radish salad, heat grape-seed oil in a medium saucepan over moderate heat. Add arugula and radishes, tossing until warm to touch. Quickly make the vinaigrette by whisking together rice-wine vinegar, grape-seed oil, and chives. Season with salt and pepper. Toss radishes and arugula with vinaigrette.

To plate, place a large circle of warm Vidalia sauce on plate. Place meat pie on top, and finish with arugula-radish salad. Serve immediately.

Recipe courtesy of Michael Taus, chef-owner of Zealous (p. 162).

Milk-Braised Pork Shoulder with Mashed Potatoes

Hearty and comforting, this tender porcine preparation from The Purple Pig was a hit—right out of the gate.

Serves 6

3 to 4-pound pork shoulder, bone removed and cut into 8-ounce portions
1½ tablespoons olive oil
Kosher salt and pepper, to taste
2 onions, peeled and quartered
1 carrot, peeled and cut into large chunks

1 rib celery, cut into 3 large pieces
1 gallon of milk
1 gallon of pork or chicken stock
1 small bunch fresh thyme
5 bay leaves

Mashed potatoes

1¼ pounds peeled Russet potatoes, cut into 1½-inch chunks
¼ cup cream, warm

4 teaspoons butter, warm
Salt and pepper, to taste

Special equipment

Kitchen string

Preheat oven to 350° F.

Tie a piece of string around each piece of pork to maintain its shape while cooking. Heat oil in a large Dutch oven set to medium-high heat. Liberally season pork with salt and pepper. When pan is sizzling-hot, sear meat in batches, turning occasionally until browned on all sides (about 5 to 7 minutes per batch). Reserve.

Add vegetables to pan, sautéing until softened (about 15 minutes). Add milk, stock, thyme, and bay leaves. Adjust seasonings and bring to a boil. Return meat to pan. Cover and place in oven to braise until tender (2½ to 3 hours).

Meanwhile, place potatoes in a large pot and cover with cold water. Season aggressively with salt. Bring to a boil and cook until potatoes are tender (about 15 minutes). Drain potatoes and mash them with cream and butter. Adjust seasonings and cover to keep warm.

Remove pork from the oven. Discard kitchen string and cover to keep warm. Discard bay leaves and thyme stalks from milk gravy. Working in batches, puree vegetables and cooking liquid. Strain puree and return to pan. Reduce over medium heat until it achieves a saucy consistency (about 20 to 30 minutes).

To plate, top mashed potatoes with a hunk of pork and finish dish with milk gravy.

Recipe courtesy of Jimmy Bannos Jr., executive chef-partner of The Purple Pig (p. 101).

Roast Chicken with Red Grapes, Caramelized Pearl Onions, & Port Pan Gravy

Simple enough for a weeknight supper, this tangy, sweet chicken dish also has celebratory appeal.

Serves 4

- 1 3- to 4-pound skin-on chicken, cut into eight pieces
- 2½ tablespoons olive oil
- Kosher salt and fresh-cracked pepper, to taste
- 2½ tablespoons balsamic vinegar
- 1 cup large red seedless grapes
- 2 garlic cloves, sliced very thinly
- 1 cup pearl onions, peeled and halved
- 3 tablespoons port
- 1 tablespoon unsalted butter

Preheat oven to 375° F. Place chicken in a large oven- and stovetop-safe roasting pan. Drizzle with olive oil and generously season with salt and pepper. Spoon balsamic vinegar evenly over the top.

Place chicken in the oven and roast for 15 minutes. Baste with pan juices and add grapes, garlic, and pearl onions, tossing with juices to coat. Return to oven and roast for another 30 to 40 minutes, basting periodically,

or until cooked through and juices run clear. Set meat, onions, and grapes on a serving platter and cover to keep warm.

To make gravy, place roasting pan on the stovetop over medium heat. Add port to the pan, and scrape the bottom of the pan to dislodge flavorful, browned bits. Simmer until reduced to the consistency of sauce (about 7 minutes). Swirl in butter to finish the sauce. Serve immediately, passing gravy.

Recipe courtesy of Jennifer Olvera.

Goat Cheesecake with Candied Fennel & Blood-Orange Curd

Pastry chef Hillary Blanchard of one sixtyblue finishes this surprising, not-too-sweet finale with candied hazelnuts.

Serves 10

16 ounces cream cheese
16 ounces goat cheese, room
  temperature
4 ounces sugar

1 whole vanilla bean, scraped
2 tablespoon lemon juice
4 eggs
1 cup cream

Candied fennel

2 cups water
2 cups sugar

2 bulbs fresh
  fennel (shaved)

Blood orange curd

8 egg yolks
½ cup blood-orange puree or
  juice
1 tablespoon orange zest

½ cup sugar
5 tablespoons butter, room
  temperature

Garnishes

1 tablespoon tarragon, finely
  chopped

1 orange, peeled, white pith
  removed and segmented

Preheat oven to 325° F. Using a hand-held mixer, beat cream and goat cheeses on medium speed until light and fluffy. With mixer running on low speed, add the sugar, contents of vanilla-bean pod, lemon juice, and eggs. Scrape side and bottom of mixing bowl thoroughly. Slowly add the cream and mix until combined.

Grease a 9-inch springform pan and wrap the bottom and sides with foil; this will protect the cake while it is baking in a water bath. Pour cheesecake batter into pan. Place in a roasting pan filled with enough hot water to reach half way up the sides of the cake pan, adding additional hot water as needed. Bake until the edges puff slightly and the center is set (about 1½ hours). Remove cheesecake from the water bath and cool completely.

To candy the fennel, bring water and sugar to a boil over medium-high heat. Add fennel and reduce heat to low., Cook until fennel is tender and translucent and the liquid is syrupy (about 35 minutes). Strain and cool completely, reserving fennel syrup for later use.

Prepare curd by bringing a pot of water to boil over medium-high heat. Meanwhile, whisk egg yolks, blood-orange puree or juice, zest, and sugar in heat-safe bowl until smooth. When water reaches a simmer, reduce heat to low and cook curd mixture in bowl set over water bath until thickened (this happens at about 170° F). Do not allow to boil. Remove from heat when it is thick enough to coat the back of a spoon. Stir in butter and strain. Cover with plastic wrap and cool over ice bath. Refrigerate until ready to use.

To serve, run a knife along the outside of the cheesecake. Release the springform pan and slice the cake, wiping knife between cuts. Garnish plate with blood-orange curd. Place a slice of cheesecake on top of curd, alongside a teaspoon of fennel and an orange segment. Drizzle plate with fennel syrup, sprinkle with tarragon, and serve.

Adapted recipe courtesy of Hillary Blanchard, pastry chef of one sixtyblue (p. 143).

Butterscotch Pot de Crème

A master of both sweet and savory, Heather Terhune of
Sable Kitchen & Bar serves her finale in a Mason jar with
brown butter–pecan shortbread and candied kumquats.

Serves 6

- 6 tablespoons water
- 8 tablespoons sugar, divided use
- 1½ cups heavy cream
- 1 vanilla bean, split and
  scraped
- ¼ teaspoon salt
- 4 egg yolks

Mix 6 tablespoons water and 2 tablespoons sugar in a medium saucepan. Stirring
constantly, caramelize the sugar over medium heat until amber in color.

Remove from the pan from heat and add the heavy cream and the contents of
vanilla bean. Heat the cream mixture on medium, stirring until the caramel
completely dissolves.

In a medium saucepan, whisk together the remaining 6 tablespoons of sugar, salt,
and egg yolks. Temper the hot cream into the egg mixture by gradually whisking
in cream a few tablespoons at a time. Continue to cook over medium heat, stirring constantly until the mixture thickens and coats the back of a spoon. Strain
mixture through a fine sieve. Divide into individual glass jars or ramekins. Set
overnight in the refrigerator. Serve chilled.

Recipe courtesy of Heather Terhune, executive chef of Sable Kitchen & Bar (p. 151).

Goat-Cheese Bavaroise with Brown-Sugar Cake & Blueberry Compote

Winner of Top Chef *season 4, Stephanie Izard of Girl & the Goat proves dessert is a centerpiece-worthy affair.*

Serves 6

4½ cups heavy cream
1 sheet gelatin, such as King Arthur brand
2 tablespoons maple syrup

5 ounces goat cheese, room temperature
1 egg white

Brown-sugar cake

2 tablespoons butter
⅔ cup light brown sugar, packed
1 teaspoon vanilla extract

⅓ teaspoon salt
1 egg
½ teaspoon baking powder
½ cup flour, sifted

Blueberry compote

½ stalk lemongrass
2 tablespoons ginger
1 lemon, juiced and zested
½ lime, juiced and zested

1½ cups water
⅔ cup sugar
2 cups blueberries
Raw sugar (for garnish)

Heat about 1 cup of cream in a small saucepan just until warm. While the cream is heating, bloom sheet gelatin in a bowl of cold water for 5 to 10 minutes. Gently squeeze water from gelatin and add to warm cream. Stir until completely dissolved.

In the bowl of a mixer fitted with a whisk attachment, combine the maple syrup and warmed cream mixture. Add goat cheese and whip until smooth. Add the rest of the heavy cream and continue whipping until smooth and fluffy. Place in a large bowl in preparation for the next stage.

Using the mixer outfitted with the whisk attachment, beat the egg white to form stiff peaks and fold into the reserved goat-cheese mixture. Chill in refrigerator.

Preheat oven to 325° F. Grease an 8-inch square glass baking dish.

Make the cake by combining the butter, sugar, vanilla, and salt in a large pan over medium-low heat, stirring until the sugar has just dissolved. Remove from heat and allow to cool slightly. Add the egg and vigorously whisk to combine, taking care that the sugar mixture is not too hot or it will scramble the egg. Add baking powder and sifted flour and stir until combined and free of lumps. Pour batter in baking dish and bake for about 20 minutes, until a toothpick inserted into the center comes out clean. Remove from oven and cool completely.

To prepare blueberry compote, add the lemongrass, ginger, lemon and lime juices, zests, water, and sugar to a saucepan set to medium heat. Bring to a boil. Remove from heat and allow to steep *for an hour. Strain, discard solids and return liquid to the pan. Add half of the blueberries and simmer 15 to 20 minutes or until thickened. Remove from heat and add the rest of the blueberries. Chill immediately over an ice bath.*

Assemble dessert in individual serving dishes as you would a trifle, beginning with a layer of cake. Top with a few spoons of blueberry compote, followed by goat cheese bavaroise. Sprinkle with raw sugar and serve.

Recipe courtesy of Stephanie Izard, executive chef of Girl & the Goat (p. 128).

Chocolate Bread Pudding

Everything a dessert should be—gooey, rich, and chocolaty—this signature sweet from Rockit Bar & Grill is a fan fave.

Serves 8

1-pound loaf chocolate bread, such as Red Hen Bread's bittersweet chocolate

7 whole eggs

1½ cups granulated sugar

2 cups heavy cream

1 teaspoon vanilla extract

Vanilla-bean ice cream

Hot fudge sauce

Preheat oven to 325° F. Cut bread into 1-inch cubes. Spread in a single layer on a baking sheet and toast in oven for 5 minutes. Allow to cool to room temperature. In a large bowl, whisk eggs, sugar, heavy cream, and vanilla extract. Grease an 8-inch square baking pan and add toasted bread cubes.

Pour egg mixture on top. Press bread down into mixture, as the bread will begin to float. Allow to soak for 20 minutes, pressing the bread down every 5 minutes until it absorbs the liquid. Bake for 30 minutes or until center is set.

Allow to cool for 15 minutes and serve topped with vanilla ice cream and hot fudge sauce.

Recipe courtesy of Amanda Downing, chef de cuisine of Rockit Bar & Grill (p. 149).

Go, Go Gadget

As any good cook knows, using quality tools makes all the difference in the world. Thankfully, you can fulfill your needs (and wants) at these spots around town.

Northwestern Cutlery Supply (312-421-3666, www.northwesterncutlery.net) sells everything from two-handled cheese knives to extra-fine strainers, cast-iron cookware from Le Creuset, and Vitamix blenders. Knife-sharpening services are provided as well.

Head to **The Chopping Block** (see page 387) for stainless-steel All-Clad pans, baking dishes, and gourmet goodies, like saffron salt.

1730 Outlet Company (773-871-4331; www.1730outlet.com) has two Chicago-area locations selling TAG products, such as cake stands, chip and dip sets, kitchen towels, and dishes at rock-bottom prices.

P.O.S.H. (312-280-1602; www.poshchicago.com) stocks everything from vintage hotel silver to flea-market finds. Visits may yield a floral ashtray from Belgium, nostalgic Schweppes "Indian tonic" nut dishes from France, or mouth-blown Italian Army carafes.

Dominic's Kitchen Store in Park Ridge (847-698-1255; www.dominicskitchenstore.com) is a chef-y shop brimming with stand mixers, graphite-gray toasters, canning necessities, and everything else under the sun.

Woks 'n' Things (312-842-0701), a Chinatown treasure trove, sells not only its namesake implements, but also professional-grade cookware, chopsticks, sushi-making supplies, and pre-seasoned woks.

Culinary Instruction

Some people want to sit and be served; others like to play with their food. For the latter, hands-on culinary instruction—from basic to specialized and advanced—is offered at formal institutions, restaurant kitchens, or cultural centers.

If you endeavor to roll sushi, want to whip up an exotic, company-appropriate curry—heck, even butcher a whole hog—there is a pro with expertise to impart.

Cooking Classes

Alliance Française de Chicago, 810 N. Dearborn St., Gold Coast, Chicago, IL 60654; (312) 337-1070; www.af-chicago.org. This cultural center is dedicated to fostering French relations, language, and cuisine, while offering a regular roster of wine- and gastronomy-related classes (cassoulet-concocting, wine and cheese pairings) and demonstrations for Francophiles, including those of the pint-sized variety.

Bespoke Cuisine, 1358 W. Randolph St., West Loop, Chicago, IL 60607; (312) 455-8400; www.bespokecuisine.com. A full-fledged boutique caterer at heart, this culinary hub also hosts hands-on cooking classes and parties for singles, couples, and small groups with varying themes—be it bourbon-based, backyard barbecue–themed, or comfort food–centric. Classes may be customized, namely for private events for 15 or more.

Beverly's Pantry, 1907 W. 103rd St., Beverly, Chicago, IL 60643; (773) 238-8550; www.beverlyspantry.com. As its name suggests, this spot is stocked with posh pantry picks and other desirables for the gourmand: Staub cookware, kitchen gadgets, and mustards from Stonewall Kitchen. But it's also the site of cooking classes beginning at 7 p.m. Tuesday through Thursday, classes for kids on select Saturdays, and culinary children's camps. Themes range from seasonal soups to seafood, with some classes highlighting recipes from food TV stars.

Cakewalk Chicago, 1741 W. 99th St., Beverly, Chicago, IL 60643; (773) 233-7335; www.cakewalkchicago.com. If you come to stock up on pineapple pastry filling, Guittard chocolates, and luster dust, you may be lured into signing up for a sugar-sculpting or cupcake-making course at this sweet spot. Professional diploma courses are taught, too.

Calphalon Culinary Center, 1000 W. Washington Blvd., West Loop, Chicago, IL 60607; (312) 529-0100; www.calphalonculinary-center.com. Both novices and experts plan private and corporate events amid sleek environs, where namesake cookware serves as backdrop decor, and a chef's kitchen—in which more intimate, multicourse, customized menus are prepared—mimics the experience of cooking like pros.

Chez Madeline Cooking School, 425 Woodside Ave., Hinsdale. IL 60521; (630) 655-0355; www.chezm .com. A labor of love from cookbook author Madelaine Bullwinkel, who has taught the techniques of French cooking for more than three decades, this haven hosts classes on day-to-day cooking, coupled with topical gatherings and food tours to far-reaching destinations like the Côte d'Azur.

The Chopping Block, 222 Merchandise Mart Plz., River North, Chicago, IL 60654; (312) 644-6360; www.thechoppingblock.net. Interactive, engaging options for the home cook abound at Shelley Young's state-of-the-art culinary confines. Offering everything from demos to hands-on instruction and wine classes with laid-back

COOKING CLASSES FROM
LOCAL LUMINARIES

Learn techniques from those you admire—while spending time in the back of the house—at cooking classes from local luminaries. **Vie** (see p. 241) features engaging options, such as a whole-hog butchery series and in-kitchen lunch with Sous Chef Nathan Sears. Meanwhile, Amaury Rosado of **Chef Amaury's Epicurean Affair** (see p. 222) teaches hands-on classes every other Tues in his kitchen, and **a tavola's** Dan Bocik (see p. 70) does, too. Heat-seekers might consider attending **Jimmy Bannos's** once-monthly Cajun cooking class at **Heaven on Seven** (see p. 131). Or, if you're looking to get closer to what you eat, make fast tracks for **Markethouse**, which hosts periodic cooking events attended by local farmers. Alternately, **La Madia** (see p. 136) offers an up close and personal chef's table series that includes six courses of seasonal, Italian-inspired fare—with or without wine pairings.

Not to be overlooked is French dining fixture **Le Titi de Paris** (see p. 212), where Michael and Susan Maddox regularly demonstrate hands-on Parisian preps for grownups and short stacks.

Want to explore further? Visit **www.chicagocooks.com**, a food-driven directory and event calendar with valuable information about not only cooking classes but also recipe contests and food-related gatherings.

and boot-camp bents, classes are both traditional (knife skills) and more complex (pasta workshops, sushi). Themes for children, couples, and gals' nights out are furthered by affairs like a Sunday supper club. There is a second location at 4747 N. Lincoln Ave., (773) 472-6700.

Cook Au Vin, 2256 N. Elston Ave., Bucktown, Chicago, IL 60614; (773) 489-3141; www.cook-au-vin.com. This French portal features an on-site bakery and creperie turning out custom-made, Black Dog gelato–filled cakes and crackly baguettes. To the point, it also holds four-course, BYOB cooking classes revolving around seven themed menus. Custom catering is offered as well, and this kitchen may be reserved for parties and events.

Cooking Fools, 1916 W. North Ave., Bucktown, Chicago, IL 60622; (773) 276-5565; www.cookingfools.net. Head to this gourmet kitchen for takeout when you're too lazy to cook, and sign on to learn the art of fish, rice, or dumpling cookery when you're not. There's also a nice selection of specialty goods for sale, such as Tupelo honey, global wines, and sauces from La Cocina.

Cooking with the Best Chefs, Various, (224) 353-3300; www .bestchefs.com. An ongoing catalog of classes, demonstrations, and events—offered at many locations by countless chefs throughout northern Illinois—is met by restaurant tours, day trips, and local and regional food forays at this one-stop spot. Online registration is required.

Flavour Cooking School, 7401 W. Madison St., Forest Park, IL 60130; (708) 488-0808; www.flavourcookingschool.com. Whether you're a seasoned cook or just starting out, Denise Norton's approachable meal-maker educates on seasonal topics, ethnic cuisines, and simply offers fun. Subjects, while ever changing, may include noodles, grilling, and chicken 101. Also, boot camps, couples classes, and instruction for kids as young as four are provided.

Give Me Some Sugar, 5442 W. Pensacola Ave., Portage Park, Chicago, IL 60641; (312) 546-4788; www.givesugar .com. Alessandra Sweeney reveals the sweeter side of life during once-monthly classes at TipsyCake, while offering private cake decorating and candy making instruction in-home. During the latter, participants can fancify a fondant cake.

Green City Market (773-880-1266; www.greencitymarket.org) features an endless array of culinary events during this indoor and outdoor farmers' market. Demonstrations—hosted by top toques— cover topics such as snout-to-tail cooking and the making of manly meat and potatoes–type dishes.

A Kid's Kitchen, 1603 N. Aurora Rd., Naperville, IL 60563; (630) 983-3663; www.akidskitchen.com. Little chefs get their cook on at this peanut and tree nut–free facility, hosting private and group lessons as well as birthday parties for those as young as age three. Kid-sized, professional-looking embroidered aprons and hats are available for purchase.

The Kids' Table, 2337 W. North Ave., Wicker Park, Chicago, IL 60647; (773) 235-2665; www.kids-table.com. Parents and kids find common ground at this family-friendly, health-minded locale, which offers a workshop for picky eaters, plus tutelage for tots, teens, grownups, and families. It also hosts parties and events.

Macy's on State Street, 111 N. State St., Loop, Chicago, IL 60602; (800) 329-8667; www.macys.com/culinarycouncil. The food-related activities are abundant at this spot with its own culinary council of big-name chefs. Workshops as well as tastings, food-and-wine pairings, and cookbook signings attract food fanatics to these digs. Afterward, stop at Seven on State—an upscale food court with celebs' quick-serve joints from Rick Bayless (Frontera Fresco), Takashi Yagihashi (Noodles by Takashi) and Marcus Samuelsson (Marc Burger). Macy's has several locations in the Chicago area.

Parties That Cook, Various; (888) 907-2665; www.partiesthat cook.com. Recognized for its corporate team-building events, this festive spot provides instruction in homes or at venues preordained by food-loving groups of families and friends. Additionally, hands-on cooking classes—some with a date-night focus—are hosted at spots like Charlie Baggs in the Belden.

HIDE AND SEEK

Chicago foragers are everywhere, unearthing hen-of-the-woods mushrooms from urban landscapes, purslane from cracks in city sidewalks, and mulberries along avenues. And while the everyday eater may not have the know-how to go it alone, foraging forays—led by experts—reveal edibles you might otherwise overlook.

Nance Klehm of **Spontaneous Vegetation** (www .spontaneousvegetation.net) hosts on-request workshops on topics such as composting; hosts cooking classes about raw cheese, pickling, and herbal tinctures; and guides 2-hour urban walks that unearth plants and their uses. Post-forage, participants sample herbal food, made from what they found. Contact Klehm at nettlesting@yahoo.com.

One Sister Inc. (www.onesisterinc.com) is an underground dining club and handmade pierogi company owned by lifelong forager Iliana Regan, who also hosts mushroom hunts in hidden locations. E-mail Regan at ilianaregan@yahoo.com for information about upcoming events.

Dave Swanson of mobile **Braise Culinary School** in Milwaukee, (414-241-9577; www .braiselocalfood.com) hosts an annual morel mushroom hunt as well as a bike-based Tour de Farms, an event that culminates in a farm dinner made from local, seasonal products.

The Second Floor, Fuller's Home & Hardware, 35 E. 1st St., Hinsdale, IL 60521; (630) 323-7750; www.fullerssecondfloor.com. Sign up for a range of educational classes—from family-style fêtes to lunch-and-learn, pizza and bunch-based gatherings—held at the upper-level chef's studio of this upscale, West Suburban hardware store.

Sur la Table, 55 W. North Ave., Lincoln Park, Chicago, IL 60610; www.surlatable.com. Those into cooking will be tempted by the electric gadgets, cutlery, and cooks' tools from this kitchen expert. Some advice: avert your eyes and sign up for the *Saveur* cooking series instead. Additional classes cover everything from global cuisine to stylish entertaining. Consider the kids' camps as well. There are locations at 55 S. Main St., Naperville, (630) 428-1110; and 100 W. Higgins Rd., South Barrington, (847) 551-1090.

Viking Cooking School and Culinary Shop, Abt Design Center, 1140 N. Milwaukee Ave., Glenview, IL 60025; (847) 350-0705; www.vikingcookingschool.com/glenview. There's plenty to salivate over at this brainchild from the name-brand appliance company. Interactive classes for teens and adults—as well as an intensive Viking University series—take place in a gleaming, stainless-steel setting. It's also the site of deluxe dinners.

The Wooden Spoon, 5047 N. Clark St. Uptown, Chicago, IL 60640; (773) 293-3190; www.woodenspoonchicago.com. Come to eye cookware from Lodge, Le Creuset, and All-Clad, but stay for the varying how-tos, which may include schooling in Latin, Caribbean, and mom-type cuisines. Private events may be arranged, and next-day knife sharpening is provided for a nominal, per utensil fee.

World Kitchen, Gallery 37 Center for the Arts, 66 E. Randolph St., Loop, Chicago, IL 60601; (312) 742-8497; www.chicagoworld kitchen.org. Explore the world—or, rather, the world by ethnic cuisines—at this program from the Chicago Department of Cultural Affairs. Whether you want to master Asian cooking, seek a hands-on history lesson on Chicago food, or ache for authentic Moroccan fare, come here to learn the ins and outs.

Young Chef's Academy, Glenbrook Market Place, 2825A Pfingsten Rd., Glenview, IL 60026; (847) 715-9474; www.youngchefsacademy .com. It's never too soon to start wee ones on a culinary regimen—especially when it's as fun as the classes, kids' nights out, birthday parties, and summer camps offered here. They'll learn about kitchen safety, food preparation, and cooking and baking techniques. Best of all, they won't leave feeling duped into hard work. Kitchens may be kept peanut-free.

Cooking Schools

Chicago's Community Kitchens, Greater Chicago Food Depository, 4100 W. Ann Lurie Pl., Archer Heights, Chicago, IL

60632; (773) 843-5414; www.chicagosfoodbank.org. Teaching career-building kitchen skills since 1998, this food-service job-training center assists unemployed and underemployed Cook County residents. Its students make over 2,000 meals daily for after-school Chicago Food Depository Kids Cafes and the elderly. Guest chefs and presenters are a source of inspiration.

Cucina Della Rosa Cooking School, 211 Park Ave., Barrington, IL 60010; (847) 650-9463; www.maryrosecooks.com. Chefs, instructors, and guest speakers form the foundation of programming at this spot, opened by first-generation Italian-American Mary Rose Hoover, who organizes classes for children, teenagers, and adults—as well as kids' camps—in a luxe, custom-tiled kitchen.

The French Pastry School, City Colleges of Chicago, 226 W. Jackson Blvd., Loop, Chicago, IL 60606; (312) 726-2419; www .frenchpastryschool.com. Expect upper-crust pastry instruction—including full-time certificate programs like L'Art de la Pâtisserie—and continuing-education courses from this cooking school, which opens its doors for tours with advance registration.

The International Culinary School, Illinois Institute of Art-Chicago, 350 N. Orleans St., Near North Side, Chicago, IL 60654; (312) 280-3500; www.artinstitutes.edu. Degree, diploma, and certificate programs—including an Associate of Applied Science in

Culinary Arts—are part of the curriculum at this hands-on learning environment. Visit its BackStage Bistro, (312) 777-7800, a student-operated restaurant, at which reservations are recommended.

Kendall College, 900 N. North Branch St., Goose Island, Chicago, IL 60642; (888) 905-3632; www.kendall.edu. Many a serious student gravitates to this culinary college, with schools of business, hospitality management, culinary arts, and early-childhood education. Its culinary instructors—who preside over degreed and certificate programs in 12 commercial kitchens and at three open-to-the-public dining rooms—have at least a decade of real-world managerial experience.

Le Cordon Bleu College of Culinary Arts, 361 W. Chestnut St., River North, Chicago, IL 60610; (888) 295-7222; www.chefs.edu/Chicago. Culinary students secure degrees and certificates adhering to European and North American culinary traditions, methods, and present-day cooking technologies at this educator. The school is also home to student-run restaurant, Technique, (312) 873-2032.

Washburne Culinary Institute, City Colleges of Chicago, 740 W. 63rd St., Greater Grand Crossing, Chicago, IL 60621; (773) 602-5487; www.kennedyking.ccc.edu/washburne. Degree and certificate programs give graduates the skills they need to advance in the culinary and hospitality industries. Taste the fruits of their labor at sedate the **Parrot Cage** (see p. 188) at the South Shore Cultural Center, and at African-inspired **Sikia** (see p. 192).

Wilton School of Cake Decorating & Confectionery Art, Chestnut Court Shopping Center, 7511 Lemont Rd., Darien, IL 60561; (630) 810-2888; www.wilton.com/classes. Providing instruction for professionals and nonprofessionals, this spot specializes in courses like artisan gelatin and fondant modeling as well as half-day workshops on starting your own cake biz. Also, check out its decorating camps for kids.

Specialty Cooking Classes

Bev Art Brewer & Winemaker Supply, 10033 S. Western Ave., Beverly, Chicago, IL 60643; (773) 233-7579; www.bev-art .com. Learn how to brew beer and make wine—or pick up the supplies needed to do it at home—at this spirited address. Its regularly offered, step-by-step classes yield batches of custom-labeled bottles (about six gallons for hops heads and 28 bottles for winos).

DANKhaus German Cultural Center, 4740 N. Western Ave., Lincoln Square, Chicago, IL 60625; (773) 561-9181; www.dankhaus .com. You needn't yodel to appreciate the definitive demonstrations—be it sausage-making or schnitzel, *krapfen,* or *rouladen* preparation—offered at this Deutsche destination, during which participants eat, drink, and receive recipes to take home.

The Fish Guy, Bill Dugan (see p. 317), rolls out intimate, monthly sushi classes in his store, which demystify the art of making sushi rice, *maki,* and sashimi using the fresh catches he sources.

The Glass Rooster, various; info@theGlassRooster.com; www.the glassrooster.com. Specializing in an age-old—if initially intimi-dating—culinary tradition, Laura McLaughlin comes to homes to teach the art of canning and preserving, bringing with her all the necessary produce and equipment, including jars, rings, lids, and cleaning supplies.

Green Spirit, 2015 W. Lunt Ave., Rogers Park, (773) 484-0937; www.greenspiritliving.com. Check notions of raw-food-as-tree-bark at the door when attending the global raw-food work-shops at this healthy hub from Living Light Culinary Arts Institute grad Linda Szarkowski. Instead, walk away with heat-free know-how, including the preparation of decadent desserts and Latin American and Italian fare.

Heat and Spice Cooking School, 925 W. Cullom Ave., Uptown, Chicago, IL 60613; (773) 742-2331; www.heatandspice.com. With several locations, this expert offers breezy to intensive instruc-tion in exotic cuisines (Mexican, Vietnamese, Thai, Indian, and Sri

Lankan). Small group, couple, and vegetarian classes are options, too. Plus, you may schedule instruction at home or even at work.

Naveen's Cuisine, 2325 W. North Ave., Wicker Park, Chicago, IL 60647; (773) 661-2696; www.naveenscuisine.com. Traveler, cook, and photographer Naveen Sachar teaches the techniques of Indian and Thai cuisines, while imparting the ins and outs of aromatic spices and cultural cooking techniques. Leave knowing how to create everything from *madras murgh* curry to vegetable *korma* and juicy kebabs.

Ranjana's Indian Cooking Class, 6730 S. Euclid Ave., South Shore, Chicago, IL 60649; (773) 355-9559; www.indiancookingclass .com. Unleash the bold flavors of Indian cuisine under the deft hand of Ranjana Bhargava, who hosts 3-hour vegetarian classes for all skill sets in her home. Opt to take single classes or a more in-depth, 4-class series. Or, arrange a custom, spice-centric dinner party based on Indian tapas or eggplant, prepared six ways.

Rebecca Wheeler, (773) 368-1336; www.rebeccawheeler.com. Rebecca Wheeler's ethnic and regional classes trot from Chinese, Punjab, and Southern Indian-style vegetarian to the cuisines of Italy, France, and Southeast Asia. In addition to stints at Trotter's to Go and Trio, Wheeler has taught classes at Williams-Sonoma and is a staff member of The Wooden Spoon. Be sure to inquire about her market tours.

Food Fests & Events

Some are charitable or themed; others prove downright strange. But whether in deference of desserts or in reverence of ribs, food gatherings are a way to unite *bons vivants,* uncover indigenous eats, and—often—revel in seasonal delights. That's true in Chicago proper—and beyond.

February

Chicago Restaurant Week, www.choosechicago.com, is an annual 10-day restaurant "week" that takes place at more than 200 restaurants. Expect specially designed, deeply discounted two- to four-course, fixed-price meals during lunch. Some spots even throw in bottles of vino.

March

Chicago Chef Week, www.chicagochefweek.com, makes a case for overindulgence. Special three-course lunch and dinner menus are available at dozens of restaurants at cut-rate prices.

April

Baconfest, (773) 257-3378; http://baconfestchicago.com, is an irreverent fête dedicated to cured meat featuring a who's who of Chicago chefs. During the event, pros whip up enough bacon-based foods, spirits, and desserts to, frankly, stuff a pig. For those who can't leave well enough alone, there are bacon-themed crafts on hand, too.

May

The **Morel Mushroom Festival,** (608) 739-3182; www.muscoda .com, takes place in the dairy state's morel capital, Muscoda, a town situated along the winding Wisconsin River. Folks may sell or buy elusive morels around town from early- to mid-May. Then, during a mid-month festival, there's a carnival, horseshoe tournament, and helicopter rides as well as fried morels at its "mushroom headquarters," the Kratochwill Memorial Building.

The **World's Largest Brat Festival,** (608) 236-2022; www.brat fest.com, takes places in Madison, WI, each Memorial Day weekend.

Celebrating Craft Brews

Chicago's beer culture is prevalent, though cold ones are especially celebrated during some open-to-the-public events. **Chicago Craft Beer Week** (www.chibeerweek.com) is one such example. Held in May in conjunction with the Illinois Craft Brewers Guild during American Craft Beer Week, the citywide bash features tastings at bars, shops, and restaurants, plus beer dinners, brewery tours, book signings, and a slew of limited-release beers. There are pub crawls and drink specials aplenty, too. Also of note is **AleFest Chicago** (www.alefest .com/chicago.htm), a craft beer tasting with a charitable bent. It highlights more than 150 craft beers from 50 breweries. Not to be overlooked is Chicago Beer Society's **Day and Night of the Living Ales** (www .chibeer.org), an annual, walk-around tasting featuring cask-conditioned ales from Chicago breweries.

In addition to lots o' brats, you'll find classic takes and veggie takes, plus plenty of milk, ice-cold soda, and brewskis to wash them down. The fête features bands, brat-themed souvenirs, an ice-cream booth, and fireworks as well.

June

The Chicago Botanic Garden Wine Festival, (847) 382-1480; www.chicago-botanic.org, kicks off summer at the verdant Chicago Botanic Garden in Glencoe. It features gourmet purveyors, wineries, cookware and cutlery specialists, and kitchen remodelers as well as grub from local restaurants.

Harvard Milk Days, (815) 943-4614; www.milkdays.com, in Harvard, IL, began with a small hay-wagon stage and street dancing. Now, it's a bona-fide bovine tribute, complete with milk-drinking contest, pancake breakfast, and grilling competition as well as an endless spread of dairy-based food. Hop atop a camel for a ride, and check out the reptile exhibit, too.

Pretzel City Fest, (815) 232-2121l; www.pretzelcityusa.org, arose after the circa-1869 Billerbeck Bakery brought pretzels to the town of Freeport, IL. (Its high school athletic team is even named for the salty snack). During the event, merrymaking includes tractor and pony rides, food galore, and a pretzel-themed recipe contest.

The **Rhubarb Festival,** (309) 582-2751; www.aledomainstreet .com, is a June extravaganza in Aledo, IL, during which over 12,000 rhubarb seeds are gifted; more than 20,000 pies filled with the stalky staple may be purchased; and samples of the sweet-tart perennial abound. Meanwhile, live music offers a diversion.

Ribfest Chicago, (773) 525-3609; www.ribfest-chicago.com, is a popular North Center jubilee that takes places each summer. Young and old converge over tangy, sauced ribs, prepared by 'cue restaurants citywide. Nearly two-dozen bands keep the vibe light, and a cook-off puts amateur grillers to the coals.

Taste of Randolph Street, (312) 666-1991; www.westloop.org, is in equal parts about cuisine from West Loop restaurants—from Veerasway to de cero—and indie rock. Dishes and beats usually drop mid-month.

June/July

Taste of Chicago, (312) 744-3315; www.tasteofchicago.us, is the city's signature crowd-thronged food festival, where sample portions of food are bought with tickets. There's also music on multiple stages.

July

The **Green City Market Chef BBQ Benefit;** (773) 880-1266; www.greencitymarket.org, is a crazy-popular, perpetually sold-out picnic showcasing farm-fresh food sizzled up by Chicago chefs. In addition to grilled grub, there's plenty of locally made beer, wine, and handcrafted cocktails. Profits support programming for the sustainable farmers' market.

Pierogi Fest, (219) 659-0292; www.pierogifest.net, takes place in Whiting, IN, mid-summer. Rife with walking, talking pastries and booty-shaking dumplings, it's presided over by a Polish princess, a dozen Rockette-esque Pieroguettes, and a Polish ambassador dubbed Polkahontas. In other words if you own a babushka, wear it.

Ribfest (Naperville), (630) 779-2702; www.ribfest.net, is a showcase of national pitmasters in suburban Naperville, luring thousands to gnaw on vendors' baby backs, tip back suds in strategically placed beer tents, and listen to live acts.

August

Brat Days, (920) 803-8980; www.sheboyganjaycees.com, pays homage to the encased sausage Sheboygan, WI, is known for. While munching on the snappy snacks, listen to live tunes, plenty of them nodding to eras past.

Burger Fest, www.homeofthehamburger.org, honors the "birthplace" of the burger in Seymour, WI. An idyllic town of 3,000 situated 15 miles west of Green Bay, it's where an 8,266-pounder was grilled. Besides mouthfuls of meat, the bash features hot air balloon ascensions as well as a run, pony rides, a hamburger-themed parade, and an eating contest.

DeKalb Corn Fest, (815) 748-2676; www.cornfest.com, is among the state's oldest and last remaining free music festivals, making it a favorite among students from nearby Northern Illinois University. Come for the inflatables, carnival, and craft show, and stay for the beer garden and sweet corn boil, yeilding free cobs during a specified time. Helicopter and biplane rides up the ante during the late summer event.

The **Mendota Sweet Corn Festival,** (815) 539-6507; www.sweetcornfestival.com, is a butter-spiked ode to Del Monte sweet corn, which is cooked with the help of a vintage steam engine in the north-central Illinois town of Mendota. During it, festival-goers consume more than 50 tons-worth of ears. There's also a beer garden and flea market jam-packed with crafts.

The **Rutabaga Festival,** (715) 822-3378; www.cumberland-wisconsin.com, is the pride and joy of Cumberland, WI, come late summer. Curiously, it includes an annual hot pepper–eating contest, too. Plus, a fly-, drive-, or walk-in, all-you-can-eat pancake break-fast takes place at the Cumberland Municipal airport. The veg that inspires the gathering can be found at a concurrent farmers' market.

Taste of the Nation, (877) 268-2783; www.strength.org/chicago, is Share Our Strength's culinary benefit, which aims to end childhood hunger. Locally, the gathering culls Chicago's top chefs, pastry chefs, and mixologists, who donate their time to prepare a belly-busting array of edibles. Ticket sales, in their entirety, support Share Our Strength's efforts.

The **Urbana Sweet Corn Festival,** (217) 344-3872; www.urbana business.com, warrants a weekend getaway. In addition to an end-less supply of hot, butter-soused corn, it features local and national acts and a wrestling show.

Veggie Fest, (630) 955-1200; www.veggiefestchicago.org, is a veg-focused food and music festival scheduled each August in Naperville. Beyond health-conscious eats tinged with Thai, Indian, and kid-friendly flavors, it welcomes speakers and lifestyle-oriented booths.

September

The **Amish Cheese Country Festival,** (800) 722-6474; www .arthurcheesefestival.com, takes place annually on Labor Day weekend in Arthur, IL. Festivities include a tractor pull, rat race, parade, and plenty of free cheese. It's also the site of a national cheese-eating competition and international cheese-curling cham-pionship, which involves scooting a cheese "stone" down a rink toward its target.

Apple Dumpling Days, (608) 462-2400; www.elroylions.org, spur competition in the town of Elroy, WI. During the event, races take place on repurposed railroad beds. However, couch potatoes also are invited to gobble up its honorary treat.

Cheese Days, (608) 325-7771; www.cheesedays.com, take place in Monroe, WI, each autumn. The event is loaded with family fun, beer, and—you guessed it—cheese, which appears in cream puffs, griddled sandwiches, and in cake form on a stick. Listening to polka bands, yodelers, and accordion players—or attending farm animal-related festivities—all quintessential ways to pass time.

Fondue Festival, (920) 921-9500; www.fonduefest.com, celebrates the world's largest fondue pot in Fond du Lac, WI, each year. Tastes of fondue varieties are on hand. There's also a bicycle ride and plenty of cheesy gift baskets displayed at downtown shops.

The **Pumpkin Festival,** (309) 263-2491; www .pumpkincapital.com, is hosted annually in the town of Morton, IL. Indulge in squash-based cheesecake, ice cream, cookies, fudge, and pies. Other events include a parade, pageant, and decoration contest as well as live banjo music.

Warrens Cranberry Festival, (608) 378-4200; www.cranfest.com, in Warrens, WI, is said to be the largest gala of its kind worldwide. In addition to a lineup of marsh tours, more than 80 food vendors tempt with treats (try the pancakes topped with cranberry syrup). Biggest berry and recipe contests are scheduled, and a parade takes place.

The **Watermelon Festival,** (608) 697-6744; www.pardeeville watermelonfestival.com, puts the fruit in the limelight in Pardeeville, WI. An open-air market, free, sliced watermelon, and a baked-goods auction are available. There's a speed-eating and seed-spitting contest as well.

September

Chicago Gourmet, (312) 380-4128; www.illinoisrestaurants.org, is an extravaganza celebrating food and wine in Millennium Park each fall. In addition to the event proper—which features speakers, sommeliers, and demos—some area restaurants offer special menus as well.

October

The **Turkey Testicle Festival,** (815) 234-9910; www.2camels .com/turkey-testicle-festival.php, in Byron IL, is about as frightful as it sounds: kooks come to down hundreds of pounds of the poultry part.

November

The **International Beer Tasting & Chili Cook-Off,** (217) 344-3872; www.urbanabusiness.com, ushers in fall in Urbana, IL, with more than 150 specialty and import beers and all the chili you can eat.

The **Wisconsin Cheese Festival,** (608) 358-7837; www.wicheesefest.com, takes place in Madison, WI, with loads of painstakingly crafted, artisan cheeses, tasting seminars, and farm tours as well as cheesemaker dinners.

Quick Index of Food Fests & Events

Appendix A: Eateries by Cuisine

RoPa Restaurant & Wine Bar, 27
Roti Mediterranean Grill, 150
Turquoise, 65
Venus Greek-Cypriot Cuisine, 159
WAVE, 109
Zaytune Mediterranean Grill, 200

Mexican
Adobo Grill, 68
Big Star, 72
Birrieria Reyes de Ocotlán, 167
Birrieria Zaragoza, 167
Bombon Café, 118
Carnitas El Paisa, 41
Carnitas Uruapan, 170
Cemitas Puebla, 80
Chilam Balam, 44
Don Pedro Carnitas, 172
El Pollo Giro, 225
El Tipico, 208
Frontera Grill, 126
La Casa de Isaac, 212
La Casa de Samuel, 178
La Cebollita Grill, 179
La Cocina de Frida, 19
La Lagartija, 180
La Michoacana, 180
La Oaxaqueña, 52
La Pasadita, 91

Las Palmas, 92
Los Moles, 54
Mexique, 140
Mixteco Grill, 56
New Rebozo, 234
Nuevo Leon, 186
Sabor Saveur, 102
Sol de Mexico, 61
Taco Grill & Salsa Bar, 239
Taqueria El Milagro, 195
Taqueria Ricardo, 64
Taqueria Tayahua, 195
Topolobampo, 158
Totopo, 240
Xni-Pec de Yucatan, 242
XOCO, 162
Zocalo Restaurant and Tequila
    Bar, 164

Middle Eastern/Lebanese/ Assyrian/Israeli
Al Bawadi Grill, 220
Cedars Mediterranean Kitchen, 170
Chickpea, 81
Couscous, 171
Istanbul, 50
Kan Zaman, 134
Mizrahi Grill, 213
Naf Naf Grill, 234

Nuevo Latino/Latin/Pan-Latin

Persian

428 App

Appendix B:
Index of Purveyors

Organizations, Food Services & Learning Centers

Appendix C: Index of Cooking Classes, Schools, Clubs & Food Forays

Index